PICASSO IN THE PRESCHOOL

FIRST EDITION

PICASSO IN THE PRESCHOOL

Children's Development in and through the Arts

Catherine McTamaney

Vanderbilt University

cognella® | ACADEMIC PUBLISHING

Bassim Hamadeh, CEO and Publisher

Annie Petersen, Specialist Acquisitions Editor

Gem Rabanera, Project Editor

Casey Hands, Associate Production Editor

Emely Villavicencio, Senior Graphic Designer

Trey Soto, Licensing Coordinator

Natalie Piccotti, Director of Marketing

Kassie Graves, Vice President of Editorial

Jamie Giganti, Director of Academic Publishing

www.cognella.com   800-200-3908

Contents

Welcome

What called you to teaching? Was it the excitement of witnessing a second-grader finally grasp a concept in math with which he had been struggling? Did you love reading and want to be a part of instilling that in new readers? Were you drawn to the energy of a classroom of small children, or did you have a great teacher (or two or three or five) who inspired you to teach? There are as many different motivations for teaching as there are teachers. As teachers and future teachers, we know that this is a deeply personal and relationship-driven work, one which is influenced every day by our own experiences, both in and out of school, and one in which the experiences of our students are both critically relevant and impossible to fully understand. We may be drawn to the work because of its humanitarian nature, or we may love the pedagogical precision of introducing new concepts. We may appreciate and want to prolong the innocent wonder of childhood, or we may realize that childhood is perhaps the best time to establish the habits and mindsets of scholarship.

Teachers assume many roles and intents, and even when our own work is very different from another teacher's work, our overarching goals and motivations often hold a lot in common. Even when we enact it in different ways, we are all drawn to the work of teaching because we think our teaching will make some difference. We think our teaching may do some good.

Consider then, the different roles you may describe for your work as a teacher: facilitator, lecturer, parent support, disciplinarian, emotional guide, bureaucrat, police officer, paper cutter, photocopier, playground supervisor, transit authority, colleague, comedian, custodian, educator.

Of the many roles that you may accept, I'll encourage you to add one more: As a teacher, you are an artist, your medium the children you serve. This text will provide supports for teaching *through* the arts. Thinking of teaching *as* an art elevates our work from the pedantic to the profound. When we think of ourselves as artists, we set both a very high standard for the evocative nature of our work and a deeper compassion for the difficult challenges we will face in pursuing that standard. This text will take the perspective, too, that the *process* of creating art is both essential to children's development and paramount to the *product* of that process. Thinking of our own teaching from the same lens challenges us to prioritize the interactions between teacher and student rather than the grade. In both art and teaching, attending to the work itself rather than the outcome of that work raises the authenticity of the outcome.

You may not naturally consider yourself an artist, or, indeed, consider teaching the arts integral to your work as a classroom teacher. Perhaps the arts have not been emphasized in your own school experience. Perhaps the arts were valued, but primarily for the product of highly talented individuals. Maybe you think the arts are for people who are "good at" theatre, dance, visual art or music and you don't think of yourself as "good at" those things. Rather than leading you to particular kinds of art-outputs, this text will challenge you to think about teaching through the arts as an integrated tool for supporting children's development across multiple domains. First, though, we should think about how the construction of contemporary views of teacher roles has developed. The role of the arts in children's education and its place in teacher education and teacher roles has evolved. Although the influence of the arts in human development has been recognized since the times of Aristotle, social norms, trends in education, and the expansion of formal requirements for content knowledge continue to impact how that influence is expressed in classroom settings.

The Teacher's Role: A Brief History of the Foundations of Art Education

From ancient times, the role of education in the arts has created two different audiences: art education intended to elevate the human experience and art experiences designed to build skills for use in everyday vocations. In *Politics*, composed around 350 BCE, the Greek philosopher Aristotle defined the importance of education in the arts. In his division of the four "formal" branches of education, Aristotle named reading and writing, gymnastics, music and drawing. "All art," he wrote," is concerned with coming into being, i.e. with contriving and considering how something may come into being which is capable of either being or not being, and whose origin is in the maker and not in the thing made." Aristotle continued, "Art is identical with a state of capacity to make, involving a true course of reasoning.[1]" In this classical understanding, art is a means by which its maker comes

---

1 Aristotle, *The Nicomachean Ethics*, Book 6

to understand the world, to build upon the momentum of nature and to suggest an evolution of thinking and of our role in the world. Teachers were primarily tutors who taught drawing as part of formal education, or musicians or dancers who taught students the performing arts for social settings. Dance, music, theatre and visual arts were taught as a means of protecting and preserving the values of the society.

With the Middle Ages' rapid expansion of Christianity, Aristotle's idea of art as a means of understanding and reflecting pure and ideal forms was replaced with a more limited and fundamental role: expanding the Church and evangelizing its stories. When Constantine, through the Edict of Milan in 313, recognized Christianity as the lawful religion of the Roman Empire, he began a transition out of the classical era of art and into one that emphasized stories from the life of Jesus. Initially, the naturalistic style of Greek and Roman arts prevailed, while eventually absorbing artistic influences from the north, west and east as the empire expanded. The arts were used both to teach Christianity and to glorify the religion and its followers. Formal education was overseen by the Church, which determined the curriculum, set standards for tutors, and decided into what fields students would be directed. Church leaders identified seven disciplines: arithmetic, geometry, grammar, rhetoric, logic, astronomy, and music. Students who demonstrated skill in these disciplines would continue their education in a university setting, including advanced study in architecture and other visual arts and in music. Art education, specifically, focused on the design of churches, frescoes and murals, or on the illustration of books including calligraphy for the dissemination of the Gospel. Teachers were often priests or other religious leaders, and the religious intent demanded precision in replication, not creativity or new thinking. The role of the teacher was to assure students had the physical skill needed to implement existing designs, to correct and refine.

During the Middle Ages, monastic workshops, craft guilds, and apprentices abounded, reflecting some of the earliest models of formal art education recorded. Artisans in guilds invited apprentices as young as 13 to begin training in the craft. These structures were formalized through the publication of workshop treatises like *The Various Arts* by Theophilus and Cennini's *The Craftsman's Handbook (Il Libro Dell'Arte)*, which served as early teaching manuals for apprentices. *The Various Arts* included over a thousand examples of metalwork and visual art techniques, from toolmaking to papermaking and including the design of stained-glass windows. *The Craftsman's Handbook* was written with young apprentices in mind, and included recipes for the handcrafted paints necessary for the design of frescos and panels in church settings.

The Renaissance marked the beginning of a new era in art education, and one which remains visible today. The role of the artist evolved from technical re-creator of religious stories and images to inspired and inspiring innovator, elevating our collective experience of beauty. The Renaissances defined the primary conflict of art education with which teachers still struggle today: Should art education focus on skills of a technical craft or on talent development for individuals with artistic "gifts"?

In the Renaissance, the emphasis fell to the latter, with the development of the skill designed to lead to the expression of genius. Students were educated in aesthetics, in drama, music, and poetry, with the classical perspective of art as meaning-making again taking prominence. Guilds were replaced by academies in which artistic geniuses were trained. Vasari's Accademia del Disegno in Florence, focused on connecting contemporary artists with wisdom and inspiration of masters, which the French Academy of Painting and Sculpture instilled a disciplined and rigorous focus in its students, who are permitted, in the academy, to explore subjects prohibited outside its walls, including life drawing. These centers emphasized the intersection of art with other disciplines—especially math—in the pursuit of perfect proportions in representation.

Art Education and the American Identity

The trajectory of art education trends followed a similar path on the American continent, although American art education emerged more slowly than its contemporary models in Europe. Early structures for formal education emphasized religious and moral limits, with art education included only to the extent that it propelled religious obedience. Puritanical laws in the late 17th century required literacy education for all children and the Massachusetts Laws of 1642 and 1647 established compulsory education for the first time on the continent. In 1647, the Old Deluder Satan Act required communities of more than fifty households to provide a schoolmaster for their children. As the economic infrastructure developed, so did the needed apprenticeships to establish tradesmen. Education in the arts, though, remained utilitarian and tied to the promotion of religious belief. Formal art education in the early settlements in America was practical and limited, with handicrafts and ornamental arts for girls and architecture for boys. Artists who sought classical training traveled to Europe for their education.

As the Renaissance gave way to the Age of Reason and, eventually, to the Enlightenment, the power of reason overtook objectives of religion both in theories of education and the role of the arts. In America, Benjamin Franklin published *Proposals Relating to the Education of Youth in Pennsylvania* (1749), supporting formal education in the arts, and lobbied for funding for the Philadelphia Academy, which opened in 1751. Abroad, Johann Pestalozzi, Swiss educator and reformist, promoted an integration of "head, hand and heart," in children's education. His series of letters, *How Gertrude Teaches her Children* (1801) elevated both the attention given to children's education and the understanding that children's formal education could not be separated from informal experiences. Pestalozzi introduced common school drawing as part of the curriculum at his institute and published *ABC der Anschauung* in 1803 to direct teachers in drawing methods. Pestalozzi's influence was felt across the world, reaching to early American theorists of both education and the arts. In 1808, his American protegee Joseph Neef authored *Sketch of a Plan and Method of Education* and founded a school for boys based on Pestalozzi's theories. Although the school quickly closed, it reflected an early effort to integrate the arts across the traditional disciplines of formal education and mirrored trends in art development in America.

Charles Wilson Peale, who remains recognized for his realistic portraits of historical figures, was a powerful force for the development of new museums and artistic centers in America at the same time. In 1786, he founded the Philadelphia Museum. In 1794, Peale organized the first collection of American artists, the Columbianum. The society held its first exhibition in 1795, focused on the representation of the American landscape in the establishment of a new American identity. In 1802, the American Academy of Fine Arts opened in New York, educating young men in classical fine art. In 1805, Peale, along with William Rush and other patrons and artists from the Columbianum, founded the Pennsylvania Academy of Fine Art. Initially, classic fine arts and realism and, soon after, life drawing classes were offered. While these efforts provided the foundation for later, expanded art education, teaching in the arts was not widespread. It was not until the emergence of the Common School movement in the 19th century that educators more regularly advocated for art education in schools, and even then, art education was largely limited to drawing, as a technical skill required to learn to write.

The Common School movement was one of a number of social reform efforts in the US intended to promote a common set of cultural values in America after an influx of large numbers of immigrants in the early 1800s. Public education at this time was identified as a cure for the idle hands that led youth to vagrancy, and drawing was emphasized as a means of promoting moral development. Prior to the 19th century, formal education had been largely limited to the children of wealthy families. Social reformists responding to the rapid growth in population in the first half of the 19th century sought to provide compulsory, free and public education as a remedy to the need to acclimate new immigrants and preserve existing social expectations. Art education, in this experience, helped to promote a common set of cultural values and norms for children from widely variant backgrounds and was intended to establish a dependable middle class.

In the late 1800s, theories of scientific rationalism emerged, establishing formal, scientifically directed institutions intended to manufacture efficiently achieved social outcomes. In 1821, William Bentley Fowle's Primary School Committee of Boston introduced drawing maps into the curriculum of the Fort Hill School, an institution charged with educating up to 200 children from poverty. In 1840, Rembrandt Peale introduced the first drawing class in a public school in Pittsburg, Pennsylvania, integrating writing as a consequence of drawing education and instituting mechanical drawing as a required skill of the curriculum. While the early 19th century saw the expansion of art as an expression of identity and genius, this perspective remained a background lens, with a wide gap between education of artistic genius and art for everyone else. Standardized art education included limited classical art experiences, and primarily mechanical ones like the instruction of technical drawing skills as a precursor to reading and writing. Fowle represents an era of theorists who struggled with the role of art in affecting social change. He argued for the equitable opportunities allowed through open access to education, and believed in education in the arts for both the poor and for girls, ultimately teaching at the Female Monitorial School, where he translated and use the French text, *An Introduction to Linear Drawing*. His 1834 *Manual of Drawing and Writing for the Use of Schools and Families* instructed in landscape, anatomy, and handwriting. Reformist Horace Mann pushed for public education as an equalizer between privilege and poverty and argued for drawing education as a foundation for handwriting and industrial work. His *Seventh Annual Report* to the Massachusetts Board of Education in 1844 argued for drawing as a foundation to handwriting and contributed to later efforts to institutionalize art education in public schools. Mann's

Common School Journal included reports on Pestalozzi's work and methods, including advocacy for state-funded teacher education in both. Again, educators duel with the core conflict in art education: practical, utilitarian skill development for the advancement of other disciplines, or individual creative talent development, especially through multi-sensory experiences.

While the 19th century did not see a resolution to that debate, it did include a rapid and unprecedented expansion of opportunities and public access to art in America. The Paris Exposition of 1867 highlighted the gap between artistic craft in Europe and in America and inspired efforts in the United States that ranged from the American Arts and Crafts movement to the expansion of training in the industrial arts. Social reforms in both education and the arts expanded during this period as well, especially in Boston, where the first public kindergarten was founded in 1870 and the Metropolitan Museum of Art opened in 1876. Public art museums like this included public art education, available for both men and women and funded by wealthy patrons. At the end of the 19th century, cultural changes from the fallout of the Civil War, the rapid development of industry and the influx of a new wave of immigrants inspired a widespread expansion of public education and intense debate over the role of school and teacher to remediate these influences.

Educators struggled with similar themes in reforming public schools that persisted in art education, such as whether practices should focus on the utilitarian or the inspired. On one end of the argument, emerging understanding about the unique nature of children's development began to creep into school and curriculum design, and the foundations for thinking of children's development in and through the arts began to appear. Especially influential were thinkers like Hermann Krusi, who articulated a link between higher order thinking and free drawing, Francis Wayland Parker, who emphasized the importance of children's construction of meaning through school experiences and Walter Smith, the first art supervisor for the city of Boston and one of the impetuses for the development of the Massachusetts Normal Art School. Between 1870 and 1876, Massachusetts, Maine, New York, and Vermont each enacted legislation requiring the instruction of drawing in public schools. Meanwhile, in 1892, the National Association of Education appointed a committee of educators to establish standards for public high school curriculum. The Committee of Ten challenged the outcomes of a highly classical model for public education, questioning its relevance for students who were not college-bound and ultimately advocating for high school standards that prepared students more directly for contributions out of school. In the dual track sequence the committee recommended, they made no mention of the arts. Art education as an open-ended opportunity for meaning-making was to be delineated to early childhood and elementary classrooms, with high school classrooms freed to focus on more important subjects.

The trajectory continued into the early 20th century, when innovations in production and manufacturing led to a prioritization of efficiency across organizations, including school settings. While progressive educators expanded their influence in early childhood and elementary schools, establishing schools that followed children's development, learning by doing and with time for reflection and community, many districts became increasingly bureaucratic, siloing knowledge into specific disciplines and often overlooking the arts entirely. In the same period as William Whitford published *An Introduction to Art Education* and Minna Beck released *Better Citizenship through Art Training*, proponents of organizational models of scientific management secured their influence in the hierarchies, regulations, and standardization of teacher education. Vestiges of the conflict, both in theory and structure, remain in schools today.

As the United States endured the Great Depression, defining the qualities of public education remained a question for public debate. An unstable economic foundation, international unrest, and an openness to social reforms opened the door for innovations that would help to resolve the disparity between factory and progressive models in public schools. Thinkers like Melvin Haggerty, advocate for community arts education, and Leon Winslow, forefather of the art integration movement, influenced new conversations in the role of the arts in schools. In 1932, the Progressive Education Association initiated an 8-year study of high schools and colleges, following students across multiple school settings to suggest that students educated in progressive schools perform at higher levels than students in more inflexible school settings. In the 1940s, publications like Victor D'Amico's *Creative Teaching in Art* and Viktor Lowefeld's *Creative and Mental Growth* helped to propel the belief that art education should help students to make sense of their world and environments, to construct new knowledge, and to integrate thinking across the disciplines. By basing their findings on evidence-based research, art advocates at this time were able to narrow the gap between utilitarian and inspirational art education.

The promise for integrated art experiences was high in the mid-20th century, but short-lived. In 1950, the United Nations Educational, Scientific and Cultural Organization (UNESCO) encouraged dialogue on the role of visual arts as a conduit for international diplomacy and understanding. In 1954, the International Society of Education through

Art was founded in response. The reconciliation, at least within the United States, was short-lived, however. When Soviet scientists, in 1957, successfully launched the Sputnik satellite into orbit around the Earth, American educators were challenged to identify quickly paths through which U.S. students could "catch up," with their Soviet counterparts. Integrated art education was dismissed in favor of emphasis on math and science education, a trend which persisted into the 1960s. Art education in schools became regimented as its own discipline, separate from other content.

The social unrest of the late 1960s and 1970s inspired arts-in-education proponents to argue for art education as an experience-based process including engaging in, observing, and reflecting on the ways in which art is made. In the early 1970s, teachers were increasingly trained in arts-integration methods and cross-disciplinary practices. At the same time, teacher education institutions and curriculum designers emphasized "units" of study, including content goals that crossed disciplinary boundaries. The discipline-based art-education movement reflects this history, with its own set of standards and best-practices influenced by theorists like Elliot Eisner and Jerome Bruner. Art experiences were linked to formal classroom materials and curricula to guide children's discussion and reflection on the arts.

By 1983, intensifying international competition and a focus on the remedial role of education to resolve economic, scientific, and political disparities led to the publication of *A Nation at Risk* and another national effort to increase achievement in public education through higher standardization. By the early 1990s, the pendulum had begun to swing again, prompted by Walter Annenberg's $500 million "challenge to the nation," which called for school reform through the arts instead of at the expense of the arts.

At the turn of the 21st century, educators found little more agreement in the role of art education in American schools. The No Child Left Behind regulations, enacted as part of the affirmation of the Elementary and Secondary Education Act included standards for theatre, visual art, music, and dance in K–12 classrooms, but high-stakes standardized testing focused primarily on student gains in math and language, leaving the arts, again, to supplement the "real" work of schools.

Almost since the origination of formal education in the United States, the role and importance of art education has been up for debate. Just as education reform movements swing between whole-child and back-to-basics models for school improvement, art education movements swing between art as the development of skills focused on utilitarian goals or art as the development of human understanding across multiple contexts.

Today, despite the increasing integration of the arts, many classroom teachers still see art education as something that comes after "real school." The argument suggests that, if math, science, literacy, and social studies standards are met, and time remains, the arts may be offered as an enrichment or supplement to "more important" curricular choices. Increasingly influenced by demands for evidence-based practices and speedy improvement in student outcomes, teachers often turn their focus to those content areas on which their students will be tested and overlook the opportunity for art education to strengthen those same areas. Art education need not be whittled to either skill development, social development, or talent development. While history suggests that we will choose between academic goals and artistic ones, the real promise may lie in the integration of both, where art experiences are valued both as in their own right and as a support to other learning. Essential to that reconciliation is our understanding of the role of the teacher in its initiation.

The Arts and "Real School"

History demonstrates an ongoing tension between back-to-basics school reform and models that focus on the whole child, a tension that is reflected on how and when the arts are integrated into "real school." When school reform efforts are focused primarily on student achievement in standardized tests, education in the arts will likely be cut. Although some studies suggest correlations between art education and academic achievement, other research cautions against casual links. Indeed, a sustained integration of the arts should not be justified by its influence on standardized tests. Such a stance leaves the arts vulnerable to other attack. There are certainly more efficient ways to develop math and literacy skills. To justify the integration of the arts through its promise to support other content is to devalue the worth of art education in its own right. The arts may support the engagement of other content and may allow for sustained attention and interest from students of all ages. The arts can enhance other learning, by integrating sensory, emotional, social, and motor abilities. They can support the complex interweaving of multiple disciplines by providing equally rich processes within which those disciplines are grounded. But there are other means to those ends and, when those means are less expensive or less time-consuming or ask less of classroom teachers than the arts do, the arts are also more likely to be sacrificed.

Our premise here is not to defend art education as a support for other learning, but to demonstrate the value of the arts in its own right, as an equal domain in constructivist teaching. The arts demonstrate the ancient human need for communication, with evidence of music, visual arts, dance, and theatre from the earliest documented societies. Because we are driven intrinsically to communicate, humans develop increasingly subtle and complicated means of doing so. The arts support our ability to communicate in nonlinguistic modes, to enrich and expand the complexity and nuances of that which we hope to communicate. Essential to constructivist models of learning is the ability to build meaning individually, to create meaning through repeated opportunities to internalize and express it. The arts allow for purposeful meaning-making. When students can integrate social, emotional, physical and intellectual understanding through the creation or experience of art, that understanding is made more personal, more responsive, and more lasting than when students receive it in through a single modality.

The arts offer experiences for learners to expand their social, emotional, and intellectual expertise, as a process of both creating and communicating meaning and understanding across a diverse range of concepts and ideas. Socially, the arts offer a pathway for diverse cultural experiences, for comparing and contrasting between multiple modalities conveying the same themes or between similar modalities conveying different themes. Experiences in the arts provide distinct opportunities for collaboration and for practical experience in working in groups with diverse contributions. Emotionally, the arts require risk-taking and courage in making visible creative and divergent thinking. Experiences in the arts give learners multiple languages for conveying understanding, building confidence, and allowing teachers more focused lenses into student thinking. The skill development that comes with disciplined practice supports learners' definition of persistence and self-capacity, and offer learners engaging paths to developing their ability to attend to new content. Intellectually, the arts allow interest-driven structures for deeper understanding. Visual arts, theatre, music, and dance require complex symbolic representation that interweave cognitive and emotional domains. Further, experiences in the arts to expand meaning-making learners to think creatively and critically, noticing and documenting patterns, practicing analysis and developing the capacity to discern subtle differences in meaning. Engaging in the arts allows learners to expand complex understanding, through adopting multiple perspectives or composing original design.

The arts, including visual arts, music, dance and theatre, comprise a discipline of their own, equal to literacy, math, science, and social studies in children's learning and warranting specific preparation in teacher education. The arts contribute to and reflect cognitive development, a phenomenon which will be described in greater detail in Chapter 2. The arts promote an understanding of multiple cultures and traditions, supporting the development of social skills, empathy, creating thinking, self-awareness, and cooperation. The arts offer inclusive learning opportunities regardless of socioeconomic experience, race, religion, gender or academic ability. We'll discuss these influences in Chapter 3. The arts respond to the current context of learner's lives, filling the gap between traditional teacher-centered classrooms and the multimodal digital environments within which users are both learners and teachers. They increase student engagement and retention. Finally, they support the kind of cognitive flexibility demanded by the pace and modalities of knowledge in a digital age, and they teach children both what and how to learn. We'll discuss these impacts in Chapter 9.

If we are to consider the arts as a discipline equal in its own right, we need also to reframe the role of the traditional classroom teacher in supporting this discipline. It would be indefensible to remove math from the everyday lives of learners or to segregate literacy to its own classroom for special lessons once or twice a week. Likewise, while we may have art specialists in the schools, classroom teachers must see the arts as a primary content of their own classrooms and see themselves as artists, too. While you may not see yourself as a Michelangelo or Pollock, you can expand your conception of teaching to see yourself as an artist. It may, indeed, be easier to integrate art in your own conception than some of the other roles teachers are asked to adopt.

The Teacher as Artist

Consider the work of the artist: to create, to reflect, to interpret, to challenge. Artists seek to make a new kind of sense of the human condition: to present image, movement, word, and sound in ways that stimulate new thinking. Whether an artist is working in a representational medium or a fully abstract one, the process intends to capture some element of our experience to make it evident and available in new ways. The artist seeks to establish new knowledge, either in the interpretation of known phenomena or in the creation of original ones.

Likewise, the teacher seeks to create, to reflect, to interpret, and to challenge knowledge in his students. Teachers seek to make a new kind of sense in the minds of their students, to present image, movement, word, and sound in ways that stimulate new thinking. Whether a teacher is working with concrete concepts or supporting the development of abstract understanding, the process intends to capture some element, some concept or content, to make it evident and available in new ways. The teacher seeks to establish new knowledge, in his students' interpretation of known phenomena or in the creation of new ideas. In our daily practice, we, too, struggle with whether our work is primarily about the development of skills needed in vocation or in the elevation of the human experience.

For many teachers, thinking of our work as art can be intimidating. Most of us don't consider ourselves artists and we may not even think of ourselves as "good at art." But if we define art as "the expression of that which is beautiful, evocative, or significant," then teaching is very much an art form and teachers become artists, in daily practice with as many "works" as children they teach. Artists observe the world, reflect upon those observations, and struggle to express the meaning they make in that reflection through their media. Artists intend to transform their media from that which is unmolded to that which expresses new meaning, to evoke abstract understanding through concrete action. Likewise, teachers observe their classrooms and students, reflect upon those observations, and struggle to express what they understand about the needs they observe through their lessons. Teachers intend to transform their students from that which is unmolded to that which internalizes new meaning, to support the development of abstract ideas through the concrete experiences of the classroom. And, like artists, sometimes the work we do inspires and sometimes we can't find our audience. Sometimes we are recognized for the profound influence we cast, and sometimes we're unappreciated and underfunded. And, like artists, while most of us may never be the next Picasso or Mozart recognized around the world for our genius, our art, our work, is essential and meaningful, even if only to individuals who enjoy it every day. In art and in teaching, it is not the celebrity that creates the value: it is the personal relationship between artist and medium, the meaning evoked through the interaction that defines its worth.

The Influence of Standards

Think, then, of the practice of teaching as carrying the same intent as any other artistry. We are bound by limits, policies and standards, in the same way that the artist must make meaning within the physical limits of the canvas, the stage, or the scale. Those limits define the space within which our artistry unfolds. They do not define the experience of the art.

Such is the influence of content standards. The standards identify the ideas with which our artistry should struggle. They give the context to the art, like a painter whose genre is pastoral painting or a sculptor who works exclusively with marble. They provide the themes for interpretation, and, like profound works of art that persist across generations, they ideally reflect universal norms of knowledge and content which we seek to make available to all students. It's easy to distance ourselves from the creative experience of teaching by pointing to standards for what we must do. When we think about teaching as artistry, however, we incorporate the standards as a necessary influence to the art. Our goal as artists is not to ignore the universal, but to make it more accessible, to deepen our understanding of it, and to make it available in new ways to other thinkers. Likewise, our goal as teachers is not to ignore the standards, but to make them more accessible and available in new ways to other thinkers through our practice.

Our challenge, as teachers, is to embrace our work as artists within the concrete boundaries of our practice, to challenge ourselves to create, to reflect, and to interpret knowledge with our students within those frames. The frame is not the art and, to say the least, a frame without some art within it lacks appeal. There is no conflict between teaching as artistry and teaching with standards. One provides the skeleton and the other the movement. You need both to dance.

Modeling Risk-Taking

If you're not quite yet ready to think of yourself as an artist, pretend you are. Your students may not be there yet, either, and it falls to you to model for them the disposition towards new knowledge that you want them to adopt. When we model an openness to play, to messiness and mistake-making, we remind the students in our classrooms that they are more interesting than the numbers that describe them. Art smudges the edges of the hard statistics that too often define and limit our understanding of children. It offers an opportunity to expand their thinking by exploring activities with more than one right answer, by seeking new solutions to common problems, and by moving away from the anxiety and perfectionism that can be implicitly suggested by high-stakes expectations. Simultaneously, art engagement requires its own sort of risk-taking, in the public expression of private thoughts. When we are willing to be brave in our own experiences in the arts, especially in those media in which we are less confident, we model that bravery for children. Knowing that children's biases, their hesitations, and self-imposed limits will be informed significantly by their school experiences, teachers who allow themselves to be held back by those same fears reinforce them in their students.

Individual Growth through Practice

Finally, an engagement with the arts strengthens us beyond the classroom. We have not chosen easy work. Teaching is exhausting and depleting. Even on our best days, we spend most of them giving of ourselves to others: to the students we serve, to colleagues, to parents, and to the policymakers who define our practice. We are challenged by contemporary expectations of the profession to accomplish extraordinary outcomes in little time with limited resources. And while we often encourage our students to think of themselves beyond the narrow parameters of GPA and test scores, we can find it hard to remember that our value, too, is determined by more than the paperwork we complete. When we engage in the arts, it offers us the same benefits our students experience: a new language through which to make and express meaning, a path through which to strengthen our knowledge of concepts and ideas, and a means to restore and expand ourselves by pushing past the deeply ingrained cognitive tracks of everyday thinking.

We can incorporate the arts into our classrooms through specific lessons that develop particular skills or perspectives, that enhance students' understanding of essential concepts, or that offer them multiple means to express that understanding. When we do so, we offer children more complex ways of engaging content, of internalizing new ideas and expressing them back to an audience. Incorporating the arts strengthens learning. We can incorporate the arts into our classrooms by acknowledging the creative and expressive power of the practice of teaching itself, one which requires courage and risk-taking, one which holds the potential for profound experiences, one which, when successful, is at once complex and beautiful and, when less so, is both heartbreaking and challenging.

Organization of This Text

In developing a pedagogical text for the support of children's development in and through the arts, certain challenges present themselves. Should we focus more on the physical development of skills? Should we focus on the integration of art activities into traditional content to support and enhance children's learning of defined content? Should we focus on the ways in which art experiences allow for children's development outside of those traditional norms, focusing on the breadth of art engagement across the whole child? Effective art integration requires us to strike a balance among multiple perspectives. If we think of the arts as an additional language through which children can express their knowledge of content, of themselves, and of their place in the world, we are bound to provide them with the opportunities to learn the rules of that language to support them as they develop their fluency. Children will need certain physical skills to be able to represent their knowledge through the arts, like the ability to manage particular artistic tools or to understand the practical structures of the relationship of actor and stage, for example. They'll also need opportunities for open-ended experimentation and exploration with those same tools and structures to be able to express themselves in new ways. This text is designed to support teachers across that spectrum.

First, we'll explore the implications of children's development in multiple domains and its interaction with the arts. Then, we'll delve more deeply into each of the major art domains: theatre, visual art, dance, and music, linking children's development to the structures of those domains. We'll expand our focus to think about the development of children's own aesthetics and their understanding of others' aesthetics, and finally, we'll consider the ways in which children's development in and through the arts can be assessed to strengthen and support teaching and learning in these modalities. I hope the organization will provide a firm understanding of how our choices as teachers are guided first by what we understand regarding children's development, then by the ways in which that development can be supported by particular types of activities, and finally by considering how to gauge our own effectiveness in the objective. We will move across the spectrum of practical to poetic an an effort to support your capacity as a teacher to do the same for the children you serve.

Incorporating the arts strengthens teaching. Engaging the arts is a change of practice and a change of mindset. I hope this text will support you in both.

Discuss

Visit the video series at http://www.learner.org/libraries/artsinevery-classroom/ and view the videos entitled, "Three Leaders at Arts-Based Schools." What are the values these leaders espouse to support integrating art education throughout their classrooms? What are the challenges to overcome in this perspective? As a future teacher, what lessons can you take from their experiences to support or challenge your existing conceptions of your work?

What content area do you feel most comfortable with or are you most excited to teach? Can you imagine means of integrating visual arts into this content area? Music? Theatre? Dance?

Discuss the ways in which you are aware of your own creativity. What are the environments within which you feel most safe to be creative? How does an audience influence your willingness to do something new? How courageous are you about similar risk-taking when you're alone or with a small group of trusted peers?

Collaborate

Visit the website http://www.nationalartsstandards.org. How does the National Coalition for Core Arts Standards organize the ways through which children can engage in the arts? Choose a grade or developmental level to consider more closely. What themes or values do you see reflected in the kinds of standards set for the age or grade you've chosen? Share your observations with a colleague who has chosen a different stage. How do your conclusions reflect your values as a teacher? How do your partner's conclusions reflect his or her values as a teacher?

Think about some common obstacles to creative and divergent thinking. Make a list of ten obstacles that could interfere with your ability to teach in creative ways. Make a list of ten obstacles that could interfere with your students' willingness to take divergent risks. What are some ways in which you could navigate around these obstacles for yourself or your students? Share your list with a colleague and rebuild your lists using each other's ideas.

Create

Create a timeline of trends in art education. Consider other historic, political or philosophical events that occurred along the same timeline. Our justification for preschool and K–12 education often follows other social values. How have social trends influenced or been reflected in trends in art education?

Think about your own experience as a learner. Which art experiences are most memorable? What qualities do your most memorable art experiences share? Do you still consider yourself an artist? Can you remember a time when you did? Using images from newspapers, magazines, or online resources, prepare a collage of your current identity as an artist.

For Further Reading

Booth, E. (2003). Art for art's sake and art as a learning tool: Achieving a balance. *Journal for Learning through Music,* 2: 19–22.

Bruer, J. T. (1999). In search of … brain-based education. *Phi Delta Kappan, 80*(9), 648–654.

Burton, J., Horowitz, R., & Abeles, H. (1999). *Learning in and through the arts: curriculum implications.* New York: Teachers College Press, Columbia University.

Burton, J.M. (2004). The practice of teaching in K-12 schools: Devices and desires. In E. Eisner & M. Day (Eds.), *Handbook of research and policy in art education* (pp.553–575). Mahwah, NJ: Lawrence Erlbaum Associates, Inc.

Dawson, J. (2003). The complete curriculum: Ensuring a place for the arts and foreign languages in America's schools. Retrieved December 12, 2015 from http://www.nasbe.org/wp-content/uploads/Complete_Curriculum_Arts-and-Foreign-Languages_NASBE.pdf

Dobbs, S. M. (2004). Discipline-based art education. In E. Eisner & M. Day (Eds.), *Handbook of research and policy in art education,* (pp. 701–724). Mahwah, NJ: Lawrence Erlbaum Associates, Inc.

Eisner, E. (1992). The misunderstood role of the arts in human development. *Kappan, April,* 591–595.

Eisner, E. (1998a). *The kind of schools we need.* Portsmouth, NH: Heinemann.

Hebert, D. (2004). Finding the will and the way to make the arts a core subject: Thirty years of mixed progress. Retrieved December 12, 2015 from http://www.nasbe.org/wp-content/uploads/Making-the-Arts-a-Core-Subject.pdf

Goldhawk, S. (1998). Young children and the arts: Making creative connections. Retrieved December 12, 2015 from http://www.artsdel.org/ArtsEducation/YoungChildren.pdf

McWinnie, H. J. (1992). Art in early childhood education. In C. Seefeldt (Ed.), *The early childhood curriculum.* New York: Teachers College Press.

Wilson, B., & Hoffa, H. (1985). *The history of art education: Proceedings from the Penn State Conference.* Pennsylvania: National Endowment of the Arts.

Wygant, F. (1993). *School art in American culture: 1820-1970.* Cincinnati: Interwood Press.

Chapter 1

Children's Development through the Arts

In order to prepare developmentally appropriate experiences for young children through the arts, we need first to understand the benchmarks and opportunities within children's development. While ample research exists about children's cognitive, emotional, social, and physical development in early childhood, this chapter will focus on the ways in which development in those domains is both an accelerator and an outcome of children's development in the arts.

It has long been established that high quality art experiences for children in the first 6 years of life can support development across multiple domains. Through the experiences of early childhood, children develop an initial understanding of the world, of key relationships within it and of their own role as contributors to it. An essential process in those experiences is the opportunity to internalize and to communicate ideas about themselves and about the world around them. Experiences in the arts offer children multimodal means of expressing those ideas, evolving and emerging with the development of the child and allowing the communication of often more complex understandings than the child may have the verbal capacity to offer. The child whose vocabulary is simple nonetheless experiences complicated emotions. The child who cannot yet read or write nonetheless learns from the world around him. Music, theatre, dance, and visual arts can and do provide a pathway for expressing those complicated experiences.

Although children's development is typically predictable and sequential, it is still highly individual to each child. Here, we will distinguish between the physical, cognitive, social, and emotional development of infants, toddlers, and early childhood children. Remember, though: a child's individual development may move more quickly or slowly through these sequences. Likewise, a child's development in one area may be advanced, while her development in another area may be more slowly paced. Finally, we know that children's development often progresses through fits and starts, with great periods of rapid growth and alternating periods of more moderate development. Here, we'll discuss the predictable sequence of children's development. In practice, teachers should be prepared for a far more dynamic expression of that development in each child.

Physical Development across Early Childhood

Children in the first 6 years of life move through rapid changes in their development, mastering gross motor skills, establishing evolving fine motor skills and engaging in near constant physical activity. Children in early childhood learn with their whole bodies, driven to explore their environments, to touch and move and lift and carry and interact with whatever is made available to them. And while this may be the most active period of a child's physical development, it is simultaneously unrefined. Dance, for example, for the youngest children in early childhood will be largely unpredictable and expansive, engaging the child's whole body with limited evidence of prediction or planning. Visual arts may record the experience of movement during the creation of the art, rather than as the product of a carefully executed design. As the child develops over these 6 years, so does the refinement of her gross and fine motor control. Thus, early stages should introduce basic skills with lots of opportunities to practice control of the body, developing over time to lessons that demand pre-thought or refined movement.

Cognitive Development across Early Childhood

Most teachers will report the limited attention span of children in early childhood, an observation supported by ample research. Children's attention in early childhood certainly is short when compared with the developed ability to attend that older children demonstrate. In comparison to the concentration in infancy, though, most children's ability to attend undergoes impressive growth in a short window of time. In preparation, arts educators offer a variety of activities to engage and sustain children's interest, understanding that interest precedes attention in the development of the young child. Because children are motivated to learn about their world, they seek experiences that expand that understanding. Children explore, and the most appropriate environments provide them opportunities to do so in an open-ended, discovery-based path. Simultaneously, children's developing understanding of how the world works requires repetition and predictability, supporting the child as he tests developing schema through repeated applications. Dance, then, is focused on repeated activities and sequences, reinforcing the child's need for repetition and predictability, with frequent opportunities for free movement and play. Music experiences will provide both simple, easy to repeat music and times when children can explore different sounds and songs and to explore with and create new instruments. Dramatic play will include repetition through easy verbal activities, like finger plays and chants, and open play with a variety of objects, costumes and props to explore. Visual art should include varied materials to respond to children's developing ability to represent images with greater and greater detail, and open-ended experiences to experiment with diverse media. Throughout the experience of early childhood, teachers should seek to balance open-ended, exploratory experiences for children within predictable, reliable and repeatable boundaries. That balance supports the increasing complexity and reliability of children's own thinking while supporting them in developing their own agency in the selection and implementation of activity.

Social and Emotional Development across Early Childhood

Critical to development during early childhood is the evolution of the child's understanding of his relationship to other people and the emotional regulation that builds as a result of those relationships. Newborns, within hours of their births, seek their mother's voices, turning toward these key relationships. Over time, the evolutionary preference for her parents expands to include an interest in other relationships, and by the time the child nears the end of early childhood, she has transferred that prioritization for her parents to the much wider and more complicated social setting of her peers. Experiences in the arts, then, mirror this expanding interest in building relationships with others, supporting children as they work and play together and by providing opportunities to work through common social and emotional challenges. At the beginning of early childhood, the arts may provide low-risk opportunities to engage with other children: toddlers finger-painting together on a large table surface, for example, or dramatic play with pots and pans as children emulate their parents' work in the kitchen. In music, the youngest children will listen to and try to match the tones of endeared voices, cooing on pitch or singing with trusted adults as they fall to sleep. In physical movement, infants may dance in the arms of an adult, connecting movement and dance with the joyful support of adults on whom they rely. As children develop, art experiences similarly expand to include peers, teachers, and other caregivers. An early childhood classroom, then, might offer a music station with a splitter for two or three friends to listen to the same music on their headphones. Teachers might incorporate more peer-reliant dances, like simple folk dances or movement games that engage friends. Visual arts pieces will begin to include images of friends together, often illustrated either reflecting upon shared experiences or imagining new ones. In later early childhood, even children's dramatic play will become more complicated and more inter-reliant on the influence of peers, expanding to include multiple characters for different children, larger group sizes at play simultaneously and more opportunities, through the creative problem solving inherent in dramatic play, to approximate the kinds of social thinking on which children will rely.

As children transition from early childhood to elementary-level development, teachers and parents can observe a more pronounced interest in their peers, in an awareness of how they fit into larger groups and more distance from the influence of their families during the school day. Art experiences across the modalities can respond to these changes, allowing for group projects that support and propel children's longer attention spans and ability to plan across multiple days, projects that demand or develop fine motor coordination, and experiences that help to strengthen talent development in artistically driven students. At the same time, elementary art experiences should allow space and time for individual reflection, balancing the child's heightened social perceptiveness with structured opportunities for personal engagement.

Regardless of age, children use the arts to explore and to make sense of the world around them, to understand complex ideas, to connect across disciplines and seemingly divergent spaces, and to establish and articulate the influence of others in their own development. The social, physical, emotional, and cognitive benefits of art experiences may be discernible in the literature, but they are integrated fluidly in the experience of art education. That is to say, a single art activity will never address only one aspect of a child's development, even if it is designed to prioritize a particular domain. For example, a visual art activity designed to build children's fine motor control with stylus tools will nonetheless impact the child's emotional, social, and cognitive development, in either affirming or countering existing schema the child holds in those areas. Likewise, a teacher who introduces a folk dance to her students because she wants to provide opportunity for social experiences in the classroom shouldn't underestimate the simultaneous physical, cognitive, and emotional needs of children as they learn and perform the dance. As we consider more closely the specific developmental benchmarks teachers may observe and prepare for in their classrooms, remember that none of these happen in isolation or without impact to the others. Children's development is integrated, fluid, and individual.

Theatre in Early Childhood Development

Theatre and its practices influence development growth across the lifetime, from formal experiences in the discipline of theatre arts to informal opportunities for play that incorporate dramatic pretending. Putting on roles, imagining new settings and telling stories is inherent in social development and spans development both in and out of school. When incorporated with intention and effective design, theatre supports children's development across multiple domains, facilitating engagement in social, emotional, physical, and cognitive growth. Because theatre as a formal discipline evolves from universal drives of human development, the discipline differs across that development and across contexts, reflecting both the age and experience of the children involved and the social contexts of the culture around them. Healthfully designed theatre practices support cognition, language development, kinesthetic growth, social engagement, problem-solving, and conflict resolution, and raise compelling questions for children in approximating social, ethical, and cultural implications of the stories and characters they portray or observe.

Infancy and Dramatic "Play"

Consider the rapid change and growth in the first year of life, when the child changes from the helpless newborn to the engaged, social, inquisitive 1-year-old. Children in early infancy absorb their environments through observation and exploration, watching, touching, tasting, listening, smelling, and engaging with everything around them. Even in these first months of life, children initiate and respond to dramatic play, the foundation of theatre arts. Dramatic play is both essential and inescapable in children's development, as babies re-enact the behaviors they see around them, doing the things they see their parents, siblings and caretakers doing, even if they don't yet understand the purpose of those actions. Imagine an infant who puts a play telephone to his ear and babbles at it, or repeats animal sounds when playing with figures or sharing a favorite book about the zoo; these are efforts to dramatize his world, to take on roles he sees executed around him and, even its simplest enactment, to understand the world into which he's been born.

Solitary Play

For children under 2, expect to see solitary play, when children are playing in and through their environment to gather new information, test schema or practice the roles they've seen enacted around them. The child's play may seem notably focused at this stage, as though the child herself fully understands the role she's playing (and regardless of whether caregivers can discern it). An infant may babble for long periods into a play telephone, engaged in "conversation." A younger toddler may struggle to balance a tote bag on his shoulder as he mimics his mother carrying a briefcase. Infants and toddlers will "feed" baby dolls, rocking dolls in their arms or holding bottles to their mouths. You may even see infants and young toddlers chiding their stuffed animals for being naughty! In these early dramatic play experiences, the child's attention may be singularly focused on his own experience, enacting and practicing roles as he internalizes them and makes sense of what he sees.

As toddlers develop, so does their interest in other children and adults. Dramatic play may expand in later toddler development to include offering a toy or prop to a parent or caregiver for them to explore or in mimicking the actions of other toddlers in their care settings. Two toddlers, for example, who are pretending to be firemen, may not distinguish the roles each plays, but they may look to each other to prompt or initiate new enactments that both adopt. So, while toddlers are less likely to choose roles in their dramatic play that require the cooperation of other players, they will often happily allow other children to fight fires with them, or also pretend to be kittens. Teachers and caregivers of toddlers should make available diverse props that reflect the venues and behaviors children experience or observe in their own lives: kitchen props, dolls with clothes to change, animal figurines and costumes for community members. Teachers and caregivers should encourage social experiences through dramatic play, but not be surprised if children are unpredictably assertive about whether they want other children to play with them. Remember: the key developmental goal at this period is the practice and enactment of the roles children see in their own experiences.

Because that enactment is primarily driven by the child's own efforts to make sense of his world, he may not enable the concurrent efforts of his peers. That interest in other children's perspective and involvement will develop as the child moves from the toddler experience into preschool development. In the meantime, teachers and caregivers can observe the lessons of belonging, identity, and community toddlers represent in their own dramatic play and take note of when those children begin to test their understandings by incorporating the varied experiences of other children.

Parallel Play

Older toddlers and young preschoolers will begin to engage in parallel play, choosing play activities that allow them to be near other children but not necessarily engaged in the same play. Teachers and caregivers may notice play which is both dramatic and parallel. For example, two children playing with blocks may both be deeply engaged in building their own designs, but may not be working on the same building together. While one child's road may intersect another child's tower, their engagement with each other will come as an outcome of their individual interest in dramatic play and their emerging curiosity about each other. Children's social drive will motivate them to play near to each other, close enough to observe and question and interact, but with their own choices directing the specifics of their own play. Look, for example, for children taking on different roles in the costume area of a classroom space. One child may use a shelf to store pretend foods for the meal he is pretending to make. Another child may use the same cabinet for supplies for her pretend medical office. They may talk with each other about their own play, orbiting around each other's play spaces without directly engaging in cooperative play.

Cooperative Play

Children in older early childhood, 4-, 5-, and 6-year-olds, will demonstrate more advanced play, developing the cognitive and social skills necessary for cooperative play, when multiple children engage in a single narrative line of dramatic play with distinct and interrelated roles. In order for this to occur, children must be developmentally ready to predict, develop and follow through with plans, requiring solid cognitive preparation. They must be able to interpret and respond to the social cues of peers, requiring social preparation. They must be able to regulate their own responses, requiring emotional preparation. And they must be able to navigate the enactment of various roles, requiring physical preparation. Playing with a friend, then, is a far more complicated task than it may first appear, and typically emerges after children have had ample practice in enacting roles on their own first.

Given, then, the complex factors that must be coordinated for peaceful cooperative dramatic play, teachers and caregivers should be especially attentive to positive social modeling and responsiveness in these activities. Individual children may be at different levels of readiness for the complex demands of cooperative play, and will need facilitation in language, conflict resolution, and problem-solving that predictably emerge in these experiences. While children's dramatic and cooperative play is essential to their evolving understanding of their role in the world and their potential for contribution to it, it's not easy. Young children require positive, proactive modeling by teachers to predict, enact and cooperate with other children while engaging in dramatic play.

Sociodramatic Play

Finally, older children, after the complicated internalization of lessons learned in their own parallel and cooperative play experiences, will be driven to sociodramatic play, those experiences that involve groups of children enacting stories and contexts together, when the engagement and selection of the group is as important as the story they decide to enact. Consider older children on a playground who are acting out the characters of a favorite movie. Some children will emerge as social leaders, selecting players and assigning roles, directing the motivation of the story and resolving (however messily) conflicts when they arise. Other children may concede to these roles or challenge them, and often the resolution becomes the most important part of the "play" experience. In this more advanced stage of development, the social implications of the play are as important as the topic or context of the play itself. Children have internalized complex rules and conclusions about their communities and the multiple roles people play within them. Building on those experiences, they begin, through sociodramatic play, to explore the nuances of relationships between people in various roles. The involvement of other children is the work of the play at this level of development, and the development and meaning-making of social norms its outcome.

Implications for Teachers and Caregivers

Between birth and age 6, dramatic play, as the precursor to formal theatre experiences, contributes to children's emotional, cognitive, social, and physical development. It fosters language and literacy skills by incorporating rich vocabulary and opportunities to make authentic the use of new words through enacted play. It supports developing empathy toward others through the adoption of diverse perspectives, provided opportunities for conflict resolution and problem solving and offers engaged practice in the nuances of relationships with an increasing scope of others. Dramatic play allows for the healthy expression of complex emotions and for playing-through possible mediations. It supports children in the abstraction of ideas as they enact increasingly complex scenarios while making equally complex choices about their own contributions to that play, demanding both the cognitive abstractions demonstrated through representational skills and role playing.

Because dramatic play is driven by children's development in early childhood, teachers and caregivers should be prepared for its influence across the many settings of a child's day. Dramatic play will not be limited to the "dramatic play area" or the "blocks area" of a classroom, although teachers should allow for ample space, time, and materials to support it in prepared ways. Rather, children will cycle between enacting the world around them, reflecting upon that world and challenging new understandings built through their own experiences and enactments. Teachers and caregivers should be prepared for and responsive to children's expression throughout that cycle, as they use dramatic play as one of many modes to understand and make sense of their world.

Music in Early Childhood Development

Children are prewired to respond to music, a phenomenon linked to language development and reflected in the abundance of research into the development of auditory and vocal skills in young children. Simple expressions of children's connection to music is evident even without a research agenda. Newborns will turn their heads toward familiar music. Babies will struggle to coo in response to an engaged adult. Toddlers will match simple tunes and intonations, singing along to music they hear frequently. As children move from the first 3 years into early childhood, their musical explorations will become increasingly adventurous, singing to themselves when they are busy in other activities and mastering increasingly complex melodies and intonations. Throughout, children will express their own personal connection to music, preferring particular songs for bath time or lullabies for bed, incorporating songs and music from favored children's media into their dramatic play and creating new, adventurous, if sometimes illogical, lyrics of their own. Music can be intertwined joyfully through most of the experiences of early childhood, and thus becomes an important contributor to the climate within which children's development unfolds.

But beyond the day-to-day exuberance for music that children often display, music development is an expansively researched field, in part because of the observable connections between different elements of music interpretation and creation and the overlap between those connections and other compelling factors in children's cognitive development.

Prenatal Development

The human ear begins to develop in the third week of pregnancy and takes shape by twenty weeks. By 24 weeks, hearing is fully developed, and the fetus can hear voices, music and other sounds from outside the womb. While sounds in the womb are muffled, the rhythm and melody of music is unaltered, and the developing brain begins to note patterns in music and changes to those patterns in differing melodies and beats. Because lower frequencies move through amniotic fluid more easily, fetuses often respond more to music with consistent, low bass sounds and percussion. The emotional reaction of the mother to different music during pregnancy will also be transferred to the infant, although there is no evidence to argue that a particular type of music is more beneficial. Jazz music and show tunes have just as much impact as Mozart and Beethoven. The pace of music, however, does matter. Whatever the choice of music in pregnancy, fetuses are calmed by music with regular beats and startled by music that changes rhythm or volume unexpectedly. These experiences in the womb are printed on the child's development. After birth, the infant will respond to familiar songs from pregnancy through increased movement, more active suckling or calm. Although there is limited research on the long-term cognitive effects of prenatal music experiences, the physical and emotional development that occurs within the womb does seem strongly influenced by musical experiences.

Musical Preferences in Infancy

In the first 6 months of infancy, infants' response to music changes rapidly. Rather than preferring the low-frequency sounds that transferred best through amniotic fluid, infants by 6 months of age prefer high pitched music and, over the first year, develop increasingly sophisticated responses to musical experiences. Within the year, infants can distinguish between pitches and combinations of sounds, differences in rhythm, tone, and meter in varying music. Infants can discern changes in melody, key, and voice, and notice when a new accompaniment attends a familiar melody. Infants between 6 and 12 months remember music that they've heard for at least a week, even after delays of two weeks since they've last heard it. And infants will differentiate between the accompanying responses to music, like the facial expressions of the singer, to focus on behaviors associated with the music, like clapping along, ignoring other nearby distractions. Infants will identify the relationship between sounds and their sources and rapidly develop the capacity to link musical cues with caregivers, responding and mimicking sounds from caregivers with more attention than other sounds in their environment.

Toward the end of the first year, the neural capacity for infants has developed to allow integrated sensory stimulation and processing. Infants internalize early the cultural norms of music in their lives, and at about 1 year old, prefer the tones of scales and meters reflective of their culture. Over the first 2 years, common musical qualities become familiar and known to infants and toddlers, although children remain more receptive to unfamiliar music than adults well into early childhood.

Musical Development and Auditory Discrimination

Infants in their first year are able to match the pitch and variation of sounds offered to them by caregivers, and even very young infants will coo in response to caring engagement. Children's vocal range is limited in infancy and toddler development, though. While most toddlers can sing notes within single octave, by age 6, children typically develop two full octaves of comfortable vocal range. Instruction affects this range, as children generally initiate singing at lower tones than when they are choosing a song and higher tones when they are asked to repeat a song they've learned. Throughout early childhood, children who are regularly exposed to music, and particularly those who are exposed to intentional music instruction, develop wider vocal ranges than those who are not.

Children develop increasingly complicated physical abilities to discern differences between music over the course of early childhood, a skill essential to the development of language. Infants can perceive differences in rhythm and pattern by as young as 2 months, and variations in tempo and frequency by as early as 7 months. Older infants and young toddlers will respond in an effort to keep a steady beat, although they are less likely to be able to match beats well. Toddlers are also able to recognize familiar songs and to respond to pitch concepts like "high" and "low." Indeed, being able to distinguish between timbre within music, especially during the first year of life, is an early indicator of language development, and often predicts how early children will learn to talk. Overlapping the development of language, studies reflect an expanding ability for young children to distinguish and repeat tune segments by the age of 3, expanding range and independent singing by the age of 4 and accurate pitch by the age of 5, although 5-year-olds often lack stable tonality. By the age of 6, children have internalized the rules of music sufficiently to identify when a song lacks a tonal conclusion, although the ability to sing a familiar tune may be less developed. Throughout early childhood, when children are given the opportunity to listen to music and join in when they prefer, they do so more frequently than when they receive direct instruction in phrases in a song. In other words, while it may seem simpler to present a new song to children phrase by phrase and allow them to repeat it, children adopt new music more easily and more comfortably when they hear it completely and repeatedly and can choose when to sing along.

Identifying harmony develops later in children, generally in early elementary, although children are able to recognize the contour and rhythm of music as early as 1 year and with developing complexity through age 4, around the same time that children begin to be able to reliably move their bodies on the beat. Infants' early discernment of timbre also continues to develop with more nuance, with children by the age of 6 being able to discriminate and identify changes in timbre easily, even more so than their ability to discern duration, pitch or harmony. Children in early childhood tend to refer instrumental timbre over vocal timbre, woodwinds over brass, and male voices over female voices, except in the case of popular music!

Musical Expression and Emotional Engagement

Child-initiated music making also increases in its frequency and complexity as children grow, although the rise in child-initiated music from infancy to toddler often decreases after the fourth or fifth year. Infants will initiate melodic coos and babbles, adjusting the pitch of their own voices and try-ing to match the pitch of voices of their caretakers. Toddlers will begin to repeat familiar tunes, although they will often repeatedly loop fragments of a familiar melody (much to their parents' dismay) rather than singing a song from beginning to end. Spontaneous music making, that is the fluid integration of singing and vocalizations, percussive experimentation during play and other sound play, decreases between the ages of 3 and 6, although children who are offered supportive, musically rich environ-ments in early childhood will persist in their sound play and will initiate more creative and original music than peers in less musically rich environ-ments, especially when those rich environments included opportunities for improvisation and exploration. In early childhood, children's initiated music serves multiple purposes. For toddlers, expressive music may reflect their own exploration of an environment. For older children, it may be incorporated into dramatic play or an effort to engage social experiences with other peers, or to accompany solitary play.

Throughout early childhood, children's experiences creating and responding to music reflect the rich emotional development the period. Infants and toddlers demonstrate differing emotional responses to lullabies than to playful songs, although it's unclear whether these responses reflects qualities of the music or the social cues from other caretakers and peers to differing music. Indeed, many studies support the highly individual nature of children's responses to music as early as age 3, demonstrating that when children can choose their own music, they may not make the same links between music and emotional need as caretakers may predict.

Implications for Teachers and Caregivers

The musical potential of children is universal: each child has the capacity to enjoy authentic music experiences. The development of that capacity, however, may differ based on the number and quality of music encounters children enjoy. The complex umbrella of "music" raises interesting chal-lenges for teachers and caregivers, who may not be familiar with the specific qualities of timbre, tone, harmony, pitch groupings, or vocalization. Later chapters will address practical implications for translating what a compli-cated body of research suggests about children's musical development into developmentally appropriate learning experiences. However, some general guidelines do emerge.

Ample evidence supports the importance of the first year in developing the neural pathways on which children will rely for both their music and language development in later years. Infants should hear music of differing styles, including different genres of music but also different qualities within genres. Teachers and caregivers should provide music with multiple voices: male, female, younger voices, older voices, solos, duets, and groups. Teachers and caregivers should model music-making, offering opportunities for infants to move their bodies, to play with instruments and to explore sounds in differing settings.

Toddlers' interest in timbre should lead teachers and caretakers to offer various musical instruments for exploration and choice, allowing toddlers to select the instruments they can affect independently and in open-ended exploration. Simultaneously, teachers and caregivers should take advantage of toddlers' adept receptivity to vocabulary to use the correct names of various instruments as children explore. When young children demonstrate an interest in learning to play a particular instrument, teachers and caregivers should encourage them to select an instrument based on the child's attraction to its timbre rather than other qualities.

When teaching children songs, teachers and caregivers should be attentive to the tone and pitch of the song, knowing that children's pitch varies with age and will likely be different than the most comfortable pitch for an adult. Adults should sing through a whole song multiple times, inviting children to join in when they're comfortable doing so and modeling engagement and playfulness in the process. Critically, teachers and caregivers should understand that the foundation for music literacy offered in early childhood requires multiple modalities for exposing children to that music. Developmentally appropriate musical experiences in early childhood encourage children to take some agency in their learning, giving them a rich environment to explore and multiple paths to follow. Children's experiences in and out of school, their cultural backgrounds and identities, and their individual preferences should help inform the specific lessons offered in a school or care setting. Whatever those lessons are, they should be high quality: exemplary musical sounds, instruments that are in tune and physically accessible for children, and diverse.

Just as children's development through dramatic play follows the child across multiple settings, so does children's interest in and development through music. Children should have formal areas for music making, like a music corner in a classroom or a listening and playing center. But music should also be accepted and encouraged across the child's day. Learning about music and learning through music are most effective when they involve opportunity for play, communication, imagination, enactment, and reflection. Understanding that children's development through music will be both complex and individual, learning environments should be musically diverse, offering opportunities for sophisticated musical experience and expression over simple sing-songs or worksheets. Teachers and caregivers should note when children initiate music making, as an indicator of the ways in which children make sense of their world through the songs they create and the ones that they choose to repeat. Music should be available to children that reflect multiple genres and cultures, and children's music-making should be encouraged as yet another modality through which they can question, reflect and express their understanding of the world and their potential to contribute to it.

Dance in Early Childhood Development

Dance offers a critical tool to human development, both within our own lives and across generations and cultures. It requires no language skills, evoking a fundamental understanding of body and message, inherent in children from birth and essential for self-expression. Children move from before their births and children whose ability to move is limited by context or culture experience limits to other elements of their infant development as well. Children move with a wealth of motives: to build coordination among the muscles of their body, to practice concentration, to become independent, to achieve social goals, to express complicated emotions. Not all movement is dance, but in early childhood, the relationship of move-ment, dance and development is deeply entwined.

Dance is a cultural expression, intentional coordinated efforts to convey a particular message. Just as language evolves across cultures, so does dance. Its universality as a form of communication spans cultures and ages. From folk dances to faith-based ritual dances, from pop dance to high culture, dance is an integrated reflection of development and values.

Dance, from infancy through early childhood and beyond, is an aesthetic modality, concerned with that which is beautiful and as a symbolic expres-sion of that beauty. It is both propelling to and reflective of the physical development of the dancer, with influences to the child's social, emotional and cognitive growth as well. Of the arts, dance is the most easily adaptable to open-ended creativity, allowing for social connections between peers and between learner and teachers. It allows for enacted problem solving and critical thinking and supports the development of a positive self-image and strong self-efficacy. Although children's movement is not rightly defined as "dance" until the cognitive, social, emotional and physical precursors are in place, that development occurs earlier than many caregivers or teachers may presume and, some studies suggest, is itself a precursor to the child's self-organization of the world around him. In other words, when children can dance, they can begin to make all manner of other predictions for the coordinated efforts of their bodies, and can use those bodies to make sense of their world.

Infant Development and Dance

While we may not think of teaching dance to infants, research suggests that infants are nonetheless predisposed to dance. Of the multiple qualities of music infants can discern, the beat is the most likely to evoke a response, even in the womb. Infants respond to changes in beat and are driven to try to move their bodies on a beat from as early as 5 months old. Infants will move their bodies in an effort to match the steady rhythms they hear, beginning first with the large muscles of the torso, arms and thighs, wiggling their upper bodies and flapping their arms and legs. In fact, the more infants succeed in coordinating the movement of their bodies to the beat of the music, the more positive affect they demonstrate. A beat you can dance to makes even babies smile! Infants will pay close attention to others who are dancing in their view, leaning in toward dancers and often moving along if music is audible. And while babies initiate early their own efforts to synchronize their bodies to the beat of music, they can discern dancers who are off the beat by as early as 8 months, watching off-beat dancing more intently and for longer periods of time than when they are watching dancers who stay on the beat.

Which is not to suggest that teachers or caregivers should avoid dancing with infants if they are not good dancers themselves. Infants build trusting relationships with caregivers through joyful movement together. Teachers and caregivers should dance with infants in their arms to music of all genres and dance on their own when infants can observe them and enjoy watching. Infants will attend to dancing cues they experience by dancing in the arms of a caregiver. In a caregiver's arms, infants will connect the pace and tone of the music to the emotional affect of the caregiver, developing her own association between the rhythms of diverse music and the universe emotions some rhythms convey. A gentle lullaby, then, becomes associated with the softer settling in of sleep time, while an active pop beat becomes associated with vivacious play. These early associations will persist for infants as they become toddlers.

Toddler Development and Dance

Up on their feet and ready to move, toddlers will explore how their bodies respond to music and rhythm of all kinds. The period between 1 and 3 years old is one of near perpetual motion, when children's curiosity about the world is matched by a developing ability to encounter it. Toddler coordination is limited, however, and, while toddlers will respond quickly and vibrantly to the music they hear, dance at this age is often erratic and kinetic, weaker in full-body coordination but rich in vibrant bursts of energy.

Sensorimotor experiences are keystone for the constant movement of the toddler years, and dance offers full-body sensorimotor engagement. While some toddlers develop in a deliberate and predictable sequence through walking, running, and jumping, others will walk just long enough to feel confident moving faster, and then will explore all the other directions in which their bodies can go. Because toddlers are both physically emergent in regulating their own bodies and process information more slowly than older children, toddler movement can seem untethered and frustrating for teachers and caregivers. It's important to remember that the ability to control and coordinate her own body is a developing skill for the young child. Falling down, bumping into objects and people, and misjudging the dimensions of her own body are predictable challenges to the developing toddler (and to the teachers and caregivers who support them).

Toddlers typically respond naturally and without much encouragement to music, squatting, wiggling and dancing as their own coordination allows. As a result, dance offers promising opportunities to guide toddlers in practicing the coordination of their bodies in motion. Dance at this age develops gross motor coordination, establishing pattern sense and kinesthetic memory and offering an outlet to the high activity needs of toddlers, essential as they develop their ability to self-regulate that activity. In preparing for and responding to that development, teachers and caregivers should be mindful of the short attention span of most toddlers and the notable need for structure and predictability. Toddler dance classes should be focused on simple, repetitive patterns that allow toddlers to practice moving their bodies bilaterally—tapping one foot but not the other, for example. They should provide simple instructions for actions that allow the toddler to cross her midline, reaching across her body, for example. Because toddlers' cognitive development requires ample time to process information and instructions, responsive toddler dance instruction will be equally paced and deliberate. At the same time, most toddlers embrace movement with great joy and enthusiasm and want to move their bodies in explorative, expansive ways. Dance opportunities at this age should offer structured practice in small, managed movements of the body, balanced with opportunities for open dance and improvisation.

Dance in Early Childhood Development

After the first 3 years, children typically develop the ability to move their bodies with far more coordination than when they were younger, although the need for movement remains quite high. Child-initiated dance at this age will include more intentional movements, galloping and skipping, holding weight on one foot, or mimicking dance styles they've observed in others and through media. Three- and 4-year-olds become fascinated with opposites and will practice extremes through their own bodies: moving up and down, to one side and to the other, forward and back, quickly and slowly, etc. They are beginning to move out of the heavily sensorimotor stage of toddler dance and into more intentionally representational dances, dancing "like snowflakes" or "like elephants" or using dance to express emotion and mood. At the same time, 3- and 4-year-olds become much more interested in exploring diverse roles through dramatic play. Dance at this age is likely to incorporate role-playing, with children re-creating dances they've seen in the media or exploring roles and relationships between characters in narratives and stories they enjoy. By 5 or 6, children may not be able to choreograph specific dances, but they can direct the roles for larger groups of friends to dance together. As children move out of early childhood and into the first stages of elementary development, teachers and caregivers may notice them designing more intricate and complicated dances that intentionally promote some peers or exclude others. In early childhood, however, children are often welcome to enter or withdraw from dances without any social implications.

As children move through early childhood, they also develop increasingly self-aware responses to feedback around their dance. Teachers and caregivers may notice children verbalizing observations about their own dancing or the dancing of their peers, or taking quite seriously the feedback of observers. Dancing with an audience becomes a social motivator, allowing for social interaction and cooperation among multiple bodies at once. Children learn to work with peers to coordinate movements and choreography, even in simple dances between two or three children. Thus, dance provides a concrete, body-based way for children to explore relationships with others, coordinating intents and navigating complicated roles in larger groups. Because children in early childhood learn most effectively through concrete, hands-on experiences of concepts, dance allows an opportunity for the child's body to make sense of abstract ideas like concepts of time and emotion and of awareness of others' experiences and perspectives.

Of equal importance is the influence of dance to later literacy development. In infancy and toddler years, teachers and caregivers can easily observe the connection between the child's thinking and her movement. When she wants food, she reaches for it. If she is sad, her body reflects that. In early childhood, movement continues to precede expressive language, even though the child may have established vocabulary for many of her ideas. Children can use their bodies to express complex emotions and understandings for which they do not yet have words to describe. A child who is dancing as the character in a book, for example, may represent a more complex understanding of that character's emotions and motivations then she could express with the vocabulary she's mastered.

Implications for Teachers and Caregivers

Dance development in the first 6 years of life evolves from early lessons about the coordination of bodies and beat to far more complicated social opportunities to express and explore complex symbolic representations. Teachers and caregivers should be aware of that progression, both as it relates to the types of activities they'll prepare for children along it and for the implications it has for children's ability to be successful with increasingly complicated dance expectations. Instructions or expectations in dance may seem far simpler to adults than they are to children in enacting them. Err on the side of simpler skills to master individually, and then allow children to combine them for more complex steps.

In early dance experiences, teachers and caregivers should offer energetic opportunities for full-body engagement, during which children can explore moving their bodies in new ways, test associations they have made between certain qualities of music and the emotion they are likely to convey, and develop the regulation to control their own movement. At the same time, teachers and caregivers should provide deliberate opportunities for children to practice repetitive movements with select muscle groups, supporting their development of gross and fine motor control and coordination. Offer dance opportunities that include relevant applications to expand children's vocabulary about their bodies and about the ways in which they can move. Incorporate opposites in language and movement, like pointing and flexing one's feet or opening one's arms out and in from your body. Movements that support the child in coordinating along and across his own vertical and horizontal planes, like bending, stretching, jumping with both feet, touching your fingers to your opposite toes, and the like support the establishment of neuropathways, patterns for how movements are routinized and internalized.

Because dance will express concretely children's understanding of abstract ideas, teachers and caregivers should offer opportunities for imaginative dance, exploring imagery, narrative, vocabulary, and games with simple rules. Dances may be highly imaginative enactments of stories children have read together or individualized opportunities to take on the movement of another person or animal. Social dances are particularly appealing to young children and a means through which children can be introduced to cultural norms and practices from around the world. Provide ample space for children's dance, and expect children to struggle with self-regulation as they develop the coordination and control to dance within particular spaces and to stop and start on cue.

Dance opportunities should be literacy-rich, with experiences for children both to express emotions and ideas for which they do not yet have language and to give language to emotions and ideas they already understand. Teachers and caregivers should incorporate rich descriptive language to describe and direct how children move, expanding vocabulary in immediately applicable ways. Ask children to melt their bodies like ice or to move frenetically like a water bug. Guide them in exploring heavy steps and light steps, moving rapidly and slowly, drawing their attention both to the language and to the ways in which moving bodies can be described.

In early childhood, children's ability to receive, understand, and enact complex directions is emergent and evolving. Use simple one or two step instructions in repetition until children are able to quickly match language to movement, and model movements for children.

Dance in early childhood engages the development of the whole child—physical, emotional, social, and cognitive—and is one of the few learning experiences that reliably uses the child's own body as a tool for understanding. While dance standards exist for early childhood, because dance reflects children's development across multiple domains, teachers should expect wider variability in children's dance ability than they may observe in other artistic expressions. Some children may be physically well coordinated, but have more frustration in regulating their emotional engagement in an active dance. Other children may struggle with how to appropriately engage the physical or social space of their peers, pushing past physical and social boundaries to want to dance with children who are not receptive. Language development and the pace of processing may vary for children, creating challenges for enactment of directions that may seem simple to an adult.

Finally, because dance activities involve the child's whole body and are, by design, different ways of moving and interacting than the child experiences when she is not dancing, teachers and caregivers should be especially attentive to practicing and establishing norms for starting and ending a dance and should allow extended, quiet transitions for children moving out of dance and into other learning settings. Dance asks children to develop their self-awareness and awareness of others. As such, it is also a fertile space for children to begin to compare their own performance with the performance of their peers and to be discouraged easily if differences in their development are responded to as intentional misbehaviors. Teachers and caregivers should be cautious to prepare children for success in dance by allowing them opportunities to practice the boundaries of the art form, including where they can move their bodies and with what intensity, and when they should start and stop.

Dance is both inherent and essential in human development. Our bodies move from before we are born, and over the course of our lives we refine the ability to move them in more intentional and elegant ways. Dance celebrates children's enacted understanding of their world and offers them a powerful language to express emotions and ideas beyond their verbal vocabulary. And yet, of the arts, it is often the one from which we feel the most detached and the discipline which seems most distinct from our everyday lives. As our ability to coordinate our movements evolves, so does our awareness of how that movement differs from others' and how it differs from the aesthetic we expect to represent through dance. Teachers and caregivers, then, have a special obligation in supporting children's development through dance: to protect the intrinsic motivation to move our bodies in expressive ways and to do so without hesitation how that expression may differ from others'.

Visual Art in Early Childhood Development

Early childhood is a period ripe for children's development in and through visual arts, which can support children's physical, social, cognitive and emotional development in both isolated and integrated ways. In early childhood, children are driven to understand their environments, to make sense of their experiences and to represent those experiences in new ways. Indeed, this drive is inherent in human development and universal across the evolution of society. Early humans created visual art, with some of the first examples of human's artwork dated to as early as 1.5 million years ago. Cave painting, decorated burial sites and remnants of early sketches suggest that our ancestors used visual art to enhance and manipulate their own thinking and to record their experiences for others. More contemporary research suggests that humans are still motivated by the relationship between art and thinking, and seek art experiences as a means through which they can organize and refine their own ideas. Development in visual art is the result of a vast array of human experiences, physical development, cultural influence, cognitive structuring. While the physical development we'll focus on here emphasizes the development of children's visual discrimination and fine and gross motor skills, there is debate in the field about what factors most significantly influence children's development in the visual arts, and a growing body of evidence suggesting that development continues into early adulthood.

The complexity of art has evolved with the complexity of our social structures, and evidence exists that the visual arts became far more complicated at about the same time as the advent of spoken language. The relationship between language and visual arts persists in human development today, as visual art, like other modalities, can convey more complicated ideas than verbal or written language alone. In contemporary development, our spatial sense allows for all manner of large scale of engagements, from being able to capably drive a car to understanding how far to hit a golf ball to reach the green. Human development in the visual arts includes our ability to discern and represent relationships in space, to interpret and reflect abstract understandings of concepts and ideas and to manage the physical tools and media to communicate our intended messages.

Visual Art and Infant Development

Early infancy includes critical periods for the development of visual discernment. Before children intentionally move their hands, they explore their world by looking carefully at it, with precision that becomes more refined over time. At birth, babies' vision is erratic and unfocused. They are unable to discern between two objects or to coordinate the movement of both eyes simultaneously. Until about 3 months, infants can only focus on objects about 8–10 inches from their faces.

In the first month, infants' eyes begin working in tandem and they are rapidly able to see far more than they could in the first few days after birth. Within that same time, children demonstrate early eye-hand coordination, tracking movement with their eyes and initiating early efforts to reach. However, they still lack the muscle development to be able to coordinate those efforts effectively. Indeed, in the first 2 months, even the small muscles that control the movement of the eyes are unreliable, and many infants experience their eyes crossing or wandering. By roughly the third month after birth, infants typically can follow moving objects with their eyes, reach for them with their hands and discern edges, contrasts and lines of different objects.

Infants' visual discrimination continues to improve over the next few months, and by the fifth month most infants are reliably coordinating the movement of their eyes. This is a necessary developmental precursor to depth perception, the ability to discern whether objects are nearer or father from the eye, and to perceive a three dimensional view of the world. Around this same time, infants develop more nuanced color vision. The physical development that leads to infants crawling, typically at around 8 months, supports children's eye-hand-foot coordination, a skill that is sometimes lacking in early walkers.

By 10 months, children are able to discern distance, reach for and grasp objects. By the end of the first year, their experiences in pulling themselves up and trying to walk will support the development of their distance perception.

In this first year, many teachers and caregivers overlook children's need for visual art. Visual art experiences in infancy can support children's development. Infants are interested in grasping, mouthing, pounding and smashing objects, learning more about the qualities of their environment and the objects within it. This is a ripe time for sensory experiences that support the visual arts, including water play, texture and dough.

Toddler Development and the Visual Arts

Between 1 and 2 years, children's visual discrimination evolves, with children discerning more nuanced differences in distance and color. By 2 years of age, children's eye-hand coordination and their depth perception should be fully refined. Children will reach to grasp wide crayons or markers and use them to draw wide, circular lines on whatever surfaces may be available. The stage between 18 months and 3 years old is called the "scribbling stage," and provides the foundational experiences for later development in the visual arts.

At first, scribbles are erratic and uncontrolled, the result of a physical impulse rather than a cognitive intent. Young toddlers lack the ability to control their elbows or wrists. The first scribbles occur as a result of children's shoulder movements and young toddlers rarely associate their movements as creating the lines on the page. With short attention spans and a limited ability to link cause and effect, young toddlers may only scribble for a minute or two before losing interest and moving on.

Through scribbling, children refine their eye-hand coordination, build fine and gross motor control in their arms, hands, and fingers and learn to manipulate their hands with intent. They may name objects in their scribbles, reflecting a developing cognitive link between symbol and object. By scribbling, children create visual products through which to engage other adults and children in conversation. They develop the ability to hold and manage a stylus. They learn to increase or decrease pressure to create particular strokes and they build fine muscle control in their hands and dexterity in their fingers.

Scribbling supports toddler's emotional development by allowing them agency to create images independently. As their physical coordination allows them to scribble more intentionally and their social development incorporates the products of that scribbling in engaging parents and peers in social experiences, scribbling becomes self-reinforcing. The more children scribble, the more they want to scribble. The more children scribble, the more skillful they become in the nature of that scribbling. The more skilled, the better the conversations they can inspire, supporting their social development, the more opportunities for symbolic representation, supporting their cognitive development, the more refined their gross and fine motor control, supporting their physical development and the more positive reinforcement they receive from teachers and caregivers, supporting their emotional development. Scribbling, then, is evidence of an important, if often oversimplified, progression of toddler development.

Early Childhood Development and the Visual Arts

Older toddlers typically move through the scribbling stage to the pre-schematic stage, when drawings become more complex, if no less realistic. Children generally will remain in this stage of development through age 4. A key indicator of this transition is in children's desire to name and label their drawings, even when the objects they are naming are not clear to other observers. Children in this stage of development will prefer particular colors rather than colors accurate to the subject of their drawings, creating a picture, for example, that includes images of parents, pets, and trees using only blue and purple markers.

When children try to draw specific objects in this stage, they do so in simple ways with few details. Initially, people may look like sunbursts, composed of a large circular center with four lines to represent arms and legs. In time, children begin to represent people as "tadpole figures," composed of a large circular head, a small body and arms that extend straight from the body. Interiors and exteriors of objects and people are illustrated at the same time, so an image of a cat in a box may show the cat surrounded by the walls of the box, but will not hide the cat within the image. When humans are drawn in this stage, they are not grounded to a horizon line, but seem to float across the page.

These repeated shapes become increasingly detailed and refined, and children's attention span increases with their absorption in drawing. By age 3, children can generally attend to a single piece of art of up to 15 minutes. They understand that drawings are representational. They develop their ability to observe, to make choices about how to represent what they've observed, to solve problems resulting from the limits of the media, and to feel increased agency.

Older 4-year-olds and younger 5-year-olds typically demonstrate evidence of the beginning of the schematic stage of development, when children's visual art increases in its complexity and detail. Drawings of people become increasingly distinct. Children may draw multiple details of the face and body, for example, instead of only eyes and a mouth. They will place features of the body in their accurate location and include groundlings of the horizon and skyline, with the feet of their subjects touching the ground. At the same time, children will express particular drawn schema for repeated objects. A dog, for example, will be drawn in the same way across multiple drawings. Colors become more realistic, if stereotypically reflecting common understandings rather than specific subjects. A tree, for example, will look like any other tree, composed of a brown trunk and green leaves. The sun will be a shade of yellow. The sky will be blue.

In the schematic stage, children will imagine narratives to accompany their drawings and are able to describe the activity captured in one of their drawings to adults or peers. Children exploring the visual arts will develop skills in persistence as they work through representational challenges, in patterns and number and in articulating their own interpretation of their art. They'll be drawn to patterns and shapes and will begin to include labels of their drawings.

Implications for Teachers and Caregivers

Children in early childhood are active learners, demanding physical movement, concrete manipulative and extended time with concepts to repeat and explore their qualities. Children are also typically social, with complex, if sometimes unspoken, narratives defining their activities and motivated by an intrinsic desire to understand the world and their place within it. Art experiences should offer children in early childhood a means through which they can make more complex and more explicit their conceptions of the world.

Children from 0–6 learn best when learning is modeled for them, and when lessons include opportunities for open ended practice. As in the other arts, children need structured, predictable experiences and exploratory self-initiated expression. Teachers and caregivers should remember that children from 0-6 are largely concerned with the process of art exploration and will show less connection or importance with the products of that exploration. It's common for children to be unable to identify their own artwork in early childhood or to leave it behind without concern when they're done creating it.

For younger children, artistic experiences will be largely focused on the child's gross motor skills, as the fine motor skills necessary to control a pencil or paintbrush have not yet developed. Experiences that allow for large, fluid motions controlled by the shoulders and torso are more manageable than experiences that require the refinement of the small muscles of the hand and fingers, although children will be interested in holding crayons and markers as they mimic the kinds of creative expression they see in adults. Art materials should be diverse and should allow for equally diverse interactions: paint with a variety of tools or body parts to manipulate it, clay, blocks, crayons of varying widths and dimensions, knob-handled brushes and markers, and the like. Art-making in early childhood emphasizes the experience and experimentation of media more than the effort to represent a particular subject.

Teachers and caregivers can support children's exploration in visual arts by balancing open-ended exploration within the safe parameters of a structured and predictable environment. Offer a prepared space for art exploration, with reliable and well-maintained materials. Keep the art supplies well stocked and tidy, removing paints and markers that are dried or other materials that have been damaged or misused. Because children are just beginning their explorations with art, they may lack the persistence to struggle past poorly maintained materials and media and may confuse the weaknesses in the materials for their own capacity for creativity. As in other areas of the arts, prepare children to transition into art experiences through predictable routines, putting on a smock, placing a mat down on the table, etc., and prepare them to transition back to less messy activities by setting predictable times for exploration and returning the materials to their tidy conditions before moving on.

Materials and media should be developmentally appropriate for children lacking fine motor control. Look for knob-headed crayons or paint brushes for toddlers, allowing them to hold the tool with the palms of their hands rather than their fingers. Offer blocks of different sizes and weights. Include paints that can be manipulated with their hands or large brushes, and paper sizes that allow for the full spread of a child's arm span.

Once children have access to the materials, however, let their explorations be open-ended. Model how to use the tools available, but avoid modeling particular products for children to create. Rather than matching their design to a predetermined model, by placing precut pieces on a paper snowman, for example, allow children to explore materials with their own inquiry. Teachers and caregivers might pose interesting questions or ask children to talk or think about their art explicitly, but they should avoid dictating what that art should look like. Let art experiences be an opportunity to tune in to children's natural curiosity and to support their ideas and questions about new experiences.

Take care not to appropriate intent to young children's art experiences. Art at this age is most often a physical experience and not an expression of intended subjects. Rather than asking a child, "Oh! What have you drawn?" ask open-ended questions that allow the child to describe his process. "Tell me about playing with the dough," or "Can you tell me how it feels to paint with the large brushes?" Teachers and caregivers should avoid prescribing intent to the product of children's artwork, when children are mostly concerned with the process. It is part of the nature of the adult to see patterns in the environment, and to ascribe symbolic connections to color, placement and spatial relationships. Children have not yet developed that perspective, however, and may be confused by questions about their artwork or specific instructions about what to draw.

Finally, teachers and caregivers should model engagement and meaning making through the visual arts by allowing time and conversation with children about art they view together. With infants, allow infants to pay attention to the objects that draw their gaze, and wait patiently until they look away before moving on to new subjects. As children become more mobile and their receptive language increases, take them to see art in public spaces. If visiting a gallery, you may want to be prepared to view a single room or a small area of the larger space, allowing for children's short attention spans and for the time it will take for children to process the new things they see. Select art books that are designed for children and represent common themes from their own lives: food, family, home, and other children. Engage children in age-appropriate conversations about what they see in the art they view and how it is similar or different from their own experiences. Remembering children's propensity for narrative, imagine together what might be happening in a work of art, allowing the child to attend to the aesthetic and to make sense of it through conversation with trusted caregivers.

Weaving It All Together

Children's development through and in the arts is a fluid, individualized experience, predictable through particular common sequences, but varied in pace and trajectory to each child. Teachers and caregivers should attend to the sense-making of art experiences for children at this age, and take particular note to the common disparities between children's cognitive, social and emotional development and their ability to enact those understandings with limited physical development. Children will express their understanding of the world when they have means available to them: visual art media, musical instruments, costumes, and props. But they will use whatever means they have, including their own bodies and voices, even when other materials are available.

Children's development is best matched by striking a developmentally appropriate balance between predictable, structured experiences that support children's comfort and security with open ended, creative opportunities for imaginative play. In each area of the arts, children need models of initiation, engagement and resolution. Teachers and caretakers should act as responsive models for children and curious observers to engage children's thinking and communication about their experiences.

Most importantly, while we consider the areas in specific modalities (theatre, dance, visual art, and music) and aligned with specific domains of development (physical, social, emotional, and cognitive), children's experience and expression in and through the arts is fluid. Each modality and each domain will influence the other, and the most developmentally appropriate response is the one that allows for that influence in structured, supportive ways that encourage thoughtful and individual meaning-making in each child.

Discuss

What are your earliest memories of your own art experiences as a child? Were they supportive or discouraging?

Discuss the ways in which expression through the arts was a part of your own school experience. Were the arts integrated into your regular classroom settings or set aside for special times of the day or within special spaces in your school? How did your own art education reflect what we know about developmentally appropriate art experiences?

Most children experience a time in their development when they become increasingly aware of the art acumen of their peers. Was there a time when your art experiences taught you that you were either "good at" or "not good at" art? How do those experiences influence your receptivity to the arts as an adult?

Do you see artistic creation as a valuable part of your life as an adult? What are the ways in which you embrace or avoid the arts?

Collaborate

With a partner or colleague, identify a children's book you would use in your classroom. Discuss the ways in which you could use the book as a prompt for children's dramatic play.

Share a favorite song with a colleague. What do you know about children's development that supports you in selecting this song to share with children? Consider the themes, musical accessibility and range in selecting your song.

Identify two common children's dances, like the "Hokey Pokey" or "Head, Shoulders, Knees and Toes." With a partner, describe in what ways the physical, emotional, social and cognitive development of a child may be strengthened by dancing this dance. Describe what physical, emotional, social and cognitive benchmarks the child would have to have meet in order to dance each dance successfully.

Create

Prepare a timeline demonstrating observable benchmarks in children's physical, emotional, cognitive and social development in the first 6 years and the ways in which that development would influence children's artistic experiences.

Consider the age of the child you anticipate teaching. Design a graphic you could display in your classroom to emphasize overarching goals for artistic experiences for children in your care.

Imagine you are leading a parent education program to help parents understand and support children's artistic experiences from infancy through early childhood. Prepare a visually engaging handout that includes the key concepts you hope they'll take away from your program.

For Further Reading

Abrams, R. M., Griffiths, S. K., Huang, X., Sain, J., Langford, G., & Gerhardt, K. J. (1998). Fetal music perception: The role of sound transmission. *Music Perception* 15(3), 307–317.

Berger, A. A., & Cooper, S. (2003). Musical play: A case study of preschool children and parents. *Journal of Research in Music Education* 51(2), 151–165.

Berke, M., & Colwell, C. M. (2004). Integration of music in the elementary curriculum: Perceptions of preservice elementary education majors. *Journal of Research in Music Education*, 23(1), 22–33.

Bodrova, E., & Leong, D. J. (2005). Self-regulation: A foundation for early learning. *Principal*, 85(1), 30–35.

Bond, K., & Stinson, S. W. (2007). 'It's work, work, work, work': Young people's experiences of effort and engagement in dance. *Research in Dance Education*, 8(2), 155–183.

Bowman, B. T., & Stott, F. (1994). Understanding development in a cultural context: The challenge for teachers. In B. Mallary & R. New (Eds.), *Diversity and developmentally appropriate practices: Challenges for early childhood education* (pp. 119–34). New York, NY: Teachers College Press.

Bucek, L. E. (1992). Constructing a child-centered dance curriculum. *Journal of Physical Education, Recreation & Dance*, 63(9), 39–42, 48.

Boyce-Tillman, J. (2004). Towards an ecology of music education. *Philosophy of Music Education Review*, 12(2), 102–112.

Bresler, L. (Ed.). (2004). *knowing bodies, moving minds: Towards embodied teaching and learning*. Norwell, MA: Kluwer.

Catterall, J., Chapleau, R, & Iwanaga, J. (1999). *Involvement in the arts and human development: General involvement and intensive involvement in music and theatre arts.* Los Angeles, CA: The Imagination Project.

Drewe, S. B. (1996). *Creative dance: Enriching understanding.* Calgary, AB, Canada: Detselig Enterprises Ltd.

Edwards, L., Bayless, K., & Ramsey, M. (2009). *Music and movement: A way of life for the young child* (6th ed.). Upper Saddle River, NJ: Merrill.

Eisner, E. W. (2002). What can education learn from the arts about the practice of education? In The Encyclopaedia of Informal Education. Retrieved from http://www.infed.org/biblio/eisner_arts_and_the_practice_of_education.htm

Fauconnier, G., & Turner, M. (2002). *The way we think: Conceptual blending and the mind's hidden complexities.* New York, NY: Basic Books.

Flowers, P. J. (1984). Attention to elements of music and effect of instruction in vocabulary on written descriptions of music by children and undergraduates. *Psychology of Music, 12*(1), 17–24. doi:10.1177/0305735684121002

Gault, B. (2002). Effects of pedagogical approach, presence/absence of text, and developmental music aptitude on the song performance accuracy of kindergarten and first-grade students. *Bulletin of the Council for Research in Music Education, 152,* 54–63.

Gonzalez-Mena, J. (2008). *Foundations of early childhood education: Teaching children in a diverse society* (4th ed.). New York: McGraw-Hill.

Heidemann, S., & Hewitt., D. (2010). *Play: The pathway from theory to practice* (2nd ed.). St. Paul, MN: Redleaf Press.

Humpal, M., & Wolf, J. (2003). Music in the inclusive environment. *Young Children, 58*(2), 103–107.

Isenberg, J., & Jalongo, M. R. (2001). *Creative expression and play in early childhood* (3rd ed.). Upper Saddle River, NJ: Merrill Prentice Hall.

Izumi-Taylor, S., & Morris, V. G. (2007). Active play and cooking activities for toddlers. *PlayRights, 29*(3), 7–10.

Kieff, J., & Casbergue, R. (2000). *Playful learning and teaching: Integrating play into preschool and primary programs.* Needham Heights, MA: Allyn & Bacon.

Kail, R. V. (2004). *Children and their development* (3rd ed.). Upper Saddle River, NJ: Prentice Hall.

Klinger, R., Campbell, P. S., & Goolsby, T. (1998). Approaches to children's song acquisition: Immersion and phrase-by-phrase. *Journal of Research in Music Education, 46,* 24–34.

National Dance Education Organization (NDEO). (2005). *Professional teaching standards for dance in the arts.* Bethesda, MD: National Dance Education Organization.

New Zealand Ministry of Education. (2010). The arts Nga Toi. As cited in V. G. Paley (1988). *Bad guys don't have birthdays: Fantasy play at four* (p. vii). Chicago: The University of Chicago Press.

Phillips, K .H., & Aitchison, R. E. (1998). The effects of psychomotor skills instruction on attitude toward singing and general music among students in grades 4–6. *Bulletin of the Council for Research in Music Education, 137,* 32–42.

Power, A. (2008). What motivates and engages boys in music education? *Bulletin of the Council for Research in Music Education, 175,* 85–102.

Ringgenberg, S. (2003). Music as a teaching tool: Creating story songs. *Young Children, 58*(5), 76–79.

Rogers, C. S., & Taylor, S. I. (1999). School play: Education for life. *Kindergarten Education: Theory, Research, and Practice, 4*(1), 1–19.

Santa, A. (2009). Playground as classroom. *Early Childhood Education, 33,* 154–155.

Chapter 2

Integrating the Arts in Early Childhood

"The arts have been an inseparable part of the human journey; indeed, we depend on the arts to carry us toward the fullness of our humanity. We value them for themselves, and because we do, we believe knowing and practicing them is fundamental to the healthy development of our children's minds and spirits. That is why, in any civilization—ours included—the arts are inseparable from the very meaning of the term "education." We know from long experience that no one can claim to be truly educated who lacks basic knowledge and skills in the arts."

—National Core Arts Standards, 2016

Art Integration in a Historical Context: Dewey Lost

Both the content and the scope of art education have evolved over generations, influenced by the values of the society it informs and the prominent curricular trends in education. Schools reflect the cultures they serve, and, in turn, help to influence the values of those cultures, sometimes by perpetuating them and sometimes by being the places in which social change takes root. Since the beginning of the twentieth century, when the foundations of widespread, compulsive public education were laid, the role of the arts in education has been a subject for debate. Two paths were proposed as formal, public education became the norm at the beginning of the twentieth century and despite the research to support the integration of the arts as a means toward more potent educational outcomes, the struggle for time and attention between the arts and other content for school-age children persists.

In the early days of industrialization in the United States, Edward Thorndike, a behaviorist and advocate for a scientific foundation to educational psychology, translated the applications he'd developed in industrial settings to theories of learning. His theories of social intelligence influenced early teacher educators and the organization of schools, especially the idea that learning is incremental, automatic, and identical between learners. Thorndike's influence can still be felt in the hierarchy of schools, in the segmentation of content areas and in the cataloguing of learners by grades. Although Thorndike was fascinated by individual differences, he focused his research and the implications that grew from that research on using scientifically based educational practices to diminish the impact of those differences on learning and to increase the efficiency of schools as conductors of knowledge.

Around the same time, John Dewey and his contemporaries in progressive education proposed models that emphasized the interdependence of knowledge, including an equal investment in the arts as a connector in learning. John Dewey and others argued that the experience of the learner, including the aesthetic experience, should be the basis around which other learning circled, supported by the integration of curricular content across multiple relevant experiences rather than the compartmentalization of content within stand-alone classes. As Ellen Lagemann, former dean of the Harvard Graduate School of Education and former president of the Spencer Foundation, observed in 2005, "I have long believed, as I have argued in print, that one cannot understand American education unless one realizes that Edward L. Thorndike won, and John Dewey lost."

Economic Engine of Schools and Its Influence on Art Integration

The ties between schooling and economics have driven this debate over much of the twentieth century, and were in force even in those early days of compulsory education when the pressures of industrialization helped to shape many of the school structures we still observe today. When the strength of our national economy is high, the arts are generally embraced more enthusiastically in school settings. When our national or international competitiveness wanes, the arts are often the first to follow. Although progressive educational philosophies still influence many of the *practices* of pedagogy, by the 1930s, the ideals of the progressive theorists had largely diffused, and the *structures* of an industry-based model were pervasive in public education.

By the 1950s, and despite the adoption of many elements of progressive education throughout the public school system, increasing demands to increase the competitiveness of public schools squelched the arts. Rudolph Flesch's damning 1955 publication, *Why Johnny Can't Read*, condemned the practice of context-based reading and integrated curricula. The 1957 Russian launch of Sputnik in the midst of the Cold War heightened fears that U.S. schools may be falling behind, and education reformists turned their sights on the arts as they sought to increase achievement particularly in math and science. Johnson's Great Society policies, including the Elementary and Secondary Education Act of 1965, added to the debate by increasing demands for reporting and assessment in public schools. The economic crises of the 1970s and the 1983 publication of *A Nation at Risk* marginalized the arts further, challenging arts educators to choose between abandoning the arts in schools, fighting for the arts as their own discipline separate but equal to other content, or developing models in which the arts could be integrated as a support for learning across content areas.

Countertheories

To the benefit of art integration, theorists emerged in the second half of the twentieth century who challenged more limited views of student learning and argued, instead, for more expansive and inclusive frameworks for how people learn, emphasizing art as a necessary conduit for learning. Harry Broudy contested the traditional focus of schools on the acquisition of facts. Broudy theorized that the development of the imagination trumped the retention of facts, and the evolution of imagination as a reflection of our cultural knowledge and history. Thus, the work of schools should be to support learners' ability to engage that cultural knowledge, as it is expressed through learners' understanding of the aesthetic that reflects it, toward the development of their imagination. Broudy advocated for education that increased a diversity of thought and proposed art education which focuses on aesthetic education, evoking in the learner the ability to evaluate and critique art and design across multiple cultural domains, including architecture, fashion, nature, and others. Likewise, Elliot Eisner's work emphasized sensorial education to interweave learners' emotional and intellectual development, integrating the arts as another method of meaning-making and another expression of that meaning. Both argued for the arts as equally influential to learners' ability to acquire, internalize and represent new knowledge, rather than a purely symbolic expression of content learned in more limited instruction. These theorists continue to influence models of integration in school-age settings as a counterpoint to academic expectations.

Arts as a Plus-One

Art integration advocates in the early 1990s responded to increasing efforts for standardization and testing in schools, although the emphasis shifted from aesthetic education and the development of the imagination to arguments that integration was a means through which other content could be better learned. Policy pieces spread which described the ways in which art education supported increased academic outcomes on standardized measures, defending the integration of the arts as supplemental supports to high-stakes contexts. Unlike Eisner's emphasis on the interplay of intellect and affect, policy advocates emphasized the ways in which art integration fostered higher academic outcomes. Quantitative research promoted content learning through the arts and qualitative research spotlighted traditional content teachers who successfully integrated art methods in order to foster achievement in literacy, math, social studies and science. Although art education is identified today as a core standard for public education, it is less often funded or assessed in ways that would protect it from the chopping block when districts or schools are refining budgets. More often, the arts are scheduled as "enrichment" programs, above and beyond "real school" and, thus, at risk when teachers are pressured to meet the standards that matter more.

It is important to note that, while Thorndike may have ruled the day in school-age settings, Dewey's perspective is still in prevalence in preschool development. In early childhood, our culture generally prioritizes the arts, offering rich art experiences in preschool classrooms. Most suburban and city communities offer ample resources for parents and families to engage in the arts, ranging from simple parent-child art programs for infants, toddlers and preschoolers to family events at the ballet and symphony. Art experiences are emphasized in the National Association for the Education of Young Children's *Guidelines for Developmentally Appropriate Practice*.

Early childhood advocates caution that the arts are too limited to preschool settings. While these practices may be in abundance in early childhood, as children move into school-age classrooms, they are less likely to enjoy an equal presence between the arts and other content. As NAEYC cautioned, "Standards overload is overwhelming to teachers and children alike and can lead to potentially problematic teaching practices. At the preschool and K–3 levels particularly, practices of concern include excessive lecturing to the whole group, fragmented teaching of discrete objectives, and insistence that teachers follow rigid, tightly paced schedules. There is also concern that schools are curtailing valuable experiences such as problem solving, rich play, collaboration with peers, opportunities for emotional and social development, outdoor/physical activity, and the arts. In the high-pressure classroom, children are less likely to develop a love of learning and a sense of their own competence and ability to make choices, and they miss much of the joy and expansive learning of childhood."

Why It Matters

The benefits across the lives of learners from experiences in the arts are well-documented. Learning in the arts supports both the constructs and the content of learning, especially for young children, children from economically disadvantaged backgrounds, and students in need of remedial instruction. Students who are regularly engaged in the arts outperform their peers across multiple measures, with sustained experiences in theatre and music correlated to higher achievement in math and reading. Students from the lowest economic backgrounds experience the highest benefits.

The Dana Consortium research suggests that learning *through the arts* is linked to cognitive development, including thinking, conceptual understanding, content processing, critical problem solving, and overall intelligence. It makes particular note of the development of attention skills and memory for children involved in the arts. The mental structures for children learning through the arts are noticeable in other areas as well. Hetland and Winner suggest that the links between art experiences and improved SAT scores may be a reflection of the mental habits developed through the art experiences.

Art-developed skills, like persistence, identifying relevance, observation skills, imagination skills, and innovative curiosity may generalize to other learning, making it easier for learners to excel in areas outside of the arts as a result of their experiences within the arts. Even as teachers identify more challenges to integrating the arts within the standards expectations of their classrooms, research expounds on the benefits of doing just that. Indeed, the College Board's research into the connections between the Common

Core Standards and the National Core Arts Standards finds that aligning arts education can be accomplished best without detracting from the art standards, but by using them as a "common language" through which art experts and traditional classroom teachers can collaborate.

Finding the Balance

Over time, the arts are increasingly marginalized, moved out of the work of "real school" and placed at the end of the day, or right before lunch, or at the end of the week when more highly prioritized goals have been accomplished. Art education is often the first to be cut from struggling school budgets, especially in theatre and dance, or protected only when it complements other social connectors, like schools that maintain their music budgets because they rely on the band for sporting events. Lagemann notes, "high attention to the economic purposes of schooling has tended to eclipse consideration of other priorities, including the seemingly simple act of helping children create and find meaning through drama, music, painting, sculpture and play" (1994). This doesn't have to be the case, though. Teaching creativity develops critical thinking skills, supports innovation and curiosity and engages students, all skills necessary to contribute well to today's economy. In a survey of college-educated, full time employees, over 80% agreed that creating thinking was necessary for success in their careers, and over 70% supported teaching it as its own discipline.

The challenge to determine how and when to integrate the arts, even in schools that value arts in children's development, falls often to teachers. Art integration, then, looks different between schools and between classrooms, usually added above the standards that have come to dominate the functions of schools and, less often, incorporated as meaningful ways through which those standards may be met.

Bresler's Models of Art Integration

Rather than viewing the arts and thoughtfully crafted art education experiences as supplementary to the real work of schools, research suggests that the integration of the arts can provide a powerful catalyst to learning, supporting deep understanding of the traditional academic content and propelling students and schools to better meet content standards in literacy, math, science and social studies. While there are wide ranging models for art integration, and, indeed, little consensus even among art educators of what integration might look like, at its basis, art integration includes the incorporation of visual art, music, theatre and dance within the body of content across literacy, science, math, and social studies. As social norms and workplace demands move away from the specialization and compartmentalization of knowledge, teacher educators are increasingly interested in curriculum integration, the practice of interweaving knowledge across content arts to provide relevant, learning experiences which leverage the content of multiple fields to increase the outcomes for them all. Art integration is not adding on extra art-ish activities to the end of other units. It is the full engagement of the arts as a means through which knowledge is deepened and a language through which it is expressed.

Most art integration programs fall into one of four models: *coequal cognitive integration, social integration, affective integration,* and *subservient integration* (Bresler, 1995). These often emerge in school settings as an effect of the initiative, values, and creativity of the teachers involved, and suffer for a lack of national requirements, resources, or means of measurement. Because they tend to be hyperlocalized, dependent upon individual schools and practitioners to develop and design, each mode of integration has its own values and objectives, as well as its own pedagogical methods.

Ms. Shepherd: A Mini Case Study

Dana Shepherd is a third-grade classroom teacher in a suburban school district. Her classroom serves 22 children, including 2 children who are learning English as a second language. Ms. Shepherd is the primary content teacher for literacy, math, social studies, and science, although her school community includes specialists in music, visual arts and physical education. When asked to articulate the role of art in her classroom, Ms. Shepherd reports

It's a challenge, right? Because sometimes you have to really think outside of the prepared materials to make those links and it takes a lot of time. But I couldn't imagine learning without art. It just opens up so many more ways for my kids to get engaged, to show me what they know and, frankly, often it's easier for me to see what kinds of missteps they're making when they have to create something on their own.

In high school and college, Ms. Shepherd trained as a dancer and taught children's dance classes on the weekends. She still takes classes designed for adults with a local dance school and loves attending her own students' recitals when she's invited. "Dance was always an outlet for me," she says.

It was where I went to breathe, to move my body, and to get away from the stress of the day. It was hard, but it was the kind of hard you don't notice because you're too busy doing it. I want my kids to love dance that same way … it's hard, but it's fun, too.

Ms. Shepherd's classroom is bright and airy, with one wall of windows with a low set of shelves underneath, two walls of whiteboards, and an area for student cubbies at the back of the room. She has spread her students' desks around the perimeter of the room, in a large rectangle with each desk oriented toward the center. "We move the desks sometimes to make small clusters, but I really want there to be space for the kids to demonstrate things to each other when everyone can see, and I want enough space for us to move together sometimes, too." Around the top of the walls is an evolving timeline of the 20th century, created from sheets of paper with colorful illustrations the children have designed. Each page represents two years. As the students learn about segments of U.S. history in the twentieth century, they design and add new sheets to the timeline. "I wanted the timeline to grow over the course of the year," Ms. Shepherd describes.

I think it's hard for kids to understand the concept of time, but if we can visualize it this way, it's a little easier to see how what we're learning works together. We started by inviting one of our parents in. She's a graphic designer and she creates fonts. We learned about how different kinds of lines can create different feelings in viewers. So, for every time period the students illustrate, they have to design a font to match it. We discuss the different designs and the students have to argue for which they think is a better match for the time period. Then, once we've chosen, they can add it to any written parts of their illustration.

Today, the students are practicing the Lindy in the gym with their physical education teacher. "He's been amazing about working with me on the social studies links," Ms. Shepherd describes. "I teach him the dances, then he figures out what to add or take away to match his standards. Our final dances aren't *exactly* what they might have been when they were originally popular, but the kids definitely get to see how dance has changed over the years. And some of their variations are fantastic!" The students' experiences in PE are reflected in their timeline."

The timeline is part record, and part evaluation. They have to decide what's most important in a particular window to include on that limited space. Sometimes it ends up being something really personal to them, like including the publication date for *Winnie the Pooh*. Sometimes it's something from government, like here where they've included the start of

World War I. But then, they were also really interested to realize that the "Star-Spangled Banner" wasn't adopted as the national anthem until the 1930s. They thought that was much earlier. We've been working on it since the year began, but we'll still have a couple of years left by the time the school year ends. We really use the timeline as the connector for all this other content.

Ms. Shepherd's class routine includes a large block of time after the children arrive for "scholarship," followed by lunch and then special classes in the afternoon. Children return to the classroom with about 50 minutes before dismissal for what's marked on the schedule as "Inquiries and Reflections." "That's when we wrap up whatever we've done before lunch, and think about what kinds of questions we want to tackle the next day. It's our big questions part of the day." When asked about the irregular schedule, and its lack of segments for traditional content, Ms. Shepherd explains

It took a little leap of faith with my principal, but I really wanted to see how we would do if I could think of the day as a big block of time rather than lots of little classes. We get encouraged to try all these inter-disciplinary projects, but you really can't do it if you're trying to squeeze them in these little windows. She checks in on me a lot, and every so often my students will take one of the assessments from the other third-grade classrooms so we can both make sure we're not too far off. Our district doesn't have to do the [standardized test] until fourth grade. I don't know if I'd have this much flexibility if it was a testing year.

Instead, Ms. Shepherd shifts her content focus throughout the work periods, with students moving from large group activities to content stations in the corners of the room with some individualized work at their desks. Students have personalized task lists to direct them when Ms. Shepherd is working with small groups. "It's a little harder to make the third-grade math relevant, you know, because it's a lot of skill stuff, but even there I can get a lot done with smaller groups of kids throughout the morning. And when we're in the middle of some bigger, long-term projects, it's kind of nice to have a little break to do something quieter or shorter."

Coequal Cognitive Integration

Ms. Shepherd's classroom is an example of what Bresler terms, *coequal cognitive integration*. Coequal cognitive integration finds the most support in the research, although it may be the hardest to find in practice. Coequal cognitive integration acknowledges the arts as equal to other content, and it is unique from other modes of integration by its equitable inclusion of both art-specific skills and content and art-driven modes of thinking. This model is the least common and the most difficult to implement, requiring both a rethinking of the relationship of content across disciplinary lines and an expertise in the arts in the teacher enacting the model. Ms. Shepherd's own expertise in dance, for example, allows her to bring that expertise to other content, even when some areas still require collaboration with other teachers. She enjoys the collaboration of other professionals, and the professional investment of a principal who has agreed to support an experimental model within certain parameters to maintain school norms. Ms. Shepherd is able to adjust school routines of time and the segmentation of content, both within the school day and across longer units of time. In this classroom, the arts are equal to other content and are used as a conduit for students to discover new knowledge, to demonstrate that understanding, and for the teacher to assess student learning.

In seeking out models, Bresler describes a highly effective social studies teacher who was able to incorporate lessons about composers and their musical styles within a historical context, such that the music and social studies content were fused as a part of higher-order-thinking-focused, aesthetically crafted teaching. In another example, she details the collaboration of teachers across disciplines to create an extended unit that integrated literature, music, visual arts and dance. In both instances, teachers relied on either their own personal expertise or the artistic expertise of colleagues. They had extended time to create relevant, rigorous lessons. Most importantly, they had the professional capacity to design opportunities for students to observe, interpret, and design their own representations of knowledge and to promote higher-order thinking through analysis, synthesis, and critique. While this model requires fairly common materials and supplies, it demands disciplinary expertise in the arts, advanced pedagogical competencies from the classroom teachers, and the institutional flexibility to adjust school norms to allow for extended time and more authentic interweaving of content standards.

Mr. Rickman: A Mini Case Study

Mr. Rickman is in his fourth year as a kindergarten teacher at an urban K–4 elementary school. His classroom serves eighteen children and is supported by a paraprofessional, Ms. Kinsey. About half of his children live in a nearby public housing complex. The other half live in the adjacent neighborhood, a mix of working class and middle-class families. All of Mr.

Rickman's students are native English speakers. Student skills are diverse and reflect the wide range of development visible in five- and six-year-olds. His classroom is in a new building comprised of an open-air covered walk connecting spacious classrooms with floor-to-ceiling windows. Mr. Rickman's class is at the end of the building and includes two walls of windows. The third wall of the room is covered in colorful posters labeled with words from the kindergarten word list. The fourth wall includes a built-in desk for Mr. Rickman, the door to an adjacent cubby room and another door to a bathroom Mr. Rickman's students share with the class next door.

The classroom has three large tables each seating six children. The children's chairs have soft cotton covers on the seat backs that include pockets for writing materials and notebooks and tennis balls on the feet of each chair to diminish noise. A large community carpet is in the center of the room, with spaces for each child to sit delineated by blocks of different colors, numbers and letters. Mr. Rickman has an easel nearby to the group carpet, on which he hangs the calendar and can do daily lessons. Classroom shelves are filled with boxes of small plastic blocks and other counting items, early reader books and writing materials. Mr. Rickman keeps an in-box on his desk for students to deliver their finished worksheets after each activity. Mr. Rickman is well-regarded in his school for the happy tone of his classroom.

Each morning begins with Mr. Rickman at the door to his classroom, ready to welcome students as they arrive. He greets each child and asks him or her to "remind [me] what you're going to do first," prompting them to articulate the morning rules. Students hang up their backpacks, wash their hands and choose from a book to look at, a coloring sheet to complete, or help with a simple classroom chore like sharpening pencils or watering the plant. When arrival is complete, Mr. Rickman signals the children to join him on the carpet. Morning meeting lasts for typically 30 minutes and includes: updating the calendar, recording the day's weather, recording attendance, singing a simple "good morning" song, and reading a book together before Mr. Rickman dismisses the students to their desks to begin math. Mr. Rickman teaches small group lessons in math at each table while Ms. Kinsey helps children with other thematic worksheets. Math is scheduled for 40 minutes each morning, followed by a similar balance of small-group and individual work for literacy. At 10:30, Mr. Rickman invites the children back to the carpet for group movement games. Meanwhile, Ms. Kinsey invites children individually to wash their hands, use the bathroom, and prepare for snack. As each child prepares for snack, he or she returns to a desk to wait until all the children are ready. Ms. Kinsey and Mr. Rickman distribute a simple snack. Snack lasts roughly 10 minutes before the children clean up and line up to go to a special teacher. Specials rotate throughout the week, and include Art, Chorus, and Spanish. Twice a week, students go to Physical Education. After Specials, the students return to eat their lunch in the classroom. Lunch is followed by "Quiet Choices," during which children may read quietly, draw or rest at their tables. The last hour of the day rotates between math and literacy lessons.

When asked about the role of the arts in his classroom, Mr. Rickman reports, "The kids love it. We sing together at morning meeting and we have different songs throughout the day or to welcome new people to the room. Having guests can be kind of overwhelming and wild, but when we have a performance, the kids kind of up their game. They want to impress the visitors." Mr. Rickman's school has always enjoyed a close partnership with the community. Neighborhood volunteers help monthly on landscaping and maintenance projects at the school, which also hosts established Boy and Girl Scout troops that participate in neighborhood projects regularly. A local church collects special snacks for children in afterschool. This year, Mr. Rickman welcomed a local dentist, a nurse practitioner, and a firefighter from the nearest firehouse as part of his "Helpers" unit. The children enjoyed Dr. Steiner's model tooth, listened to each other's heartbeats with the stethoscope Mr. Fleming brought with him, and tried to balance Ms. Fisher's heavy helmet on their heads. After each visit, the students drew sets of large illustrated thank-you cards. Before each helper's visit, the children prepared a special song about his or her occupation. At the end of each visit, the children sang a variation of "Consider Yourself" from the musical, *Oliver*, to celebrate their guest.

Today, Mr. Rickman's class is preparing to welcome their parents and families to a special evening event at school: Family Math Night. During the afternoon literacy period, each child illustrates a cheerful picture on the front of a blank, folded card. Inside the card, the children copy a message from Mr. Rickman's easel, "Please come to Family Math Night," and sign their names. After the children complete their invitations, Mr. Rickman and Ms. Kinsey insert a small preprinted note inside each, detailing the date, time and location of the evening and highlighting, "A Special Musical Performance by the Children." At dismissal, the class practices its "Welcome mathematicians" song together, singing, "Welcome, welcome, mathematicians. We can count. We can add. We move numbers in our heads. Turn on your math brain and turn on the fun!" At the Family

Math Night, scheduled for the following week, families are invited to the classroom at the end of after-school for pizza and math games. "We've done Family Math for a couple of years. It's an easy way to get the parents involved and I really want them to be thinking about math outside of the classroom. The math games are puzzles and logic games mostly, but they give a structure for thinking about all the places where we use numbers and operations." Mr. Rickman admits that getting parents to school to engage in math activities can be a challenge.

I tried it different ways in the past and realized that I needed something more than the time with the kids to entice parents. They're just all so busy that getting them to give up their evening time can be hard. We order pizza so it's one less thing for them to have to do that night and I always have a special performance from the kids. It might not be a parent, but grandma or an auntie or someone will make sure to be there to hear the kids singing, then they stick around for dinner and the activities. It's a great way to get us all on the same page, and then the parents get to meet each other, too.

The classroom-based performances are part of a larger, school-wide performance schedule. Full-school assemblies are scheduled bimonthly, with each grade level featured at each assembly. Prekindergarteners are matched with second-grade partners. Kindergarteners are matched with third-grade partners. First graders are matched with fourth-grade partners. For each bimonthly assembly, grade partners either perform short musical numbers, serve as hosts by greeting and seating parents, design the welcoming banner and emcee the presentation, or have their artwork displayed in the halls. The school PTO uses these assemblies to share important information about school events and fundraising. The principal offers updates about teachers and school accomplishments. Each assembly has a festive, engaged climate and welcomes about 60% of the school population. When asked about the time involved preparing for these regular community events, Mr. Rickman shrugs.

It's really not that big a deal. The older kids take the lead for music when it's our turn, or we give the art teacher some things we've done in class to hang. It's a little more involved when we host, because we have to pick kids for specific roles, but we only end up hosting once a year and the principal usually gives us the last one, so the kids are settled.

Parents describe the assemblies as "welcoming," "low-key," and "a good way to get information about school." When a previous PTO president proposed scaling them back to do only one each semester, parents objected, and the bimonthly assemblies remained. The current PTO president raves about how "quickly sign-up sheets get filled" at the assemblies.

Social Integration

Mr. Rickman's school and class exemplify what Bresler defined as *social integration*: arts-integration models that were primarily focused on building community and engagement rather than thinking or learning through the arts. In these instances, the arts are used to add color to existing school norms, to encourage participation or turnout or to increase the festiveness of school events. The arts exist here, but they are taught in isolation from other content. When they appear in the classroom, they are simple and routinized, opportunities to establish social norms and procedures. Children enjoy fun, engaging songs and the art exposure increases the warm, welcoming climate in the hallways. Parents and family members will make time to get to school for a performance, when they might not make the sacrifice of time for a purely informational meeting. In Mr. Rickman's school and classroom, the arts help to create a sense of belonging and community without intruding on time dedicated to traditional academic content.

The social integration model complements the academic objectives of the classroom without substantively changing them, using the arts to support positive social engagement at school. In a social integration model, schools rely on the arts to support the school community and connect with families. A social integration model may highlight the arts when the entire school community is involved, at PTA meetings or school assemblies, but does not use the arts to contribute meaningfully to the intellectual development of learners. That is not to say that these programs are less valued. Indeed, social integration schools often appear to be art-rich. Expecting musical performances or art installations to increase parent turnout to school events, classrooms and teachers may actually prioritize these experiences over other learning. Bresler noted school performances observed in social integration models that were "festive and varied" and expanded across the grade levels in dance, music and theatre. Content tends to be easily accessible and likely to attract a crowd: popular songs, holiday favorites, clever skits, and dances. Preparation time is minimal and lacking in artistic expertise. Content in the arts is equally simplistic and unsophisticated and little attention is paid to learners' or audience members' learning through the experience. Instead, the arts, while celebrated in this model, are a means through which other social needs were met, increasing the ties of the community and increasing turnout at parent events.

Mrs. Kennedy: A Mini Case Study

Mrs. Kennedy is an experienced first-grade teacher who has been teaching for 32 years. "I always wanted to be a teacher," she says. Her classroom is a warm and soothing environment, serving 20 children from the suburban adjacent neighborhood. Mrs. Kennedy rarely turns on the overhead fluorescent lights, preferring instead to use the variety of table lamps and pedestal lamps she's set up in the room. The classroom is in an older school building, although it has been updated and is well-kept. One wall of the room has a row of windows above low shelves filled with early readers, middle readers and chapter books, and math manipulatives. The other three walls have chalkboards and bulletin boards. Mrs. Kennedy has covered the bulletin boards with pastel paper and displays student work throughout the room. When teaching, she uses all three chalkboards, teaching literacy from one, math from another, and using the third for student examples. Student desks are blocked in groups of four or six, and one large table doubles as a small group instructional space and Mrs. Kennedy's desk.

Mrs. Kennedy's classroom schedule is posted on a large, brightly decorated sign by the front door. From 7:55 until 8:10, children listen to morning announcements. At 8:10, they come together to complete the calendar. At 8:30, they work on math in whole group lessons or individually while Mrs. Kennedy works with smaller groups of students. At 9:30, they take a break for recess and to use the restroom. At 9:50, they begin "Writer's Workshop," a time for individual writing with small group work with Mrs. Kennedy. At 11:00, they clean up and have lunch. At 11:45, they DEAR, Drop Everything and Read until 12:00, when Mrs. Kennedy leads guided reading during a literacy block. At 1:15, they travel out of the classroom to their specials, returning at 2:00 for science or social studies. At 2:40, they have a full-group meeting to review homework agendas before dismissal at 2:55.

On the counter under the windows are the cages for the classroom pets, two gerbils named Pasteur and Curie, and a variety of large houseplants. One corner of the room has been dedicated as a reading nook and includes a large papasan chair, a fluffy rug, and a smaller dedicated bookshelf. "My students spend most of their day in this room. I want it to feel comfortable," Mrs. Kennedy describes. "They can feel at ease and still get their work done."

When asked about the role of art in her classroom, Mrs. Kennedy replies:

It's so important. When I started teaching, we had art around all the time. I had an easel in the classroom and the children could choose it whenever they wanted. I had a set of headphones and a cassette player, so children could listen to music during free play. We have to do a lot more during the day now. In some ways, it's like we're doing a second- or third-grade curriculum in first grade now. I have to be much more creative to find ways to keep the arts in the classroom.

Mrs. Kennedy describes looking for opportunities to use the arts during other content times. "I want them to know math, but I also want them to know Mozart," she says, "And so we do them both at the same time." When children are working on independent work, Mrs. Kennedy plays soft classical music to accompany them. During quiet reading time, Mrs. Kennedy plays soothing contemporary music.

I try to use music to create a mood, both when the children need to calm down but also when I want them to be more energetic. At the end of every week, we play dance music while we're cleaning up the classroom. The children sing along, or dance, while they're putting things away for the weekend.

Mrs. Kennedy describes her frustration with the current emphasis on testing and content. "It's not healthy," she says.

When I started teaching, we had a lot of leeway over the course of the year. As long as they were ready for second grade, I can a lot of say in how to get them there. Now, though, we lose almost a full week to testing in the spring, and they're not going to be ready for those tests unless I keep on the state's schedule the rest of the year. I have to figure out how to make sure my classroom is still a place my children want to come. So, we do all the test prep, but we try to do it with a little flair.

Children listen to music while completing quiet work and have times when the music is more playful, and they are allowed to dance. Near the gerbils, Mrs. Kennedy has a small basket filled with coloring sheets, blank paper, and colored pencils, and children are encouraged to hang their finished drawings on the classroom walls around the chalkboards and bulletin boards.

I started using it for my more advanced children who would finish their work early. It was a nice way to stay busy but do something a little less academic. But then I realized that it was really my struggling kids who needed it most. So, now the coloring basket is available anytime someone is feeling frustrated or needs a break. Sometimes, if a child is struggling with an academic problem, I'll ask him to go draw for 2 minutes and come back to try it again. We call it "brain wiggling" and the children know that sometimes you just have to wiggle your brain for all the pieces to line up again.

Mrs. Kennedy says that she'd like more art opportunities in the classroom, but that she's "got to fit it within the system."

The Affective Style

Mrs. Kennedy uses the arts primarily for their affective influence, responding to students' emotional need and humanizing a classroom she feels is too academic otherwise. Like the social integration model, the affective style supports traditional content, but without expanding the definition of that content to include the arts or offering substantive learning through the arts. Instead, the affective style offers opportunities to change learners' moods or support learners' creativity. As a mood-stimulator, music, for example, might be used to soothe students after active periods or as a background score to quiet seat work. Visual art may be explored as a shared experience among students to discuss the feelings the artwork evoked. In the affective style, the arts are used as a context to model particular emotional conditions or to discuss those emotions. Teachers are less likely to choose art lessons that result in a particular product or the development of a specific skill. Rather, art activities expose learners to art in order to better identify and articulate their feelings. Affective style lessons offer a break to the routines of the day and help to change learners' moods to better complement academic goals. For example, teachers might play quiet, peaceful music during times when they want the classroom to be quiet and peaceful, essentially delegating the arts to a position of support for obedient behaviors.

A second dimension of the affective style includes those art integration methods that offer open-ended, learner-driven lessons to support imagination and creativity. Teachers in this model might offer diverse art materials and media, prompting learners to create visual art of their own design. In these open-ended experiences, teachers offered little expertise or specific instruction. Instead, they use the arts to balance out what they viewed as limited or narrow academic curricular experiences, to give learners a chance to develop a sense of agency within school settings that were more structured. As such, teachers adopt a supportive style void of critical oversight or authority. Teachers using this model view the arts as expressions of individuality and uniqueness and supports for the development of self-esteem.

The affective style, as Bresler identifies it, is most common in early childhood and lower elementary classrooms, through teachers who are primarily classroom or special education teachers with little formal art expertise but with a genuine interest in the arts. This model, then, mirrors teachers' personal experiences with the arts: as conduits to desired emotional states, but without specific academic accountability. Art experiences could be open-ended and process-driven, focusing on the ways in which they helped to soothe, calm, or support learners' self-conceptions, and on providing a counterbalance to academic pressures, filling in the gaps teachers perceived to be created by more limited or structured academic curricula. This model is most likely to be observed in classrooms with divergent or less rigorous academic expectations, particularly in lower elementary and early childhood classrooms and in classrooms with special populations.

Mr. Pincehorn: A Mini Case Study

Mr. Pincehorn is a fourth-grade teacher in an urban charter school. His classroom is comprised of 20 students of mixed economic backgrounds. This school was originally designed to be a high school. Mr. Pincehorn's classroom walls are cinder block, with one tall glass window in the corner. The door to the classroom is adjacent to one large whiteboard. Mr. Pincehorn has a podium at the front of the classroom, but his desk is in the rear of the classroom near the window. Students sit at one of five long tables in rows facing the front of the room, with four students at each table.

His school is described as "art-based" and teachers are encouraged to prepare an art activity to match each curricular unit. The classroom walls display children's art in abundance and of different scale. On one wall hangs a large sheet of blue paper with construction paper cutouts recording the water cycle. On another wall are 20 9x12 sheets of paper, with different designs by each student. "We just finished reading *Number the Stars*," Mr. Pincehorn relays, "and each scholar designed his or her own poster for the book at home. They're really fun." The posters are on display around a large banner that reads, "Scholars read!" On the third wall, there are 20 cut-out faces in profile. Each has been decorated with markers to represent one of the students in the classroom. Mr. Pincehorn has posted call-outs on white paper near each face, illustrating what that student is thinking or saying. The call-outs have phrases like, "Scholars listen with their ears, their eyes and their bodies," and "Math is hidden all around you. Look for it!" and "You can tell by looking at me that I'm ready to learn." Mr. Pincehorn explains, "I want to reinforce the messages about scholarship and thinking that are embedded in our curriculum. Having the student faces gives them the chance to see themselves as already owning the message. I prefer it to a list of rules."

The classroom is bright and colorful. The hallways are also filled with displayed art, and teachers are encouraged to change their hallway displays monthly. Mr. Pincehorn introduces the hallway art:

We were studying patterns. It's a standard, but it doesn't take a lot of time for the kids to pick up. Each table group had a pack of triangles, squares, rectangles and pentagons to choose from, and each scholar had one long strip of black paper. They could design their own patterns. It was interesting to see how they came up with so many different patterns even though they had all the same shapes.

The pattern strips are displayed in rows on the hallway wall, and each has a small label near it with the name of the student.

When asked about the role of art in his classroom, Mr. Pincehorn replies, "It makes our school special. We really need to get the academics met, but you've got to keep them engaged and the art stuff does that. There's a lot you can do with construction paper and markers. It doesn't have to be over the top."

Class schedules are posted on the door for every classroom here. Mr. Pincehorn's class begins with math for 50 minutes, then extended ELA for 90 minutes, followed by "community building" before lunch. After lunch, students return to the classroom for 90 minutes of "individual scholarship." The last session each day rotates to include science, social studies, physical education, art and music classes out of the classroom. On the way to lunch, Mr. Pincehorn's students sing in line. "I use the songs from *Schoolhouse Rock*. The kids love them and it's a fun way to get them where we're going." Today, the students are chanting "Conjunction Junction, What's Your Function?" as they move from their classroom to the cafeteria. "I mix it up," Mr. Pincehorn describes, "depending on how much time we've got and whether I need them to get more energized on the way back to class or to calm down a little bit after PE or whatever."

The Subservient Approach

The most prevalent model in Bresler's framework is the subservient approach, through which art experiences were secondary enrichments to "real" learning and are used instead to increase engagement or excitement about other content. In Mr. Pincehorn's classroom, for example, art experiences illustrate learning, like drawing a new front cover for a novel the class has read or singing a jingle to help memorize state capitols. Art experiences here are subservient to other content priorities. The tools available are easily accessible and craft-based. What is asked of learners is relatively low-risk and lower-cognition. Simple skills may be developed, but subservient art-integration lessons are more prone to technical implementation rather than artistic skill development. Learners might need to memorize lyrics or match a popular melody in music. In visual arts, they may be asked to complete simple cutting, pasting, or coloring activities that illustrate other content, but they are unlikely to engage with higher quality media that require more nuanced skill. Teachers here incorporate the arts as a filler, supporting other content area if time allows. In some settings, Bresler observed, teachers may use these kinds of art experiences to offer a "win" for learners who are more challenged in traditional demonstrations of knowledge, asking students with limited written language skills to draw a picture of what they know, for example, or letting learners identify songs they think are thematically consistent with a story, although they may not be able to articulate those themes with precision. The subservient approach may be the most common for practical reasons: it requires little skill or artistic expertise from teachers, it is time-limited, and does not need extended time for sense-making through the arts, and it allows teachers to meet the expectations of music and art without taking time from content with higher-stakes.

Multiple Models

Bresler cautions against presuming that any one model of art integration will exist in isolation of the others. More often, schools and classrooms experience bits of each of the four models, sometimes combining two or three at a time and, occasionally, including all four. Within each of the four perspectives, teachers value the arts, but may have different levels of expertise, time or understanding of how to use the arts to change how students learn. In some cases, the prevalence of one model over another may reflect the routines of schools and classrooms rather than the actual preference of teachers. In other words, just as in other teaching methods, the more a particular style of art integration is modeled and supported in one's teaching or in the cultural norms of a school, the more deeply embedded the structures of that style become. Indeed, while each model reflects an appreciation of the arts as a useful tool, the objectives of that integration and the qualities of art integration that teachers value will determine the model of integration most likely to be established. Understanding those values and objectives, then, may also provide a means through which advocates may expand authentic art experiences through which learners may make sense of new knowledge and express that sense-making.

The subservient approach foregrounds traditional content learning in literacy, math, social studies and math as distinct domains. Art education may be its own discipline in this model, with students leaving the classroom to go to art class or bringing in specialists in the arts during enrichment periods, but it doesn't influence more limited methods through which primary content should be taught. The content knowledge in those core content areas is valued in isolation from the arts. The objective of art integration, then, is to support that traditional content knowledge, to enrich memorization or increase engagement, but not to change the structures of school or learning. Arts here conform to traditional models of school. Classrooms may display ample art products from students. Those products are likely to be closed-ended and similar between students, demonstrating some creativity within limited parameters that conform to predetermined academic outcomes. Look for art activities that are craft-based, that require less time or complex materials, and that can fit around other academic content on the class schedule.

The affective style values a balance between those traditional structures of school and the emotional lives of learners, reflecting teachers' belief that core content does not allow for children's creativity or emotional authenticity, and integrating the arts as a means through which those otherwise overlooked domains can be addressed. The affective style doesn't question the legitimacy of traditional structures of school, but it does suggest that they are limited in their ability to respond to children's rich emotional lives and in their capacity to support open-ended creative expression. The objective art integration here is to balance those traditional norms. Like the subservient approach, the affective style identifies the arts as distinct from core content. Unlike the subservient approach, the affective style suggests that distinction is nonetheless essential to the development of the whole child. Look for art activities that support children's emotional lives, that provide "down-time" to academic expectations or that try to offer children the chance to be creative.

The social-integration style, like the subservient approach, fits the arts around the "real work" of schools, but exploits the vibrancy of art experiences and performance as a conduit for strong communities to support that work. The social-integration style accepts the traditional norms of school and learning, and values the arts as a special tool through which social reliance can develop. The objective of art integration, then, is to supplement the work of school by creating a culture of engagement and participation among the communities that support it. Look for activities in which groups of students come together to perform or create public installation, typically outside of the regular school day or calendar, and with audience members of either other students or families.

The subservient, affective and social integration models share certain key values: each conforms to the norms of traditional schooling, identifying core content areas to be prioritized and using the arts to engage, supplement or balance that content. To the degree that school is a place that perpetuates social norms and transmits specific content knowledge, these models edify those structures, requiring little change to teacher presumptions or conceptualizations. In each, art comes after other content, affirming existing models for school and learning and reinforcing teacher presumptions about the nature of learning and their role within it. As school life is largely informed by the larger values of the society it serves, it is little surprise that these models reflect those values as well. In a current context that emphasizes specific academic outcomes, the most common models for art integration are those that work within the limited definition of knowledge those specific academic outcomes require. These three models ask little of teachers, little time, few resources, and very little change to the presumptions about the nature of learning or teaching. That is not to say that the teachers value the arts less. Indeed, they may hold art and its processes as essential components of a balanced life. Within the parameters of extant school expectations, however, these models integrate art in ways on top of other school expectations without fundamentally changing the way teaching or learning unfolds.

The coequal cognitive integration style, however, demands different presumptions about the work of teachers and the nature of knowledge. This model values the cognitive construction of knowledge across disciplinary boundaries, even when that construction may lead to outcomes teachers did not yet predict. In the coequal cognitive integration style, teachers must understand the disciplines of various arts with enough fluency to use them as conduits for foundational learning, and not merely supplements to the real work of the classroom. It unmoors the foundational presumptions of content and learning, shifting from predetermined content in limited and distinct domains to education as a means of identifying new questions to be asked. The boundaries between traditional content areas are diminished and the degree to which learning designs must be relevant, multidisciplinary and authentic rises sharply. This model demands a reconceptualization of the role of the teacher, from a manager of content to a catalyst for questioning and understanding. As a model, the coequal cognitive integration model requires more time, is less predictable, and less succinct, requiring more planning, more expertise, and more collaboration among diverse perspectives and stakeholders. While these demands may limit its prevalence, they nonetheless raise new issues around the role of the arts in learner development, suggesting that art education may be best enacted through longer term, content-integrated lessons and counter to the established norms of school. Look for schools and classrooms that function in observably different ways, with longer units of time, integrated projects across many days or even weeks, and open-ended products. In other words, the most effective integration model may be the one that is the most challenging to accomplish.

Finding Resolution

Enacting a coequal cognitive integration may be aspirational for most schools, as it requires paradigm shifts and changes to professional expertise beyond the capacity of many districts to employ and larger, cultural shifts that are unlikely given the history of the last century. There are means, however, to integrate the arts more authentically and to protect arts disciplines from marginalization or subservience to other content. Appel (2006) argues for ongoing, reinforced, and explicit connections between content standards, made clear within the language of the curriculum and supported by well-defined, specific goals. Students should see their work in the arts as equal to their work in other content areas, with modeled experiences that demonstrate knowledge in multimodal ways. In other words, if most assessments are traditional written responses, the occasional assessment that incorporates the arts will reinforce the belief that the arts are tangential to real learning. Content lessons and artistic experiences should have equal time, preparation and assessment.

Meanwhile, art integration advocates can defend the importance of art education to the same goals valued by science, technology, and literacy driven reforms. Americans for the Arts publishes regular updates to their report *The Arts and Economic Prosperity*, tying the arts in schools and communities to over $60 billion invested in the U.S. economy each year. The President's Committee on the Arts and Humanities supports high poverty schools in districts across the country through the Turnaround Arts program, designed to fund high-quality art programs to change school cultures and outcomes. Although the program is relatively young, it reflects a shift in perspective: from using the arts to supplement other academic goals to using the arts as a conduit to intellectual and community transformation through academic success. These efforts seek to shift the cultural expectations of the relationship of learning to the arts, a transformation necessary for long-term change. Aprill (2010) suggests that, in order to move away from the pendular swings in education reform that move back and forth between standards-based and whole-child instruction, school leaders need to first reexamine the relationship between the whole-child and the standards. If they are seen as opposite sides of the same spectrum, their differences are less likely to be reconciled. The conflict may be best resolved through the efforts of individual teachers and schools, like Ms. Shepherd, working within flexible systems to demonstrate the effectiveness of art integration.

Discuss

Visit the President's Committee on the Arts and Humanities' Turnaround Arts website at http://turnaroundarts.pcah.gov. Read the section on "What We Do." What resources are available at the school level to change the culture and climate of the school? What resources are available to increase teachers' capacity to integrate the arts? In what ways does this model seek to reconcile academic standards with the affective benefits of the arts?

Visit Americans for the Arts' ArtsU at https://artsu.americansforthearts .org. Follow the links to Arts Education and view the "Encourage Creativity" PSA videos. Consider which integration model these PSAs seem most aligned to.

Download the Kennedy Center's Alliance for Arts Education Network Community Audit for Arts Education at http://education.kennedy-center. org/education/kcaaen/resources/CAudit6-9.pdf. Discuss means by which a classroom teacher could make use of this resource to influence conversation about the role of the arts and art integration. What challenges or opportunities may be evoked in such an effort? If you were to undertake it as a classroom teacher, what stakeholders would you seek out first for professional support?

Collaborate

The Kennedy Center's Changing Education through the Arts' (2019) definition of art integration reads, "Arts integration is an approach to teaching in which students construct and demonstrate understanding through an art form. Students engage in a creative process which connects an art form and another subject area and meets evolving objectives in both." With a colleague, discuss examples of art integration projects you have seen that you think meet this definition. How did the teachers you observed reconcile the sometimes contradictory demands of their classrooms while integrating the arts?

Think about your own experiences as learners. What art integration experiences from your schooling stand out as memorable to you? Share them with a colleague. Discuss what qualities of the integration process made these experiences lasting. If the experience was positive, discuss what ways in which it met the many goals of classrooms. If the experience was not, discuss how your teachers might have adjusted the experience to create a more effective lesson.

Choose a literacy standard from a grade level you hope to teach. Design an integrated art experience in each of the four models of integration. How do the questions you have to ask yourself as a teacher change depending on the model of integration you're trying to use? Discuss with a colleague.

Create

Presume the first step in changing the effectiveness of art integration is changing the values of policy makers. Design a PSA in a modality of your choosing that you think would change your principal's mind and present it to your colleagues.

Consider how the content of this chapter would have been different if you had learned it in Coequal Cognitive integration model. Select an aspect of the chapter to translate into an integrated art experience. What media would you choose? What experts may you need to consult to design your experience?

For Further Reading

Appel, M.P. (2006). Arts Integration across the Curriculum. *ERIC, 36*(2)14–17.

Aprill, A. (2010). Direct Instruction vs. Arts Integration: A False Dichotomy. *Teaching Artist Jo urnal*, 8(1), 6-15, DOI: 10.1080/15411790903393004

Asbury, C. H., Rich, B., & Gazzaniga, M. S. (2008). *Learning, arts, and the brain: The Dana Consortium report on arts and cognition.* New York: Dana Press.

Bickley-Green, C. A. (1995). Math and Art Curriculum Integration: A Post-Modern Foundation. *Studies in Art Education, 37*(1), 6.

Bresler, L. (1995). The Subservient, Co-Equal, Affective, and Social Integration Styles and their Implications for the Arts. *Arts Education Policy Review, 96*(5), 31–37.

Bredekamp, S., & Copple, C. (n.d.). Developmentally appropriate practice in early childhood programs.

Burnaford, G., Aprill, A., Weiss, C. (2001). *Renaissance in the Classroom: Arts Integration and Meaningful Learning.* Mahwah, NJ: Lawrence Erlbaum Associates.

Clawson, H. J., & Coolbaugh, K. (2001). The YouthARTS development project. Washington, DC: U.S. Dept. of Justice, Office of Justice Programs, Office of Juvenile Justice and Delinquency Prevention.

Deasy, R., Catterall, J. S., Hetland, L., & Winner, E. (2002). *Critical links: Learning in the arts and student academic and social development.* Washington, DC: Arts Education Partnership.

Dewey, J. (1934). *Art as experience.* New York: Perigee.

Dobbs, S. M. (1998). *Learning in and through art: A guide to discipline-based art education.* Los Angeles, CA: Getty Education Institute for the Arts.

Eisner, E. (1982). *Cognition and Curriculum.* New York: Longman.

Fiske, E. B. (1999). *Champions of change: The impact of the arts on learning.* Washington, DC: Arts Education Partnership.

Freyberger, R. M. (1985). Integration: Friend or foe of art education. *Art Education, 38*(6), 6.

Gelinear, RP. (2012). *Integrating the arts across the elementary school curriculum.* Belmont, CA: Wadsworth.

Lagemann, E. C. (2005). Does History Matter in Education Research? A Brief for the Humanities in an Age of Science. *Harvard Educational Review, 75*(1), 9–24.

Lagemann, E. C., & Herbst, J. (1991). And sadly teach: Teacher education and professionalization in american culture. *The American Historical Review, 96*(1), 246.

Leonhard, C. (1993). The challenge. Bulletin of the Council for Research in Music Education.

Lichtenberg, J., Woock, C., & Wright, M. (2008). *Ready to innovate: Are educators and executives aligned on the creative readiness of the U.S. workforce?* New York, NY: Conference Board.

Ryan, J. (1994). Art & society: Containment or integration? Art in context. *Circa, 70*, 50.

Silverstein, L.B. and Layne, S. (2019). *The Kennedy Center: Arts Edge*. Retrieved from https://artsedge.kennedy-center.org/educators/how-to/arts-integration/what-is-arts-integration

Wallace Foundation. (2009). Increasing arts demand through better arts learning. (2009). New York: The Wallace Foundation. Retrieved from https://www.wallacefoundation.org/knowledge-center/Documents/Increasing-Arts-Demand-Through-Better-Arts-Learning.pdf

Zhou, M. Y. (n.d.). Art Integration Ideas and Activities. Music, Art, and Physical Education in the Elementary Curriculum, 2060–2462.

Chapter 3

Integrating Theatre

"The stage is a magic circle where only the most real things happen, a neutral territory outside the jurisdiction of Fate where stars may be crossed with impunity. A truer and more real place does not exist in all the universe."

—P. S. Baber, *Cassie Draws the Universe*

Dramatic and Sociodramatic Play in Early Childhood

From the earliest instances of intentional play, young children pretend. They "make believe," mimicking sounds of animals or objects in their environment almost as soon as they are able to construct words. They ask their parents and caregivers to "pretend I am ..." any number of identities, taking on roles and perspectives from their home lives, their favorite books and images and their communities. We know that, for the very young child, dramatic play is an integral part of sense-making of the world, an opportunity to take on multiple roles in an effort to better understand the rules and norms of their society, to explore possible ways of being and to connect with others.

Ms. Shondra Patterson teaches in a playschool, in a classroom serving 10 three-year-olds. Shondra's classroom includes a dramatic play area, in which children can practice putting on different clothes and costumes. She also offers a small play kitchen with a wooden stove, sink, and refrigerator. In another area of the classroom, baskets with small figures of dinosaurs, construction workers, and zoo animals are available. "There's not really one area for dramatic play," she describes, "although I've got the dress-up box. It really happens all over the place. The kids are always pretending."

Smilansky and Shefatya (1990) distinguish between *dramatic play*, when children engage in imitation and mimicking on their own, practicing the relationships they observe around them, and *sociodramatic play*, when two or more children engage in role-playing together, including the negotiation and compromise that emerge as a result. Both are naturalistic and observable in early childhood development.

Social-Emotional Learning and Sociodramatic Play

When children engage in sociodramatic play, they have the chance to practice social engagements, supporting their social and emotional growth. Children's social development is enhanced by the negotiation and compromise inherent in sociodramatic play; if there are multiple children enacting other roles, each child must consider and engage the others' perspective for the sociodramatic play to remain relevant to them all. Children also practice both the range and regulation of emotions through dramatic play. By taking on someone else's perspective, they can practice empathy in manageable scenarios, a skill which is then transferred to other real-life contexts. Dress-up areas, figurines, and pretend spaces make these opportunities explicit, but young children will engage in sociodramatic play across the classroom as a natural reflection of their development. Listen in at the snack table and you may overhear two children pretending to be at a tea party. Listen to a child playing with blocks and you may find that each block represents a specific vehicle, and each vehicle has its own agenda and personality. Through the endless examples of child-driven dramatic and sociodramatic play, young children are motivated to explore their worlds, to take on roles within that world, and to make better sense of their contribution to it.

Research suggests that engaging in dramatic and sociodramatic play involves a complicated interplay of understandings, as children develop the ability to discern between what is real and what is magical, what is alive and what is animated, and how their own emotions and the emotions of others influence each other. Because sociodramatic play is often cooperative play, it supports children's development of healthy peer relationships.

Physical Development and Dramatic and Sociodramatic Play

Dramatic and sociodramatic play also supports children's physical development. As children take on pretend roles, they challenge their bodies to do the things those characters do. Firefighters climb trees to save kittens. Doctors hold stethoscopes to listen to their patients' hearts. In playing dress-up, children learn to move their bodies in different ways, to manage fasteners, to put on jackets and socks, to tie shoes, or manage big boots. Motivated by the pretend games, children push themselves to manage the props associated with that play and, in doing so, develop the fine and gross motor skills they'll need when they're managing their own needs in "real life."

Because dramatic play is intrinsically motivating to young children, teachers can make use of that motivation in and out of the classroom. Providing areas for dramatic and sociodramatic play with ample costumes, props and set pieces is useful even with the very young child. Children will manage large crates or blocks to build thrones, to create kitchens, or to design their own homes. They will use art supplies to create simple puppets and set pieces. They'll turn outdoor climbers into trucks or castles in their minds to support their dramatic and sociodramatic play. The absence of these tools will not deter children from dramatic or imaginative play, but access to them will expand children's parameters of what might be.

Cognitive Development and Dramatic and Sociodramatic Play

Dramatic play is symbolic play—an opportunity for children to think abstractly and to use their memories and imaginations. Dramatic and sociodramatic play offers relevant opportunities for problem solving, applied math skills, practical living skills and literacy. Imagine a group of children pretending to run a bank. They have to imagine the bank scenario, assign roles, understand the different intents of each character, operate tools like a cash register or calculator, count out change, and understand a variety of social cues. Even when their content knowledge is lacking (and a child gives a "million dollars" in change for a ten-dollar bill), children are learning that some tools (e.g., money) have value in some settings and others (e.g., goldfish) do not.

Children's dramatic and sociodramatic play is cognitively complex, demonstrating their emerging understanding of the world and giving them opportunities to resolve dissonances in that understanding. With support, these activities provide a springboard for developing skills of inquiry, problem solving, classification, and concept resolution.

Language Development and Dramatic and Sociodramatic Play

Cooperative play offers children meaningful opportunities to practice new language skills, to explain what they're doing to other participants or to observers, to ask and answer questions about other's play, and to acquire new vocabulary. When a block becomes a lion, someone needs to describe it to others who might think it's still a block. Dramatic and sociodramatic play allows children to incorporate new language they've learned from scenarios they can only access through play. Astronauts or tyrannosauruses become necessary words. Literacy materials incorporated in the play, like signs illustrating labeling different shops or marking the cost of apples in a pretend market, reinforce the relevance of the written word. Dramatic and sociodramatic play that's linked to stories engages children in reading and being read to, expanding the connection to books and literacy.

Adults and Sociodramatic Play in the Early Childhood Classroom

Differing curricula will support differing roles for adults in sociodramatic play in early childhood classrooms. Waldorf classrooms, for example, may encourage adults to assume roles in children's play while Montessori classrooms will encourage children's play separate from the influence of teacher. Despite these differences, any early childhood teacher who wants to include sociodramatic play will need to allow time for it, to provide materials that are appropriate for play and, most importantly, to acknowledge that dramatic play is a natural reflection of children's development and intrinsic to their sense-making of the world. Even when classrooms do not have specific areas set aside for dramatic or sociodramatic play, that play nonetheless occurs. The most critical role of the teacher is in acknowledging the developmental importance of role-taking for young children. Offer high quality materials that support children's emerging understanding of the world. Providing quality books with interesting stories and illustrations to engage children's imaginations. Ask questions about children's play to allow them to articulate their imaginations and constructions. Especially in the critical age window of 0–6, children's dramatic and sociodramatic play allows them not only engaging, fun experiences. It is an essential component to their development across multiple domains and a necessary tool to building their sense of themselves and their contribution to the world around them.

Sociodramatic Play in Early Elementary and Beyond

The benefits of sociodramatic play don't end in early childhood, although they may be more often facilitated and evoked by classroom teachers. Drama activities support children's development of written and oral language, their social and emotional understanding, and their cognitive growth. As a means of understanding new content, drama activities make immediate and relevant content that may be foreign to children.

Dramatic Play in Elementary Classrooms

While some practitioners may only think of dramatic play as an element of early childhood classrooms, incorporating it into elementary classrooms sustains and expands similar benefits to children's development. Oral and language development emerges as a necessary tool for drama experiences. Literacy emerges purposefully through the development and design of props, inquiry into informational books to develop details for sets or to resolve conflicts between contributors, and organizing, preparing, and presenting scripts, among others. The social power of drama activities gives children a chance to rely on each other, to contribute to projects in which each participant's role is essential, to appreciate the diversity of experiences and capacities in their own classroom, and to try on diverse perspectives from other cultures. Dramatic play, sociodramatic play, and drama exercises can all be integrated in ways that support children's learning across the curriculum and the development of agency, self-awareness, and social skills.

In early elementary classrooms, drama exercises may begin to take the place of dramatic and sociodramatic play, although kindergarten and first-grade classrooms can still incorporate stand-alone dramatic and sociodramatic play spaces. In the classroom, teachers may allow a designated space, costumes and props, or centers for children to choose according to their own interest or in response to content objectives. In school-age classrooms, these opportunities require more intentional interweaving by the teacher.

Thinking about Drama in the Elementary Classroom

Elementary teachers may make use of simple, teacher-structured activities that encourage students to take on the perspectives of characters and players across the curriculum. Drama supports children by facilitating their language skills and increasing their reading comprehension. It offers opportunities to challenge presumptions, solve problems, and generate critical and alternative points of view. It supports learners' cognitive and affective development, refining the relationship between self and others and developing empathy and cooperation. It requires students to develop their ability to imagine, both as performers and audience members, a skill necessary to develop innovative solutions in the sciences and arts. It develops the ability to interpret new information and to retell information for a new audience, deepening the learner's own understanding of the content. It provides immediate access for diverse learners, by allowing students to "show what they know" through a combination of movement, language, intonation, and physicality. Learners who need to move, who are stronger in spatial skills, interpersonal skills, linguistic skills, or intrapersonal skills than they are in the written word will find access in drama that was not immediately apparent in more traditional demonstrations.

Further, drama is hands-on and experiential, engaging the mind, body, voice, and emotions to interpret and convey new information. Each sense that is engaged provides an opportunity to remember new information through that experience. Connecting students emotionally to the content they're learning increases their ability to recall and retain that content, and the emotional and energetic nature of drama provides a personal connection to the material, one that embeds it firmly in the mind. The Boston Tea Party takes on an entirely new importance when students have to act it out. Comprehension and retention of content increase greatly by using drama.

Drama and improvisation support learners' understanding of literature, influence children's writing, and offers children multiple languages to demonstrate their understanding of content. In retelling content through performance for their peers or a larger audience, learners internalize character motivation, increase their retention of details, and enact relationships that may be more abstract on the page. In imagining content across different settings, children use what they know from their experiences to expand on the original knowledge. By applying what they know to new scenarios, learners develop a more sophisticated and nuanced understanding of the original source. Drama activities may be process-driven, including adding new characters to a story, placing known characters in new scenarios, building out a "back-story" that is not included in the original text, shifting players in history or context, or incorporating other new challenges to demonstrate rich knowledge. They may be opportunities to retell content, to interpret it for a new modality, and to determine which components of the content are essential in enactment. In thinking about engaging drama in the elementary classroom, we need to ask the same questions we ask when we select other pedagogical tools: What do I intend to teach? How is it best taught, and how will I know if my students have learned what I intended?

Lifelong learning skills are also supported through competence in drama. Concentration, imagination, cooperation, collaboration, and listening skills are essential for the enactment of dramatic play and generalize to other settings. Drama experiences increase self-confidence, empathy, and communication skills that are invaluable in the work place and in every day interactions with other people. Students exposed to theatre training perform better in school, have more consistent attendance, demonstrate more empathetic behavior toward others, and demonstrate greater self-esteem. And, as Bakari King, award-winning choreographer and youth-theatre teacher from Nashville, TN, describes it, "Theatre is the ultimate team sport." It requires students to work together toward a common goal, to appreciate the equal important of contributions that may look very different from each other, and to cooperate in a way that makes their entire group stronger. In Mr. King's school, students return two weeks early before school begins to rehearse a full-length multi-grade musical theatre production that is performed during the opening weekend of school each year. With over 120 young performers and only two weeks to prepare, Mr. King's programs thrive because they engage students in working together quickly, so the students themselves understand that every minute they have together counts. The social benefits for the students involved are evident: students begin the year with a strong network and community of other players that help make the start of each year much smoother.

As a tool for teachers, theatre has practical advantages over other community-driven learning. Theatre is portable, often requiring nothing more than the space for the learners to gather. It is highly adaptable, with easy adjustments to games to allow them to be revised and molded to the particular needs and population of any classroom. They are universal, easily played by learners of different backgrounds, cultures and learning styles. In creative enactments, each player has the opportunity to bring his or her own background, prior knowledge and experience to the activity.

Drama activities are easy to implement, usually only requiring a room and a facilitator. Preparation is minimal, and costs are low. Finally, they are easily repeatable. Because students enjoy playing their favorite games again and again, teachers can make small adjustments to familiar structures to apply them to new settings or content. Skills, confidence, and creativity improve as players replay the same games. The same players can produce very different material or results each time they engage. Creative expression rarely repeats itself.

Basic Tools: Practicing Listening and Collaborating

In order to use drama in ways that support other content learning, first students need to be comfortable with the tools they'll engage. Before engaging in drama enactments, teachers should take time to model the parameters of those engagements. Consider some basic rules for dramatic games:

+ During class meetings or before beginning a new game, take the time to talk with students about positive engagements. Explain that sometimes dramatic play can get very energetic and the classroom needs ways to settle down during and afterward.
+ Ask students to name ways in which they can make sure everyone is able to participate in a way that is safe and fun. Suggest positive alternatives if students offer what *not* to do. In other words, if a student suggests, "Don't be wild," ask, "If you're not being wild, what are you doing instead?" Let students name the behaviors they hope to engage in during more active play.
+ Ask students to collectively identify a classroom signal to freeze activity. Practice using the signal.
+ Ask students to identify basic assurances, like touching only their own bodies, making eye contact with other players and affirming each other's efforts. Practice and model friendly, warm responsiveness to each other before tackling content-based play.

Teachers can establish norms for drama games without much planning, providing improvisation games as a regular part of classroom meetings or within other content areas. Imagine a morning greeting in which each child was asked to say good morning in the style of a character in their text, or a science expansion that allowed children to act out how they'd hold a kite in the doldrums or in the tropical easterlies. If improvisation is included regularly in classrooms, extended drama games or enactments that last over full class periods, over days, or even over months will be more easily managed.

Almost any new concept can be engaged in improvisation first. Simple engagements in improvisation offer the chance to develop children's confidence in speaking in front of their peers, a comfort with the idea of improv as a "safe" social enterprise and a memorable way of exploring new concepts. By engaging in these activities with learners, teachers model a healthy risk-taking to public enactment, the absence of which may discourage students. Look for links to content standards that ask students to "read and comprehend," "enact," or "model" information. When content standards specify that students should be able to "interpret" new information or "apply" it to new settings, theatre exercises are a natural match to that demonstration. Even in traditionally structured classrooms, teachers can encourage students to enact concepts with their bodies or to improvise simple interactions as a means of making them comfortable with the structures of drama.

Engaging Extended Theatre Learning

Theatre-based learning is, at its simplest, an expansion of improvisation over time and at greater depth. Researchers have long considered its influence in the development of literacy and cognitive and socioemotional skills in elementary classrooms, supporting their understanding of content and increasing the detail and complexity of their own writing. Although ample resources exist for teachers to find ideas and prepared units for process drama across the curriculum, teachers should know how to design these models themselves, in order to respond to the individual development of the students in their own classrooms and to integrate drama as a meaningful component of a comprehensive curriculum. There are ample examples of prepared theatre-based units available for teachers, especially through readers' theatre and other professional resources. Teachers should understand four general modes through which extended theatre learning might best compliment classroom goals, organized by the length of time dedicated for each: holistic drama, linear drama, process drama, and interpretive drama.

Holistic Drama

Unlike theatre-based learning that requires learners to research or prepare for an enactment over time, the holistic method asks students to drop into their roles at a "gut-level" response. This model requires careful listening skills and engages a level of surprise, often leading to a different internalization of the concept being enacted.

In a holistic session, the teacher or facilitator asks students to adopt the role of a particular contributor to the enactment. In a literature or social studies unit, this might be a particular fictional or historical character. In a science or math unit, this may be a structure, element, or phenomenon that influences others. The objective of holistic drama is to construct a deeper knowledge of concepts by embodying those concepts, to foster group collaboration and cognitive skills and to support affective growth.

1. Preparing your character: After identifying a theme or idea the teacher wants students to understand more deeply, students sit with their eyes closed as the teacher explains the scenario they have selected. For example, the students may be considering the life cycle of a butterfly. The teacher guides them through a visualization of the stages of the life cycle of a butterfly, inviting them to imagine their own bodies changing in the same ways.
2. Playing with other actors: After students have imagined their transformation individually, teachers may invite a small group of them to play for each other. Students may be invited to find a space where they are visible to their peers and silently transform along the life cycle.
3. Evaluating the enactments: After practicing with their peers watching, students gather together to discuss what elements of the enactment matched their understanding of the life cycle of a butterfly or to offer feedback on more evident enactments. The teacher may use this time to ask students about specific theatre choices they've made as well.
4. Replaying: Individual students may be invited to add more animation to their enactments. At this stage, the teacher may invite two or three students to enact the changing life cycle but may signal for students to freeze at different parts and open their role up to questions from the audience. Other students may ask questions about the characters' affect like, "How do you feel about your change so far?" or "Are you frightened or anxious about what's coming next?" or they may ask more basic needs questions like, "How much did you eat today?" or "How many nights will it take for you to transform?" Both the questions and the responses require students to think more deeply about each stage of the transformation.

The holistic drama framework allows students to assume characteristics of a role or concept, to display those characteristics to others, and to reflect on their understanding and the enactments of their peers. Teachers may play roles themselves in these enactments, prodding characters or scenarios by interacting with other players, modeling engagement for students who may be more hesitant.

Linear Drama

The linear drama framework is more prescriptive that the holistic drama framework and, as a result, may be more attractive to teachers who are thinking about incorporating drama for the first time. Because each segment of this model is prompted by the teacher, the teacher has greater control to link student play to specific learning outcomes. Each stage of the enactment is prompted by the teacher with closer parameters for physical engagement, sound and interaction. In this model, the teacher acts as a narrator or coach, orchestrating the players and helping them to remain focused.

1. Preparing your character: The teacher asks the full class to find space in the classroom consistent with the class guidelines for dramatic play, being mindful of each other's personal space and of the physical choices of our own bodies. After determining which learner will enact which role, the teacher supports the students in visualizing their transformation into a moving statue of that role, in which their bodies may move but their feet stay planted. Verbally direct the students through the parts of their bodies as they transform into their role. Teacher prompts might include language like, "Think first about the top of your head. How is your role's head different than your real head? Show with the muscles of your face that you are becoming your role. Now, think about your torso and arms. How will they change to become more like your role?" Guide students through the transformation of their bodies, reminding them to keep their feet still, until their entire bodies have transformed. Signal the class to freeze. Model describing the choices you can observe students making with their bodies. Signal the class to relax.
2. Playing with other actors: After students have had a chance to practice their roles as statues, the teacher can offer scenarios in which they will interact. Imagine, for example, a fourth-grade classroom in North Carolina, studying the state's role in major conflicts between pre-colonial times and Reconstruction. The teacher may assign students to enact key stakeholders. One small group of students may enact women at the time. Another may enact Confederate soldiers. Another may enact loyalists or patriots. Individual

students may be assigned particular historical players like Zebulon Vance, Nathanael Green, or Penelope Barker. After preparing these individually, the teacher might create smaller combinations of students to engage in scenarios in which they interact with each other.

    a. Initial enactments: Building off the character preparation, students interact in their small group, introducing themselves to each other and practicing moving in the space as their characters

    b. The teacher proposes a scenario for each group to dramatize. This may be the same scenario for all the groups, or a different one for each. Groups are given a short amount of time to develop their interaction and practice it.

    c. Finally, the small groups enact their scenarios for each other.

3. Evaluating the enactments: After the enactments, the teacher and students gather to discuss the experience, focusing on the interpretations each actor or group made and how each characterization showed what the actor understood about the concept. This is also a ripe time to discuss what dramatic skills supported actors' enactments, allowing students to learn over time how to implement effective dramatic choices around sound, movement, concentration, cooperation, and listening.

4. Replaying: After reflecting as a group, the class may be given additional scenarios or given the opportunity to reconstruct their original scenario. In reflecting on these new enactments, learners can discuss how their understanding has grown and changed from their initial enactment.

Each of these stages may reflect class-based learning, or students can be assigned roles early in the unit to pay closer attention to and learn more about. Allowing students to assess the enactments supports reflection and self-analysis, leading too to the ways in which an enactment in science may require skills learned in language arts or other connections. The replaying stage offers further development, clarification, and self-correction. Linear drama activities can be integrated over different time frames, too, growing and shrinking in their time-demand to best respond to classroom needs.

Process Drama

Process drama activities are teacher-directed, sequenced experiences that, like holistic and linear drama, allow students to take on new roles and engage in new contexts, but on a deeper and more extended level than the other two. Process drama is like fan fiction: it allows students to create new contexts for familiar content, to learn more about characters and concepts from one area of the curriculum by placing them in new areas or addressing them in new ways.

1. Source selection: Process drama can be matched to any original content source appropriate for your students. Select a source that you think compliments enactment well, that allows a rich thematic focus and that would support multiple actors. For example, third-graders often read *Bud, Not Buddy* by Christopher Paul Curtis, the story of 10-year-old Bud Caldwell, an African American 10-year-old boy on his own during the Great Depression. *Bud, Not Buddy* deals with themes of poverty, race, honesty, perseverance, and home, and invites students to consider these issues within both a historical context and across the safety of time.

2. Focus identification: Select a thematic focus from your source. Ask yourself, "What problems evolve from this source? How could we explore those problems? Who might be involved in solving them?" For example, a teacher may choose to focus on definitions of home for a process drama experience of *Bud, Not Buddy*. But she may realize that students may not understand what train travel is like or have a context for life in a shanty town, or understand the distances between important locations in the novel, like Flint, Michigan, Grand Rapids, or California. The teacher will have to consider the implications of each of these locations for students who are attempting to dramatize them. After consideration, the teacher will identify a core question to articulate the focus: What would have happened if Bud hadn't missed the train?

3. Expand the context: Consider activities that allow your students to expand the original context of their focus. Ideally, look for new contexts that allow students to think about their own roles by challenging them in new ways. New contexts should identify the original roles, identify the new situation and identify the conflict or problem the actors will have to solve in that next context. In *Bud, Not Buddy*, Bud's efforts to reach California fall short. But what if they hadn't? How would the story be different in Bud didn't miss the train? What other characters would be encounter? The teacher can split students into groups representing major cities along the rail to California. For each group, students will determine their own roles inside those new cities. One group may decide to be workers at a train station in one city. Another group may decide to be individuals from a town adjacent to the train station, with distinguished roles and relationships between them.

4. Establish a narrative thread: Begin to develop the narrative thread—that storyline that will take students and their roles through a beginning, middle, and end to their characters addressing the new context, responding to the conflict, and resolving it. The teacher will help students to craft a narrative

thread that refines the original theme of "Home." In each city, what tensions might exist to push the story along? How will those tensions be resolved?

5. Offer "poetic" enrichments: As students are working on their narratives, develop short poetic activities that help them to deepen their understanding of the concepts beyond a base representation. Push students to think about the symbolic meaning of the narrative and to make emotional connections to the work. The teacher here might take a break from the narrative construction to introduce poetry that addresses the theme of home, like Anne Bronte's "Lines Written from Home," or Robert Louis Stevenson's "To Friends at Home." The teacher may introduce great works of art, like Jan Olis's *Dutch Family in an Interior* or Jennifer Hunold's *The Visual Dynamic* that present images of home. Through these enrichments, the teacher should look for opportunities to expand the students' symbolic repertoire.

6. Offer reflective supports: Throughout the process, offer specific times to interrupt the work to allow for collective reflection. Activities should invite students to come out of their roles to talk about the narrative they are constructing and to accept feedback on its unfolding. At this point, the teacher may help students to create a single outline that shows the narrative thread through each of the small group inquiries. Together, they may imagine ways of resolving the story after each group's contribution is experienced.

7. Review for engagement and diversity of interactions: Make sure you have designed opportunities for the entire group to participate, when everyone receives information they will all need, opportunities for smaller groups to work together to solve specific problems, opportunities for pairs of students to work closely and activities for individual preparation, enactment or reflection. In designing their own enactment, learners can benefit from times with the full group and with individuals, contributing to the narrative thread and constructing a deeper understanding of their own characters.

8. Review for objectives: Consider your plan to be sure the teaching goals you've designed will be met in this model and to identify the specific ways in which you'll be able to tell if students have mastered them. Different groups may be challenged to meet different standards or groups may have different tasks within them to explore. With careful teacher involvement, students can be prompted to incorporate themes and content from across their curriculum, using process drama as a truly integrative model of art education.

For complex models like this, the teachers may choose a teacher-in-role engagement, where she enacts a role of her own, linking the work of the smaller groups. She may be a train conductor if she wants to engage with Bud and the other characters directly, or she may serve as the narrator. Process drama relies on student imagination and improvisation, with thoughtful planning and teacher-prompting to connect the experience to content goals beyond the affective or socioemotional benefits of the play. Although time intensive, it allows for deep connections between students and the content and across disciplinary boundaries. Because students can identify their own roles, it allows students to engage in new social roles outside of the biases engendered by race, ethnicity, gender or ability. A well-constructed process drama may take a week or more of extended work, but, with careful crafting, it can address multiple standards within that window, making content more relevant and memorable to the learners.

Interpretive Drama

Interpretive drama is the type of school-based theatre learning probably most familiar to teachers. Interpretive drama supports children in using their bodies, minds and voices to internalize and represent written text. In this model, learners use their own experiences and perspectives to enact the story, developing concrete representations of the meaning of a text. Interpretive drama draws on the traditions of reenactment, reader's theatre and choral poetry to connect students to literature in rich and personally relevant ways. But it is not without its cautions. Interpretive tools should be matched to the needs of the learner, not to the appeal to particular audiences.

Reenactment of Stories

Imagine a first-grade classroom. The teacher is directing a class performance of *What Do You Do with a Tail Like This?*, the Caldecott-winning picture book by Steve Jenkins and Robin Page. She began by reading the book aloud to her class, then assigned an animal represented in the book. Each family has prepared a costume for their child's animal and each child has memorized the lines of text appropriate for his or her character. After two weeks of preparation, the children invite their parents, families, and grandparents to school to see their show. They gather in the auditorium, where their teacher welcomes the families and cues the children to begin the performance. Each child is on stage, in line and in costume, to step forward as his or her line is said. Parents snap their cameras and grandmothers ooh and aah at their grandchildren's overwhelming cuteness. The lines aren't particularly clear, and each child recites his or her line with a mechanical intonation, but the families are delighted.

Perhaps the most commonly performed interpretive drama is the reenactment of stories like this, when children perform plays based on familiar stories. In this common process, teachers identify stories to be enacted, directing children in the casting and performance of the story, usually for an audience of family members or other community. Reenactment that is focused on memorization of lines and complicated adult-prepared costumes has little to offer to children's real learning, and sometimes teaches lessons we did not intend, discouraging learners from participating in public performance in the future. While there are ways to make this process more learner-centered, like selecting stories with multiple characters, double- and triple-casting larger roles to allow multiple children to play, and selecting stories with engaging plots that are easy for children to follow, often reenactments end up being for the benefit of the audience and not the learner.

Drama education research suggests that these kinds of reenactments may limit students' opportunities to use their own critical thinking and imaginative skills, undervaluing the role of meaning-making in theatre-based learning and replacing it with a focus on product—in this case, the performance. Memorizing lines and blocking, waiting quietly during other actors' scenes, and understanding the norms of theatre may be beyond the capacity of most young children, despite how adorable they may look on stage dressed as one of the three little pigs.

There are some structures that help avoid this potential pitfall. For example, teachers should choose stories that have plots that are manageable for young children to understand. Young children can be involved in creating a script of a familiar story, allowing them to develop their own dialogue and lines that are comfortable and accessible to them. Encouraging children to design their own costumes, to select a special prop, or to identify a tag line unique to their character can make reenactments more personally relevant and meaningful to the learner. Performing for their peers or other classes rather than family can also decrease the confusion and self-consciousness students feel when their family lives and school lives converge. Finally, reenacting stories through other props, like puppets, shadows, or felt boards, can support children in interpreting stories independently and without pressure to participate in a product-driven performance.

Readers' Theatre

Readers' theatre is an increasingly popular way to apply theatre-based learning to classroom settings. Research suggests that readers' theatre improves reading fluency and comprehension, allows students to interpret text more carefully and supports vocabulary development. When readers' theatre includes strong reader models, the benefits increase. Because readers' theatre includes interaction, communication, and modeling between and among students and teachers, learners engaged in readers' theatre are exposed to multiple models to mimic and learn from.

Readers' theatre supports student fluency by encouraging students to read at a manageable rate, and to incorporate phrasing, smoothness, and volume. It supports reading rate and accuracy, matching students to readings within their appropriate range while allowing for full-group involvement. Readers' theatre supports appropriate volume and expression, connecting oral reading expression and comprehension by challenging students to put together words in meaningful ways, and developing the connection for readers between the text and the meaning.

It is not hard for teachers to find examples of readers' theatre, although older students can be invited to identify stories on their own that they think would be usefully translated into readers' theatre. Lacking most of the technical aspects of theatre, the structures of readers' theatre prioritize vocal interpretation. There are no sets, no props or costumes. Instead, readers sit in front of the classroom on chairs or stool and read from their scripts. Readers' theatre is usually played toward the audience, relying on actors' intonation, pitch, volume and other vocalizations to bring the story to life.

By incorporating a narrator or set of narrators, almost any classroom text can be translated into readers' theatre and adjusted to allow for multiple reading levels to participate at once. Because lines are written for each character, teachers can create scripts that include characters at each reading level in their classroom. When students write the scripts themselves, appropriate reading levels are necessarily incorporated into the script.

Students may engage with the same script over multiple days for readers' theatre, receiving feedback from their peers throughout to improve the vocal interpretation of their reading. As such, the process allows for multiple readings of the same text, a method that is linked to increased fluency, without decreasing student interest.

Choral Poetry

Finally, choral poetry is a powerful tool for connecting children through drama to new forms of literature. Both drama and poetry rely on the craft of oral performance. Poetry, then, can be easily matched to theatre-based learning. Poems that include stories or narratives are particularly strong for choral poetry, although any extended poem can be incorporated this way. Consider the poem, "A Bird's Lesson," (author unknown):

A BIRD'S LESSON
A little bird, with feathers brown, Sat singing on a tree;
The song was very soft and low, But sweet as it could be.
And all the people passing by Looked up to see the bird
Whose singing was the sweetest That ever they had heard.
But all the bright eyes looked in vain; For birdie was so small,
And, with a modest dark brown coat, He made no show at all.
"Dear Papa," little Gracie said, "Where can this birdie be?
If I could only sing like that I'd sit where folks could see."
"I hope my little girl will learn
A lesson from that bird;
And try to do what good she can—Not to be seen nor heard."
"This birdie is content to sit Unnoticed by the way,
And sweetly sing his Maker's praise, From dawn to close of day."
"So live, my child, to do some good, Let life be short or long;
Though people may forget your looks, They'll not forget your song."

This simple poem, often used with third graders, supports children's interpretation of poetry through their bodies and their voices. Considering questions about performance can help to introduce elements for both poetry and vocal performance. For example, students can better understand the concept of mood if they're asked to identify how they want their audience to feel when they hear the poem. They can articulate the theme of the poem by discussing which couplet carries the most important message of the poem. In thinking about vocal elements, learners can make decisions about when to pause, when to increase or decrease their volume or pitch, when to have multiple readers read at the same time, and when to have only a single voice. Unlike readers' theatre, choral poetry encourages children to memorize the poem to perform without a script, to incorporate movement if appropriate, and to receive feedback from their teachers and peers before finalizing their performance.

Planning for Theatre-Based Learning

Selecting a model of theatre-based learning depends on your objectives for your teaching. Different models will match particular teaching goals more precisely. National theatre content standards are articulated for classrooms throughout early childhood and elementary. In addition to the enactment-driven standards in social studies, literacy, math, and science, teachers should be aware of the standards for theatre content. It's interesting to note, however, that the national theatre content standards spiral between kindergarten and fourth grade, presuming that the same skills can be addressed at increasingly sophisticated levels of development. In other words, there is no time when children are too young or too old to incorporate theatre-based learning. Instead, the American Alliance for Theatre and Education names these eight standards across the K–4 spectrum:

Content Standard #1: Script writing by planning and recording improvisations based on personal experience and heritage, imagination, literature, and history Achievement Standard (AATE, 2018):

    a.   Students collaborate to select interrelated characters, environments, and situations for classroom dramatizations

    b.   Students improvise dialogue to tell stories, and formalize improvisations by writing or recording the dialogue.

Content Standard #2: Acting by assuming roles and interacting in improvisations Achievement Standard:

    a.   Students imagine and clearly describe characters, their relationships, and their environments

    b.   Students use variations of locomotor and non-locomotor movement and vocal pitch, tempo, and tone for different characters

    c.   Students assume roles that exhibit concentration and contribute to the action of classroom dramatizations based on personal experience and heritage, imagination, literature, and history.

Content Standard #3: Designing by visualizing and arranging environments for classroom dramatizations Achievement Standard:

a. Students visualize environments and construct designs to communicate locale and mood using visual elements (such as space, color, line, shape, texture) and aural aspects using a variety of sound sources

b. Students collaborate to establish playing spaces for classroom dramatizations and to select and safely organize available materials that suggest scenery, properties, lighting, sound, costumes, and makeup.

Content Standard #4: Directing by planning classroom dramatizations Achievement Standard:

a. Students collaboratively plan and prepare improvisations and demonstrate various ways of staging classroom dramatizations.

Content Standard #5: Researching by finding information to support classroom dramatizations Achievement Standard:

a. Students communicate information to peers about people, events, time, and place related to classroom dramatizations.

Content Standard #6: Comparing and connecting art forms by describing theatre, dramatic media (such as film, television, and electronic media), and other art forms Achievement Standard:

a. Students describe visual, aural, oral, and kinetic elements in theatre, dramatic media, dance, music, and visual arts

b. Students compare how ideas and emotions are expressed in theatre, dramatic media, dance, music, and visual arts

c. Students select movement, music, or visual elements to enhance the mood of a classroom dramatization.

Content Standard #7: Analyzing and explaining personal preferences and constructing meanings from classroom dramatizations and from theatre, film, television, and electronic media productions Achievement Standard:

a. Students identify and describe the visual, aural, oral, and kinetic elements of classroom dramatizations and dramatic performances

b. Students explain how the wants and needs of characters are similar to and different from their own

c. Students articulate emotional responses to and explain personal preferences about the whole as well as the parts of dramatic performances

d. Students analyze classroom dramatizations and, using appropriate terminology, constructively suggest alternative ideas for dramatizing roles, arranging environments, and developing situations along with means of improving the collaborative processes of planning, playing, responding, and evaluating.

Content Standard #8: Understanding context by recognizing the role of theatre, film, television, and electronic media in daily life Achievement Standard:

a. Students identify and compare similar characters and situations in stories and dramas from and about various cultures, illustrate with classroom dramatizations, and discuss how theatre reflects life
b. Students identify and compare the various settings and reasons for creating dramas and attending theatre, film, television, and electronic media productions.

Connecting these standards to your own teaching requires purposeful planning, thinking ahead to integrate theatre-based learning in meaningful ways across the curriculum. Ask yourself what the big ideas of your content are. What do students need to know how to do and how will they apply that knowledge? Are there applications that can be met through theatre-based learning? Are there concepts that are best managed holistically? Through extended linear drama? Through process drama? Through one of the interpretive modes? Where will you look during the *process* of theatre-based learning to see evidence of concept mastery, and what qualities or understandings of concepts may be evident through enactment? Are the benefits of enactment best matched to your intended content as a measure of prior knowledge, as a means of predicting and assessing content in the middle of a unit, as an evaluative model, or throughout the teaching?

Establishing a culture of theatre-based learning requires specific attention as well. Deep engagement with content in this manner requires more time to plan, process, and reflect than a simpler, rote lessons may. Student behavioral norms may change, as students leave their seats to engage in enactments, to observe each other, or to work together on planning and feedback. The noise level in the classroom will likely rise. Consider the stakeholders whose support you'll need to enlist to implement these models of teaching. Are there ways to secure space for heuristic models of learning within standards-driven cultures?

Integrating theatre-based learning into your teaching may include some small steps, like timely holistic improvisations or affective lessons during morning meetings and group times. Or, it may include more authentic, deep learning, like the internalization that evolves in linear drama or process drama experiences. It may provide simple tools to make students feel heard and known, like a morning greeting that allows for some playfulness, or more complex models that cross curricular boundaries and increase multiple skills, like readers' theatre or choral poetry. None of these models are likely to be successful without the buy-in of the teachers enacting them. Start first with the models that appeal most to you, and work through your comfort level to challenge yourself towards more involved, multilevel, and higher-order driven practices. That's exactly how children grow in their comfort in theatre-based learning: in small steps of increasing risk until they've grown accustomed to the skills and expectations.

Discuss

What are your own memories of theatre-based learning? What are the ways in which your theatre experiences either supported or undermined your willingness to engage at school? Discuss your experiences with a colleague and try to identify the characteristics that you would preserve or prevent in your own teaching?

Which of the models of theatre-based learning is initially most appealing to you? Why? Discuss with a colleague what you would need personally and professionally to feel comfortable trying a model that you're not yet comfortable with. How are your fears as a teacher similar to the hesitations students may feel if you were to institute these practices in your classroom?

Collaborate

With a colleague or small group of colleagues, compare the theatre content standards with a unit you currently teach or plan to teach. Identify immediate links between expectations across content boundaries. Identify links you could make with slight modifications. Identify links that you could make by using one of the techniques described in this chapter. Present your analysis to other colleagues or faculty members as a model of interweaving theatre-based learning.

With a colleague or small group of colleagues, analyze a unit you currently teach or are planning to teach that includes some theatre-based learning. What model of integration does it best reflect: subservient, affective, social integration, or coequal cognitive integration? What adjustments could you make to the unit to increase the authenticity of the integration? What resources do you have in your school, in faculty or instructional supports, to help you translate the unit?

Create

Choose a favorite children's book and construct your own readers' theatre script. Identify at least three different reader levels in your script. Share your script with other teachers for feedback.

Identify an epic poem you think would be ideal for choral poetry. Identify the literacy standards met by learning about and through the poem. Design a lesson to share with colleagues introducing them to this poem. Approximate teaching it to students in your classroom through practice with your colleagues. Consider volume, gesture, intonation, emphasis, rhythm, pitch, pauses and phrasing. How will you evoke thinking in your students to have them master these concepts through their own choral poetry practice?

Identify a concept from science standards for a grade you currently teach or intend to teach. Consider ways in which you can introduce it through holistic drama and prepare a lesson that incorporates holistic drama. Approximate your teaching with colleagues for feedback and reflection.

For Further Reading

American Alliance for Theatre & Education (AATE). (2018). The National Standards for Theatre Education, Grades K–4. Retrieved from https://www.aate.com/grades-k-4.

Ashiabi, Godwin S. (2007). Play in the preschool classroom: Its socioemotional significance and the teacher's role in play. *Early Childhood Education Journal*, 35(2), 199–207.

Betts, J. D. (2005). Theatre arts integration at a middle school: Teacher professional development and drama experience. *Youth Theatre Journal*, 19(1), 17–33.

Bhroin, Máire Ní. (2007). A slice of life: The interrelationships among art, play, and the "real" life of the young child. *International Journal of Education and the Arts*, 8(16), 1–24.

Bodrova, Elena. (2008). Make-believe play versus academic skills: A Vygotskian approach to today's dilemma of early childhood education. *European Early Childhood Education Research Journal*, 16(3), 357–369.

Bodrova, Elena, & Leong, Deborah J. (2005). The importance of play: Why children need to play. *Early Childhood Today*, 20(1), 6–7.

Bretherton, Inge. (1984). Representing the social world in symbolic play: Reality and fantasy. In Inge Bretherton (Ed.) *Symbolic play: The development of social understanding* (pp. 3–41). Orlando, FL: Academic Press.

Burns, Susan M., & Brainerd, Charles J. (1979). Effects of constructive and dramatic play on perspective taking in very young children. *Developmental Psychology, 15*(5), 512–521.

Dau, Elizabeth. (1999). I can be playful too: The adult's role in children's socio-dramatic play. In Elizabeth Dau (Main Ed.) & Elizabeth Jones (Consulting Ed.) *Child's play: Revisiting play in early childhood settings* (pp. 187–202). Baltimore, MD: Paul H. Brookes.

De la Cruz, R. E. (1995). *The effects of creative drama on the social and oral language skills of children with learning disabilities.* (Unpublished doctoral dissertation). Illinois State University, Bloomington, IL. DuPont, S. (2002). The effectiveness of creative drama as an instructional strategy to enhance the reading comprehension skills of fifth-grade remedial readers. In Richard Deasy (Ed.), *Critical links: Learning in the arts and student achievement and social development* (pp. 22–23). Washington, DC: Arts Education Partnership.

Friedman, Ori, & Leslie, Alan M. (2007). The conceptual underpinnings of pretense: Pretending is not "behaving-as-if." *Cognition, 105*(1), 103–124.

Gassner, J. (1954). Theatre arts in a free society. *Educational Theatre Journal, 6*(3), 191.

Gourgey, A., Bosseau, J., & Delgado, J. (1985) The impact of an improvisational dramatics program on student attitudes and achievement. *Children's Theatre Review, 34*, 9–14.

Harley, Elspeth. (1999). Stop, look, and listen: Adopting an investigative stance when children play. In Elizabeth Dau (Main Ed.) & Elizabeth Jones (Consulting Ed.), *Child's play: Revisiting play in early childhood settings* (pp. 16–27). Baltimore, MD: Paul H. Brookes.

Harris, Paul L., & Kavanaugh, Robert D. (1993). Young children's understanding of pretense. *Monographs of the society for research in child development, 58*(1), 1–92.

Hughes, Fergus P. (1999). *Children, play, and development* (3rd ed.). Needham Heights, MA: Allyn & Bacon.

Iannotti, Ronald J. (1978). Effect of role-taking experiences on role-taking, empathy, altruism, and aggression. *Developmental Psychology, 14*(2), 119–124.

Kontos, Susan. (1999). Preschool teachers' talk, roles, and activity settings during free play. *Early Childhood Research Quarterly, 14*(3), 363–382.

Lillard, Angeline. (2001). Pretend play as twin earth: A socio-cognitive analysis. *Developmental Review, 21*(4), 495–531.

Lindqvist, Gunilla. (2001). When small children play: How adults dramatise and children create meaning. *Early Years, 21*(1), 7–14.

Oliver, Susan J., & Klugman, Edgar. (2006). Play and standards-driven curricula: Can they work together in preschool? *Exchange, 170*, 12–14.

Rademaker, L. L. (2003). Community involvement in arts education: A case study. Arts Education Policy Review, 105(1), 13–24.

Performing Arts Research Coalition, (2007). The value of performing arts in five communities 2: A comparison of 2002 household survey data for the greater metropolitan areas of Austin, Boston, Minneapolis–St. Paul, Sarasota, and Washington, D. C.

Smilanksy, S., & Shefatya, L. (1990). *Facilitating Play: A Medium For Promoting Cognitivie, Socioemotional And Academic Development.* Gaithersburg, MD: Psychological & Educational Publications.

Taylor, M. (2009). Integration and distance in musical theatre: The case of Sweeney Todd. *Contemporary Theatre Review, 19*(1), 74–86.

Chapter 4

Integrating Visual Arts

"I found I could say things with color and shapes that I couldn't say any other way—things I had no words for."

—Georgia O'Keeffe

Visual Arts in Early Childhood

Pablo Picasso suggests, "every child is an artist," a belief affirmed by every proud parent who has hung his or her child's scribbles up on the refrigerator door. Crayons, pencils, markers, paints, paper, easels, walls, tables—give a small child a tool for marking and a tool that marks and the child's art will quickly follow. And while we may be frustrated by the all-inclusive definition of "canvas," and the clean-up it requires, we nonetheless take joy in the marks and circles and lines our children create.

That enthusiasm is mirrored in early childhood classrooms, which regularly include opportunities for children's exploration in the visual arts. The National Association for the Education of Young Children includes standards for the implementation of visual art activities in accredited classrooms, and recommendations for the specialized preparation in teaching through the visual arts for licensure programs for Early Childhood education.

Beth Harrington has been a pre-K teacher for eight years. Her classroom is a well-lit space in the annex of a church building. The cinder-block walls are painted bright white and the children enjoy a wall of windows that overlooks the church garden. Harrington offers a large easel in the corner near a window. "I like the children to paint by the natural light," she observes. "Some of the children would stay at that easel all morning if I let them!" The classroom is rich in other art experiences, too. A set of colored pencils and a magnifying glass are placed near a classroom plant, where children fill a journal with drawings of the details of the plant. Scissors, markers, crayons and watercolor paints line the top of the art shelf, with ample paper in different shapes and sizes for the children to choose. A large table that seats six is available near the art shelf, where there is a regular crowd of 4-year-olds chatting, drawing, and cutting. "I used to worry about getting the children to sign their work," Beth describes, "Because I'd be left at the end of the day with so many unidentified drawings. Then I thought, if they can't remember drawing the picture, maybe the finished picture isn't so important to them." Children can put finished work in their tote bags to go home, or they can place them in a basket labeled "Art to Share" near the front door. Beth uses these papers to create classroom stationery or to illustrate newsletters.

Children's development in visual art is a complicated process of sense-making, influenced by the culture within which that development unfolds and collective of that experience. It is difficult to predict, nonlinear, and often unlinked to the age of the artist, beyond the physical capacity to control tools. While we may still lack the research to define sequences of artistic development, we do understand that there are environments that are more supportive of development than others, and that particular kinds of experiences can lead to expanded experimentation in the arts. As teachers and parents consider the design of these kinds of environments, it's important to consider the impact of process and product-based art experiences, and of child-centered and teacher-centered art.

In early childhood, children learn through activity, needing to touch, move, and manipulate the world around them to understand it. They explore their environments as freely as they are supported to do so, learning about their world and their role within it through repeated experiments that begin to cement that understanding. They are active both in their bodies and their minds, often easily distracted and curious. As infants and toddlers, they look to their parents and caregivers as validators, affirming their contributions or guiding them toward others. In later childhood, the social strength of their peers will take an increasingly larger role. Throughout early Childhood, children benefit from open-ended, repeated opportunities to explore media and modalities in visual art. Simultaneously, their developing fine and gross motor control, cognitive, and language skills can be strengthened by well-defined exposure to artists, tools, and perspectives. Experiences, then, need to be both exploratory and defined, supporting children's need to practice new skills and incorporate new knowledge but to do so in a way that allows open-ended investigation.

Children's development through and in visual arts often follows sequenced appearances of skills and modes of representation, although the pace and trajectory of that development may vary widely between children, reflecting each child's cultural norms and personal experiences. A child whose family quilts together, for example, may have more opportunities to practice tessellation and fine motor control than a child whose experience is limited to large markers and paper. For both children, development will move from simple to complex, from concrete to abstract, and from uncontrolled to refined, but the pace of that development and the resulting skill the child shows in differing media may be less predictable.

Teacher Guidance and Feedback

Teachers and caregivers can support the individual pace of each child's development through some careful preparation. We'll consider in greater depth children's physical, social-emotional, cognitive, and language development later in this chapter. Throughout the domains, however, teachers and caregivers should take care to offer experiences and feedback that represents an understanding of the sequential and individual nature of children's development through the arts. Avoid correcting children's artwork, even when the work omits traits you identify as essential. A child who has not yet included a torso in a figure of a person, for example, has not forgotten to do so. His development does not yet include that detail in its representation. Accept children's artwork as a complete reflection of their development at that moment in time. Remember that, even in presumably "fun" activities like visual art, children need consistency, reliability, and repetitions. Allow children access to common materials every day to support them in repeating experiences that develop growth. Offer children open-ended materials that allow for individual discoveries, like play-dough, blocks, wood, paint, and crayons. Avoid coloring books or other limited presentations. Offer children feedback on what you've observed about how they've created their artwork rather than the artwork itself. Exchange responses like, "That's so beautiful!" for "Tell me more about why you chose to use these colors." Ask children about relationships you see in their work to evoke more conversation. "I notice you put your mom right here next to you. How did you make your mom different than your drawing of yourself?" Avoid asking the child, "What is that?" Instead, use language like, "Tell me more." Avoid drawing examples for children, even when they ask for them. Instead, prompt the child to include details in his own drawing. "You're drawing a puppy. How many legs does a puppy have?" Finally, when children notice and compare their work to the artwork of their peers, avoid comparing them as well. Instead, affirm that each child is working at his or her own pace, even when they make disparaging observations about each other. Instead of ignoring a comment like, "He can't draw a house. He's just scribbling," offer children alternative ways of framing what they see. "Max is drawing his idea. Max, can you tell me more about what you're drawing?"

As you explore children's development in and through visual arts, remember that the most important outcome for the art is the child's ability to make meaning from his experiences and to express that meaning. As such, whether a child's artwork is profound or pedestrian is not as important as the meaning the child intends to convey. Ask open-ended questions that allow the child to describe his intent. Probe with follow-up questions about the child's choice of proportion, line, color, and composition. Demonstrate your faith in the child's capacity by providing companionship as he explores new artistic challenges rather than defined models for him to copy.

Consider this simple overview of children's development in and through visual arts, specifically in the development of representational drawings:

AGE	STAGE	CHARACTERISTICS	DEVELOPMENTAL BENEFITS
18 mo. –3 years	Scribble	Children scribble at random, using large sweeping strokes that originate at the shoulder. Scribbles over the course of this development will move from unintentional and uncontrolled marking to increasingly more controlled. Early indications of hand-dominance may be notable. As the child matures, she may identify some scribbles as representing particular objects or people, although they may not be apparent to viewers.	• Practicing hand-eye coordination • Gross motor development • Fine motor development • Hand development • Naming and labeling • Finger dexterity • Agency • Independence • Initiative

2–4 years old	Pre-Schematic Stage	Children create complicated drawings, including a preference for favorite colors rather than accurate colors. Look for "tadpole people," represented by a large head with extended arms and legs but few other features. Objects "float" without a common horizon line.	• Practicing hand-eye coordination • Gross motor development • Fine motor development • Hand development • Naming and labeling • Finger dexterity • Agency • Independence • Initiative • Observation skills • Problem solving and prediction
5–8 years old	Schematic Stage	People are represented with more detailed proportions. Colors take on common stereotypes (blue skies, green grass.) Horizon lines are included. Children begin to demonstrate individual schema for their own drawings, making them easier to identify as one child's art or another. Children may describe a story before they begin to draw, and often have complicated stories they can detail about their drawings before, during, or after they're complete.	• Practicing hand-eye coordination • Gross motor development • Fine motor development • Hand development • Naming and labeling • Finger dexterity • Agency • Independence • Initiative • Observation skills • Problem solving and prediction • Exploration, trial and error • Patterning • Geometrical understanding • Number sense

Social-Emotional Learning and Visual Arts

In dramatic play, children's emotional and social understanding is enacted in real-time, a model easily observed by teachers and parents. Children's emotional and social understanding is no less influential to their experience in visual arts, although that understanding may be more difficult to observe. A child who draws a picture of her family in a garden has no less complicated an understanding of the included concepts than a child who acts out the same scene. In the child's mind, the experience of mother, father, sibling, flower, rest, play, and family may be just as potent. She may understand that the family has just arrived from a long car ride, or that this garden is in their neighborhood. She may imagine that the family has gone to the garden for some needed time together, or because the parents have decided the children have had enough time in front of the TV, or because her older brother has an assignment for school to identify leaves. Children's visual art holds wide, rich meaning, creating an external representation of an internal understanding. Even when children engage in art activities independently, their engagement reflects an understanding of social norms and relationships.

Recent research suggests that children offered high quality visual art experiences develop other prosocial behaviors, including sharing, empathizing, and helping others. For infants and toddlers, these experiences often occur in the company of a parent or caregiver, environments which allow modeling of supportive behaviors and increased attachment between parents and children. Quality integrated art experiences in classroom settings are correlated with increased emotional regulation, and participation in visual arts has been connected with children's emotional expression throughout early childhood. Because visual art experiences allow children to represent emotions for which they may not yet have language, these experiences provide a conduit for expression and emotional processing that children may otherwise lack.

While earlier research suggested that children in early childhood were essentially egotistic, more recent studies reflect the expansive ability children have for empathy, cooperation, care for others, and perspective-taking. Visual art can be used as a tool in early childhood to support the expression of these tendencies, to increase children's social awareness and for conflict management and resolution. Young children often lack the self-regulation to manage emotions, despite equal complexity of those emotions. Healthy classroom spaces, then, should be places which recognize this developmental state and help narrow the gap between a child's self-regulation and the expression of their complicated emotional lives. For example, a child who experiences great frustration in waiting for another activity to be available might be encouraged to draw himself playing with that activity while he waits. A child who is developing the ability to express remorse may create an image to express what he lacks the words to say. Likewise, investigating great works of art with children offers opportunities to consider what the figures displayed are thinking, feeling or experiencing, allowing time to talk through the wide variety of expressions of emotions from a safe distance.

Khanni Foster's toddler classroom serves eight children from 20 to 30 months old with two teachers. The classroom, in the living room of a converted home, is a warm and welcoming space. "I want it to feel like they're coming to my home," Khanni describes. She has made creative use of the architectural remnants of the house. Large floor pillows line the space of what had been the fireplace, creating a soft, quiet space for looking at books or observing the classroom. Window boxes installed on the inside of the window are filled with moldable sand, and children will stand at the boxes exploring the sand as they look outside. Khanni has removed the legs from a large easel and propped it against a wall, allowing children to paint from the floor to above their heads in large, sweeping movements. She's installed plexiglass on the wall behind the easel to facilitate clean up. "I'd rather spend more time cleaning after the children leave than not have this available for them." Near the door, Khanni has a coffee table with drilled holes that fit containers of children's play dough. "I use this space when children are coming in in the morning," she explains. "Some mornings, it's harder to come to school. The dough has different scents that I can use to engage the children. And because it's the right height for standing at, it's easier to approach than if they really had to come all the way into the classroom and sit down."

In the same building, Khanni's husband, Derek, is the lead teacher in a classroom of five- and six-year-olds, a shared kindergarten/first grade. "These guys are a handful!" Derek exclaims, "There's a big difference between the beginning of kindergarten and the end of first grade. Of all the things I think they need to learn, I don't think any of it happens if they can't figure out how to get along." Derek responds to this expanding influence of peers and the increasingly complicated social interactions by directing students toward what he calls, "draw-it-outs." A simple table for two is set in a corner of the room, complete with paper and thin-line markers, where Derek facilitates children drawing when they're frustrated or overwhelmed. "We talk about why we use markers. I don't want them to be able to erase their drawings. Emotions are messy and sometimes expressing our emotions is messy, too. But it feels safer to be messy on paper than in person." Sometimes children will choose the draw-it-out table independently, "especially if they can't choose what they want to do next, or if they're planning something really big and they want to think it through first." Often, children are encouraged to go to the table to draw their perspective on a conflict with a friend, after which Derek talks with children about what they've drawn and what they wanted to express. "It's less confrontational somehow," he explains. "The kids may draw themselves sad when they've been acting angry. That gives me a chance to talk about how sad sometimes looks like angry and how we can manage it together."

Working within a school that values the role of visual art in supporting children's social-emotional development, both Khanni and Derek have identified developmentally appropriate models to match the needs of the children they serve.

Physical Development and Visual Arts

Children's physical development undergoes extraordinary changes in the few short years of early childhood. From the first months of life, when infants lack the ability to coordinate their own limbs, to the careful demonstration of refined fine motor skills possible for a six-year-old engaged in cross-stitching, children's physical development influences and is influenced by their art experiences.

Consider, for example, newborns, who lack the visual discrimination to see distinctions of line or subtleties of color in their environment. Children in early infancy need art environments rich in strong lines and contrasting color. Black and white graphic images with a single contrasting color will hold children's fascination longer. Quickly, though, typically developing infants will be able to distinguish more details, identifying different faces and attempting to match the expressions they see through smiling, cooing, or babbling at caregivers and parents. As they begin to be able to coordinate their limbs, infants' coordination will move from their shoulders to their fingers, at first exploring their environments with sweeping movements of their shoulders and arms and only after time developing the ability to grasp, grab, and manipulate with their hands and fingers.

As the infant grows into toddlerhood, so will her ability to coordinate the actions of her body more carefully. While she may still need large-handled brushes or crayons with knob-heads for drawing and painting, the shapes she creates will be more intentional. Large circles will come to reflect bodies in space. Ultimately, straight lines will offer more complicated images of family members or beloved caregivers or pets. Art experiences at this age should allow for open-ended exploration with different sized tools and media, allowing children to practice their gross and fine motor development without expectation of clearly representational art.

This refinement can be supported in early childhood by increasingly narrow tools that support the child's pincer development or increasingly subtle media that respond to pressure and stroke in more nuanced ways. For example, while a toddler may not intend the difference between a hard stroke and a soft one, and therefore will be satisfied with markers and crayons, children in later development can practice how stroke influences the intensity of color with colored pencils, water colors or other more variant media. Likewise, younger toddlers may be satisfied with moldable sand and play dough, while older children will be attracted to sculpture materials that hold their form more reliably, like clay and sculpting bricks. Children with more refined fine motor development can explore other handicrafts, including cross-stitch, latch hook, and knitting.

Throughout early childhood, children's physical development in the arts is cumulative and sequential. A child cannot draw a circle with a crayon unless he has the ability to hold a thin crayon, and he will not develop the ability to hold a thin crayon without the opportunity to manage wider tools first. Children's physical development becomes more refined from the large muscle groups to smaller muscle groups, from the torso to the shoulder to the arm, from the arm to the hand to the fingers. Because children's development across domains is often less predictable, a child may have advanced cognitive development, with specific intent for her drawings, but less developed physical skill, resulting in drawings that "don't look right!" This disparity is common and managed through experiences that carefully support children's physical development.

Devon Pickren teaches in a Montessori classroom serving children from three through 6-years-old. "I think of art as one thing and physical development as another," she describes as she tours the Practical Life area of her classroom. "These materials are physical development: coordination, fine motor, gross motor." Each shelf includes a number of small trays, and each tray includes an activity focused on a specific skill: snipping paper, cutting on a line, cutting on curving lines, drawing on lines, drawing geometric shapes, coloring gradients of colors, matching colors and shades, etc. In another area of the classroom, Pickren offers a set of cards illustrating great works of art. "These are great conversation starters. We talk about what the artist has included in the image. We can organize them by period, or by images that include families or pets, or by the origin of the artist. There's lots to think about." Pickren also offers open-ended art applications throughout the classroom. A tall director's chair sits near a window with a clipboard and sketch pencil for drawing. A child-friendly digital camera allows children to compose pictures of their friends or classroom. A palette of acrylic paints and different sizes of paintbrushes are available as a free choice, for use with either the floor easel or to take to a table. I cycle out some of the more involved media, like making clay pots or when we take out the floor loom. Those are projects that we can all contribute to, so any one child may choose it for some period of time, but they don't have to finish a project on their own if they don't want to." Children choose activities from throughout the classroom, and the time and attention they commit to any one activity varies as much as the children involved.

There is a symbiotic relationship between the experiences in a classroom like Devon Pickren's, which benefits from an understanding of all the included skills necessary for a child to convey a complicated idea in a symbolic image. Children's physical development leads to particular kinds of art experiences. Likewise, differing art experiences contribute to children's physical development. Children, even those whose cognitive development is advanced, cannot express complicated thoughts symbolically if they lack the physical development to manage the tools for that expression. Efforts to do so will be frustrating and discouraging to the young child and can be mediated by early, low-risk activities that help to develop the gross and fine motor skills the child will need later. Healthy classrooms offer art experiences which both match and extend the current development of the children they serve. Basic, skill refinement activities are essential, but so are open-ended opportunities for children to use art for meaning-making.

Cognitive Development and Visual Arts

Children's physical development, especially in early childhood, influences their cognitive development, as physical experiences both reflect and lead to advancements in cognitive development. This sequence of development affects children's ability to engage in visual art as well as the purposes of that engagement. For infants and young toddlers, art experiences are largely exploratory, investigating the way media feels in their hands or moves on a page. In these early experiences, children explore to gather new information about the world, but lack the ability to reflect upon that information or to plan complexly for new experiences. Without the cognitive development to intend symbolic expression, their "art" experiences are best understood as the unintended outcomes of their exploration of a new environment. So, a toddler may be able to hold a marker and swirl on a paper, but he or she will not initially intend a representation in that experience.

Here, the influence of parents and caregivers is easily observed. Children who are encouraged to describe their drawings will often express different meaning, as their descriptions are more likely to be of the connections the child makes to her thinking at the time the question is posed than to her thinking at the time the drawing was created. In the first few years of life, as children develop increasingly complex schema to define their world, the encouragement and reassurances of parents and caregivers reinforce that refinement. A child, for example, asked to draw a picture of her family, offers her mother a crayon drawing, comprised mostly of lines and swirls. The mother replies, "Oh! You've drawn our family!" Parents and caregivers model drawing figures, common shapes and figures, demonstrating for the child that images drawn on paper reflect objects in our environment. Exposure to well-illustrated books and conversation about those illustrations further suggests to children the qualities of commonly understood artwork: dark colors to reflect nighttime, a yellow circle to symbolize the sun. Over time, children incorporate these symbols into their own illustrations.

Teachers, parents and caregivers can support this development by understanding the stages of children's cognitive growth through visual arts. Children from birth through 3 months, for example, can benefit from well-crafted mobiles, which support an awareness of space, and contrasting illustrations to stimulate the coordination of the eyes. Infants through seven or eight months will begin to connect stimuli with particular reactions, matching cooing noises, turning toward objects they can see and touch, and responding to varying tones of voice. This point in development is well matched by distinct textures and sounds, developing children's tactile discrimination and auditory discrimination. Early board books allow for time on a parent or caregiver's lap, connecting the emotional responsiveness of nurture with the experiences of reading and observing illustrations.

Young toddlers up to eighteen months develop new abilities to plan behaviors and responses, to understand language, and to follow instructions. They are able to hold crayons and move them on a paper, to build with sturdy blocks, and to manipulate play dough. At this stage of development, caregivers can provide beautiful pictures hung at the child's eye level to explore, begin naming shapes and colors, and explore tactile media like finger paint and dough.

Older toddlers, between 18 months and 2 years, begin to demonstrate the first evidence of mental imaging, associating verbal labels with concepts, and developing more complex thoughts. At this critical window, children begin to internalize common aesthetic norms, like painting trees green. Caregivers should offer ample exploratory exercises using different media. Nontoxic paints, shaving cream, watercolors, crayons, play dough, and blocks should be available for open-ended play. More complicated books, and books with more complex illustrations are especially well suited, although caregivers will still need to consider children's short attention span when choosing these activities.

Children from 2 to 3 years old begin to develop symbolic thought, development reflected in the initiation of representational drawings. Caregivers can support that growth by talking with children about the meaning they make of their own drawings. Understanding that the story a child tells about his or her drawing may change, caregivers can engage children in conversation about their own illustrations as well as illustrations and art they see in their environment. This is a particularly opportune time to introduce children to child-friendly museums and libraries.

Children from 3 to 4 years old begin to understand the range of artistic expression, to notice how their art is different and the same from others, and to remember their intent after a drawing is complete. This development can be seen in the use of more common artistic notions, like placing the sun in the top corner of a page or placing figures of people along a common landscape line rather than floating in space on the page. Children will be able to match colors, shapes, sizes, and patterns, to draw faces and bodies with noticeable details, and to show an interest in printing letters, especially their names. Children's spatial awareness is also growing and will be demonstrated in their intentional placement of figures on a page, the proportions of qualities in their constructions in play dough, and the complexity of their built structures with blocks and other items. This is a useful time to introduce cutting, snipping, gluing, and collage.

Between 4 and 5 years old, children will be able to match geometric figures, to explore overlapping figures and to fit shapes together. This is an opportune time to introduce tessellation and mosaic to children. Their expanded understanding of their world can be explored through strong questioning, encouraging children to plan, enact, and reflect on their art-work; to describe its meaning and detail; and to provide a context for their designs. Because this is a ripe time for the development of memory, it is also appropriate to introduce artists by name, style, and period to expand children's understanding of visual arts as both an expression of their own sense-making and as a separate discipline for study.

Children in the oldest years of early childhood can use visual art in complex ways, exploring styles of art, mirroring the techniques of great artists, or illustrating their own work. The expanded ability to problem solve allows visual art to be used as a planning tool for other design work in science and math, for explaining understanding of concepts in social studies and literary arts, and for taking a more purposeful role in conflict resolution in their social groups.

As children's cognitive development becomes more complex, so does their visual art. Simple understanding will be represented simply. More complex understanding may be represented more complexly. Likewise, children's ability to interpret and reflect on other people's visual art, from the great masters' to their classmates', will grow in its complexity as their ability to understand complex relationships develops. Remember, though, that this is not a direct link: children may have the ability to understand more complicated concepts before they have the fine motor control to illustrate them. As a result, the conversation and questioning that accompanies children's experiences in visual art is a critical component of both assessing and propelling their cognitive growth.

Language Development and Visual Arts

Children's language development provides a critical link, connecting their physical, cognitive, and social-emotional development as it is expressed through visual arts. For infants and toddlers, caregiver talk can help to define what a child sees and experiences in visual arts. Language should be complex and accurate, describing with precision what the child is observing or experiencing. As children grow, however, their use of language to express the meaning behind their visual art also grows, as does the opportunity presented through the arts to support children's expanded vocabulary, problem solving, attention to detail, understanding of complex relationships, and comfort with advanced thinking skills.

Visual art experiences offer ripe opportunity for the development of new vocabulary, to define qualities of artwork, to compare between visual art works, and to describe the techniques and skills a learner is using herself to create new art. Talking with children about their own art and the artwork of others allows an authentic context for complicated concepts. Children often understand ideas in a visual context sooner than they understand the verbal vocabulary that defines those ideas. Looking at and talking about art together, then, can help to create the links between what a child sees and understands and what that child can express.

Children also can be encouraged to talk about art in three dimensions: realistically, emotionally, and aesthetically. Rich conversation in each area provides meaningful application of new vocabulary and linguistic constructs. Looking at art realistically, the child can be asked to describe exactly what he sees. Looking at art emotionally, the child can be asked to describe what feelings the artwork evokes. Looking at art aesthetically, the child can discuss the elements of art that help to support the artist's intent: color, texture, pattern, balance, composition, line, and balance.

Dianne Plummer's classroom is rich in both visual art and language. Serving sixteen five-year-olds, Dianne's class supports children who are ready for a more traditional school day, but not yet ready for the expectations of the kindergarten at her school. Her "jumpstart" classroom looks very much like an exploratory preschool, but Dianne tries to match her children's learning to the intended content standards for kindergarten.

Really, the art is like my magic sauce. I haven't found a standard yet that there isn't some piece of art to match it to. We use Pollock to talk about line and emotion. We try to estimate the number of swirls in Van Gogh's *Starry Night*. We look at Delacroix' *Liberty Leading the People* when we talk about our American heritage. We love looking at the artists whose work looks childlike, like Picasso and Matisse, and artists who use bold geometry like Mondrian. We do an entire unit on Charles Demuth, because they love thinking about the fire engine and creating their own inspired works with numbers and symbols.

Dianne uses great masters to inspire small group conversations, which the class calls, "salons." She models analytic and sense-making questions for the full group, then lets children work together on different works of art, eventually creating their own individual pieces in the style of the artist they've studied. "It takes time, but it means that the art is really central to everything else we do. Talking about art comes naturally to the kids, so if I can start with the art, then the other stuff falls into place."

Trends in Early Childhood Education and Visual Art

In the past century, as our understanding of early childhood as a distinct period in human development has grown, so has the relationship of visual art to traditional schooling. The progressive approach, influenced by Piaget and his contemporaries, prioritizes art education that connects art experiences directly with what we know about children's development. The progressive approach encouraged child-centered art education, including a stage theory of children's development in visual arts, and a hands-off approach that would reflect the natural unfolding of children's skills and behaviors. This child-centered model is still evident in many schools today, in which the art classroom is a special place, a sanctuary from other school rules or norms, within which children can "let down their hair" without fear of assessment or judgment.

In the mid-20th century, art education moved from child-centered to subject-centered experiences, largely through the development of Discipline-Based Art Education, advocated by Elliot Eisner and others. DBAE responded to the challenge to provide a rationale for teaching art in school, reflecting the efficiency and competitiveness of school focus in a post-Sputnik America. DBAE emphasized the study of art as its own discipline, including art history, critics, and aesthetics. Because DBAE also reflected distinctions based on the development of the child, it affirmed the National Association for the Education of Young Children's Guidelines for Developmentally Appropriate Practice.

Toward the end of the 20th century, art experiences in early childhood were seen to hold new promise as a means of social justice and transformation. DBAE gave way to the CBAE or Community-Based Art Education model, which incorporated diversity, multiculturalism, pop culture, and feminist critique in art experiences. CBAE prioritized the human and cultural experience over art experiences that had emphasized western culture.

Currently, a number of curricula for early childhood emphasize art education, including Project Approach, museum-based art education, and the Waldorf model. The most prominent current model, however, is the Reggio Approach, based on the atelier schools of the Reggio Emilia area in Italy. In this model, art is understood as another language through which children can express their understanding of the world and their role within it. This model emphasizes art experiences, including the media, tools, and processes of art-making, as essential to the development of symbolic thinking and foundational for other learning. This perspective presents art-making as an ongoing, process-driven experience. Artwork, whether it is the child's or another artist's, is one type of expression, to be questioned, challenged, and refined as the learner grows in his or her own development.

Process-focused or Product-focused Visual Art

The developmental benefits of children's experiences in visual art are a factor of the degree to which those experiences challenge, strengthen or expand a child's initial development. Choosing art experiences, then, caregivers and teachers should think about what the experience will provide developmentally, rather than how the art will look when it's complete. Product-focused art experiences have limited variation in the outcome. A classic example is the cotton-ball snowman, in which children paste cotton balls onto precut circles until they've completed the body of a "snowman." Add a precut orange triangle for the nose and two black circles for eyes and each child's work will be almost identical to every other. Product-focused art activities tend to support specific physical skills like the development of the pincer grip or visual discrimination, or defined cognitive skills, like sequencing. They are useful means to assess children's development or to

Table 4.1   National Core Arts Standards for PreK

STANDARD	ANCHOR STANDARD	ENDURING UNDERSTANDING	ESSENTIAL QUESTION
Creating	Generate and conceptualize artistic ideas and work.	Creativity and innovative thinking are essential life skills that can be developed.	What conditions, attitudes and behaviors support creativity and innovative thinking? What factors prevent or encourage people to take creative risks? How does collaboration expand the creative process?
Presenting	Select, analyze, and interpret artistic work for presentation.	Artists and other presenters consider various techniques, methods, venues, and criteria when analyzing, selecting, and curating objects, artifacts, and artworks for preservation and presentation.	How are artworks cared for and by whom? What criteria, methods, and processes are used to select work for preservation or presentation? Why do people value objects, artifacts, and artworks, and select them for presentation?

build basic fine motor skills, but they lack the authentic engagement afforded by process-focused experiences.

Process-focused experiences, alternatively, are open-ended and reflect the child's thinking. They are investigative or reflective, providing interesting prompts, media or processes for children to explore. There is no teacher-created sample to match, because the focus of the experience is how the children engage the media rather than the exact product they create. As a result, children's creations are more unique and reflective of the development of the individual child. They tend to be more calming and affirming. They encourage risk-taking and develop agency. Children who are allowed process-focused visual art experiences develop a different understanding of the potential uses of media, allowing them to explore that media in more creative ways.

Product-focused art often leaves little to the imagination, and, not surprisingly, does little to support children's imaginations. Research suggests that the more specific models children are shown for how their

Table 4.1   National Core Arts Standards for PreK—Continued

STANDARD	ANCHOR STANDARD	ENDURING UNDERSTANDING	ESSENTIAL QUESTION
Responding	Perceive and analyze artistic work.	Individual aesthetic and empathetic awareness developed through engagement with art can lead to understanding and appreciation of self, others, the natural world, and constructed environments.	How do life experiences influence the way you relate to art? How does learning about art impact how we perceive the world? What can we learn from our responses to art?
Connecting	Synthesize and relate knowledge and personal experiences to make art.	Through art-making, people make meaning by investigating and developing awareness of perceptions, knowledge, and experiences.	How does engaging in creating art enrich people's lives? How does making art attune people to their surroundings? How do people contribute to awareness and understanding of their lives and the lives of their communities through art-making?

own artwork should look when they're finished, the less explorative and original the children's self-initiated art becomes. Children take fewer risks when they are encouraged to match a teacher sample. They demonstrate less persistence and they increasingly see themselves as "not good at art." Teachers may feel compelled to "fix" mistakes before sharing the child's work with another audience, and comparisons between one child's work and another are easy to make. Children may be frustrated by whether they can do the project exactly as it's been modeled, within the amount of time allowed, or identically to their peers.

In its healthiest application, the integration of the visual arts is a conduit for children's meaning-making, a means through which they can explore, reflect, and express complicated ideas and concepts. For that to happen, children must be offered experiences which allow individual meaning to be constructed: open-ended explorations of process through which children's own ideas or understanding can be conveyed. In short, the more limited the possible outcomes for a child's art, the more limited the complexity of understanding that will be reflected in it. Use product-focused experiences as limited skill building for physical development, like snipping paper, controlling the pressure on a pencil, or learning to adjust the intensity of water-colors. Use process-focused experiences to support children's cognitive, social-emotional, and language development, offering open-ended, child-driven expressions that evoke and inspire conversation about what the child intended to convey and how he went about the process.

Current Standards for Early Childhood Visual Arts

Teachers should understand that although some art is created to convey meaning, some for enjoyment, and some for function and use, all art reflects the context within which it was created and communicates meaning unique to that context. Toward that end, the National Art Education Association (2016) publishes National Standards for visual arts. NAEA defines visual arts in an expansive list, including, "drawing, painting, print-making, photography, and sculpture; media arts including film, graphic communications, animation, and emerging technologies; architectural, environmental, and industrial arts such as urban, interior, product, and landscape design; folk arts; and works of art such as ceramics, fibers, jewelry, works in wood, paper, and other materials." NAEA further distinguishes between what individuals can learn about visual arts and what it means to be "*artistically literate*," that is, the ability to engage in the creation of art directly through the use of appropriate materials, in appropriate spaces. "For authentic practice to occur in arts classrooms, teachers and students must participate fully and jointly in activities where they can exercise the creative practices of imagine, investigate, construct, and reflect as unique beings committed to giving meaning to their experiences." The NAEA standards offer high-level goals for creating, presenting, responding, and connecting art experiences across children's development (Table 4.1).

State-based standards, including the 21st Century Skills and Readiness standards offer more specificity for classroom practice, defining Early Childhood standards into four primary strands: Observe and Learn to Comprehend, Envision and Critique to Reflect, Invent and Discover to Create, and Relate and Connect to Transfer. Like the NAEA standards, the 21st Century standards avoid product-centered experiences in preference for visual art explorations that provide teachers and families insight into a child's understanding and abilities. The *Observe and Learn to*

Comprehend standard looks for evidence that learners can identify their own preferences in images when offered a variety of different modalities, can use age-appropriate vocabulary to talk about art, and can recognize basic characteristics and expressive features of art as it reflects every-day life. The *Envision and Critique to Reflect* standards emphasize learners' ability to explain that works of art convey ideas and to tell a story about art. The *Invent and Discover to Create* standard prioritizes learners' ability to use trial and error to create art that matches their intent, to use art materials safely and with respect and to create visual narratives from familiar stories. Finally, the *Relate and Connect to Transfer* standard suggests that learners should be able to explain what artists are and who can be an artist, identify common experiences of artists and name some of the art materials artists use.

Consistent among the standards for art education is the presumption that the visual arts, as its own discipline, engages learners through their physical, language, and cognitive development toward their social-emotional development. At the same time, visual art can be a tool for learning in other disciplines; for expressing understanding in literary arts and social studies; for exploring mathematical relationships, especially through geometry, spatial reasoning, and design; and for investigating scientific principles, through the visual representation of complex science concepts.

Preparing Visual Art Experiences

Just as in the preparation of any other content, teachers and caregivers should consider what they know about the development of the children they serve and what they hope to accomplish through the new experience. Well-designed experiences will closely link the teacher's goals with the child's development and will have observable qualities to demonstrate the effectiveness of the experience in meeting those goals.

Remember that children are active learners who construct their understanding of the world from their experiences within it. Consider what the children in your classroom understand, how they learn best, and what new experiences you can offer to support that learning. Specifically, match open-ended art experiences to children's development.

For infants and toddlers:

+ Emphasize simple elements: line, color, shape
+ Offer rich language in one-on-one activities with a trusted adult
+ Present the child's immediate environment and everyday life
+ Use encouraging language that describes the child's engagement
+ Include different and distinct sensory stimuli, including texture, color, temperature, and form, with an awareness for the sensorial responsiveness of the child
+ Mirror child's action with adult response and repetition

For preschool children:

+ Provide child-initiated choice
+ Offer process-centered activities with open-ended opportunities to explore, create, and reflect on those experiences
+ De-emphasize product by asking probing, open questions about the kinds of choices the child made in his or her process and about his or her meaning, rather than evaluative praise like, "Good job!"
+ Look to children-initiated games for themes of art
+ Consider child-appropriate opportunities to share work with peers and to discuss choices in process
+ Identify the skills necessary for each new art experience and provide opportunities for children to practice those skills in isolation
+ Connect art experiences to children's prior knowledge
+ Offer repeated, untimed opportunities for engagement that allow child to create for long periods of time or to use the same tools or media in repeated or innovative ways
+ Look to children's literature as source material for art styles and content
+ Provide language-rich dialogue about the process of art-making and meaning-making

For early-grade children:

+ Offer child-centered and child-initiated choice of activity, media, and modality
+ Implement a plan, create, reflect, present cycle for children's art-making and for soliciting peer feedback
+ Identify art links to curricular goals

+ Identify the skills necessary for each new art experience and provide opportunities for children to practice those skills in isolation
+ Look for interdisciplinary links across curriculum to weave through visual art
+ Look to children's literature as source material for art styles and content
+ Provide language rich dialogue about the process of art-making and meaning-making

Young children explore nontraditional learning through visual arts, supporting their physical, social-emotional, cognitive and language development, including their abilities in spatial and logical thinking, mathematic and linguistic knowledge, and social skills. Because children's development varies widely, so should the kinds of experiences you provide. Throughout early childhood, some common qualities should define those experiences. High quality visual art experiences should be:

+ reflective of both child- and adult-initiated themes; including both time to take action and time to think and reflect; indoor and outdoor; and in groups and as individuals
+ ample with opportunities for child-directed choice and agency
+ sensorially stimulating with quality materials, including high-quality illustrated children's books and high-quality reproductions of great works
+ designed to allow time for repetition and practice
+ focused on children's process instead of isolated tasks or products
+ supportive of children's expression and creativity
+ flexible in implementation
+ supportive of spontaneity and child-directed engagement
+ varied in media, modality, genre, artist, period, and form

Role of the Adult in Supporting Young Children's Development through Visual Arts

As a model, enactor and learner in visual arts, the approach of the teacher or caregiver in engaging visual arts carries special importance to the child's developing understanding of art in his or her own experience. Supportive adults:

+ work with art specialists and working artists to expand the quality and diversity of art experiences available for children in their care
+ plan activities that reinforce learning goals, including a wide variety of cultural experiences that link home and school
+ reflect best practices and knowledge of early childhood development
+ model risk-taking and comfort and support children when they are anxious about new art experiences
+ value the role of play, including play through visual art, in children's development
+ provide guidance for process but not specific models of products
+ provide opportunities to practice using materials, tools, and media
+ offer open-ended opportunities to problem-solve through visual art
+ draw attention to fine art in the environment, including quality illustrations in children's books, examples of great works of art, and quality design across modalities
+ engage children in conversation about their process and effort without emphasizing the product of their art experience
+ communicate children's development in visual arts to parents with equal emphasis to other content
+ model listening and curiosity about others' art processes

Discuss

Pablo Picasso said, "Every child is an artist. The problem is how to remain an artist once he grows up." Most children are open to the arts in early childhood, but many adults are hesitant or resistant to thinking of themselves as "artists." What is it about the transition to adulthood that influences our perception of ourselves as artists? Have you become more or less open to art experiences as you've gotten older? Why? What influence might your own perception of your life as an artist have on your preparation of learning experiences for children?

What are some common obstacles to integrating visual arts in your classroom that you might expect to encounter? How can you frame the value of visual art experiences to an administrator who wants you to emphasize more traditional learning models? How can you frame the value of visual art experiences to a parent who wants the same? Brainstorm how you would discuss the ways in which traditional learning goals can be met or enhanced by visual art experiences.

Many teachers rely on product-centered art experiences for classroom displays. Given what you've learned in this chapter, what impact would displaying product-centered art likely have on your students' disposition toward visual arts? How would you explain your choice to display or not to display children's art this way to another teacher?

Collaborate

Choose a masterpiece from an online search of visual art masterpieces. Without sharing your choice, describe your masterpiece to your partner. Detail what kinds of things you see in the painting. What kinds of lines, shapes or colors do you see? How would you describe the people or objects? Next, relate what you see. What does this painting remind you of? What connections can you make to your own life? What questions are you interested to answer? Next, analyze the painting. How do the colors affect the tone of this painting? How does the composition of objects or people relate some meaning to you as a viewer? What do you think the most important part of this painting is? Why do you think the artist made it? Finally, evaluate the painting. If you didn't know the painting's title, what would you name it? Why do you think it is included in a list of great works of art? Do you agree? After you have described, related, analyzed, and evaluated the piece, ask your partner to try to identify the painting you chose from the original list of masterpieces. What did you detail that led your partner to choose the painting he or she chose? How might your partner have answered the questions differently?

The Caldecott Medal is awarded annually to the "most distinguished picture book for children" of the previous year. Look at the medal and honor recipients for a year of your choosing. With your partner, design an exploratory art experience for young children that reflects the artist's style from that book. How would you draw children's attention to the artist's choices when you first read the book together? What foundational skills would a child need to develop to be able to explore the lesson you design? Present your lesson to your peers for feedback.

With a partner, review the content standards for math, language arts, science, or social studies for an age or grade you intend to teach. Identify a series of standards you think you could address through visual art. Design a lesson or series of lessons that would integrate this concept into a visual art experience. What do you need to know about your learners to prepare this lesson? What kinds of outcomes would you expect to demonstrate that your students have learned what you intended them to learn?

Create

Origami is an art form often presented to children because of its seeming simplicity. Choose instructions for an origami project from an online resource, like www.origami-instructions.com. While some learners are able to create origami sculptures with ease, many others find origami frustrating and stressful. What is your experience? How would you adapt the instructions you've found to make them more appropriate or accessible for young children? What emotions does the experience of exploring an unfamiliar art form evoke in you?

Create a large-scale collage of images and quotes that you want to have in your classroom with you. What images will you choose to give you encouragement? What choices will you make about composition, placement, color or line to emphasize some images over others? How will you share your collage with other viewers and what do you expect they'll understand about you by viewing it?

Consider a location or venue within which you find comfort and peace. Using a digital camera, photograph that location from a perspective that captures or evokes an intended message. Share your composition with a peer. How does your choice of composition convey your own experience of the space?

For Further Reading

Art. (n.d.). Retrieved May 15, 2016, from http://www.teachingideas.co.uk/subjects/art

Art & Learning to Think & Feel. (n.d.). Retrieved May 15, 2016, from https://www.goshen.edu/art/ed/art-ed-links.html

Teaching art to young children 4–9. (2002). doi:10.4324/9780203577998

Bloom, P. (1996). Intention, history, and artifact concepts. *Cognition, 60*(1), 1–29.

Boston, B. M. (n.d.). Early childhood art: A series of six articles on basic principles. Auckland, N.Z.: Dept. of Education.

Brewer, T. M. (2011). Lessons learned from a bundled visual arts assessment. *Visual Arts Research, 37*(1), 79–95.

Brynjolson, R. (2009). *Teaching art: A complete guide for the classroom.* Winnipeg: Portage & Main Press.

Creative Arts | National Association for the Education of Young Children | NAEYC TYC | *Teaching Young Children Magazine*. Retrieved May 15, 2016, from http://www.naeyc.org/tyc/links/creativearts

Hickman, R. (2001). Art rooms and art teaching. *Art Education, 54*(1), 6. doi:10.2307/3193887

Kolbe, U., & O'Shea, J. (1979). *Early childhood art: Construction*. Waverley, N.S.W.: Sydney Kindergarten Teachers College, Child Study Centre.

Koster, J. B. (2001). *Growing artists: Teaching art to young children*. Albany, NY: Delmar Thomson Learning.

Landau, J. (1986). Looking, thinking and learning: Visual literacy for children. *Art Education, 39*(1), 17.

Mahowald, M. (2013). Creativity and Art: Using Process Art with Young Children. Retrieved May 15, 2016, from http://c.ymcdn.com/sites/mnaeyc-mnsaca.org/resource/resmgr/imported/C10MargaretMahowaldWebsite.pptx.

National Art Education Association. (2016, June 22). National Visual Arts Standards Handbook: Nationl Core Arts Standards. Retrieved from https://www.arteducators.org/learn-tools/articles/221-national-visual-arts-standards-handbook.

Pathways to Development encourages children to develop interests in the arts and sciences. (n.d.). PsycEXTRA Dataset.

Raleigh, H. P. (1964). The art teacher versus the teaching of art. *Art Journal, 24*(1), 27. doi:10.2307/774744

Thompson, C. M. (2005). Repositioning the visual arts in early childhood education. In B. Spodek & O. Saracho (Eds.), *Handbook of research on the education of young children* (2nd ed., pp. 223–243). Routledge.

Thompson, C. M. (2014). Lines of flight: Trajectories of young children drawing. *Visual Arts Research, 40*(1), 141–143.

Chapter 5

Integrating Dance

"There is a vitality, a life force, an energy, a quickening that is translated through you into action, and because there is only one of you in all time, this expression is unique. And if you block it, it will never exist through any other medium and will be lost."

—Martha Graham

Dance in Early Childhood

Watch what happens when an infant hears music. Watch her feet flail and her arms spread wide. Research suggests that infants respond to both the rhythm and tempo of music and, in fact, find it more engaging than human speech. For infants between 5 months and 2 years old, the better they are able to align their movement with the beat of the music, the more they smile, regardless of whether an adult is modeling movement. Indeed, infants will move their arms, hands, legs, feet, and torsos in response to music with more frequency than they will respond to the human voice. Although we may, as adults, avoid dancing in public, the tendency to dance appears to be inherent to humans and evident from the earliest stages of our development. We may or may not want to sing along when we hear music. We may be comfortable observing and appreciating visual art or theatre, but our bodies are compelled to move in response to a steady beat and an uplifting tune. The drive to dance is essential in our own bodies, as the importance of dance to the development and perseverance of our cultural values is universal across societies.

In early childhood, then, dance serves two purposes: it is the natural expression of children's wonder and connection to the environments around them and it is a tool through which we can convey cultural norms and narratives. Caregivers and teachers should be responsive both to children's need to dance as a natural reflection of their physical, social-emotional, and cognitive development, and attentive to the ways in which that natural tendency can be harnessed toward the support of other learning goals. Often delegated to special events or the end of the day on Friday, dance education and education through dance offer rich potential to support children's learning and development.

Dance is fundamental to learning. When children dance, they learn by doing. They enact their knowledge of concepts with the tools most closely connected to their intellect: their bodies. Dance integrates kinesthetic learning, that enactment of learning through the use of our whole bodies, into other classroom goals, including curricular goals and, importantly, the social inter-reliance of class members. Because dance allows children to use their bodies as they learn, it matches more closely with the concrete nature of children's thinking, especially in early childhood. Dance is an authentic learning opportunity, offering real-time problems to solve through creativity, cooperation and collaboration with peers. By solving creative movement "problems," children practice critical problem-solving, making real choices about their bodies and their engagement with other learners. This type of engagement supports children's sense of their own agency as problem-solvers and contributors, and enhances their knowledge, skill and understanding of the world around them.

Because verbal and nonverbal movement can be integrated in early childhood, dance offers the potential for a full-body expression of understanding. Children who are preverbal can use dance to express ideas that they are not yet able to articulate. Children who are verbal already can expand on the complexity of their articulation by enriching it in their body language and movement. As we'll discuss in this chapter, learning for early childhood requires both the intellect and the body. Language and dance, then, are not separate constructs, but are equal tools in a child's toolbox to acquire, internalize, and reflect on new knowledge.

Dance also allows children immediate feedback on multiple perspectives. Children build their sensory awareness, their consciousness of the limits of their own bodies and of the limits of other's bodies, and their knowledge of the expansive potential of movement to convey and communicate new ideas. By engaging in dance in early childhood, children learn early to enact multiple languages, to apply universal symbols in body language, and to contribute to experiences beyond the limits of their own bodies. Although once a prominent cornerstone for democratic education, in the past century, dance has lost its place as a relied-upon discipline for social and cultural learning, and has, instead, been delegated to enrichment despite the ample evidence of its strength as a pedagogical tool.

Trends in Dance Education

At the beginning of the 20th century, American public schools absorbed practices from our peers in Europe. Dance, especially large-group dance, was a common element of the school day. National dances were taught as a part of the child's developing physical, social, and intellectual development and with an eye toward securing the workings of the democracy. Theorists like John Dewey encouraged dance as a part of a democratic model of schooling, and other educational theorists pointed to the importance placed on dance from the ancient Greeks as evidence enough to defend its use in American schools. Dance was hardly an open-ended or experimental activity, however. Movement games were common and prescriptive, and adults directed each component of the dance as it was enacted by children. Dance served specific pedagogical goals: the transferral of democratic ideals and enculturation, secured through orderly, predetermined sequences of movement to assure efficiency.

In the 1920s and 1930s, the expanding influence of scientific theory on education lent its weight to dance education as well. Formal teacher education in dance developed and dance grew as its own discipline for study, with attention to movement, anatomy and efficiency. At the same time, dance in schools continued to emphasize its contribution to a democratic society. Concentration, preparation for work, and an understanding of physiology were foundations, with an emerging interest in children's free play and imagination as it was expressed through dance. Dance educators including Rudolph Laban published manuals on dance education, analyzing movement, and articulating a developmental plan for children's dance from birth through adulthood. These guides were highly directive, boiling down children's movements to lists of the most useful and necessary for proper health and social engagement.

In the 1950s, dance education was influenced by a growing interest in psychology and the development of self-esteem. Creative dance books guided teachers to incorporate dance for the "whole child," and began to consider child-centered methods for dance education. Dance education was more child-centered and open-ended, with specific methods engaged as building blocks and opportunities for children to develop their own extensions.

The open classrooms of the 1960s and 1970s saw the increased influence of a growing body of work on brain development, thinking of dance as essential for the integration of the hemispheres of the brain and a natural component of child-centered classrooms. Dance still held its role as a tool for social cohesion, and folk dances, especially square dancing, were common in school curricula. Simultaneously, the idea of dance as a personal expression of emotion and understanding began to evolve, as the genre of modern dance pushed the boundaries of classical instruction.

Despite 70 years of well-integrated dance programs, dance education began to wane in school settings in the 1980s and early 1990s. Changing norms for family life, including single-parent households and families within which both parents worked led to less time outdoors for children and more sedentary entertainment. Fitness and aerobics took the place of dance in school settings. As school became relied upon to assure the physical healthfulness of students, dance was relegated to special events in exchange for more active PE curricula. Dance curricula began to replace the word *dance* with *movement*, and emphasized fitness over the social or democratic benefits of dance.

In the early 21st century, dance was further separated from the norms of the school day, and even the physical fitness and movement curricula that had been in place was sacrificed for more instructional time on traditional content areas, especially in literacy and math. While previous generations had enjoyed physical education or recess every day, many districts limited their physical education programs to an hour or two a week, if that. Ironically, although current research best supports the perspectives on dance education first proposed over a hundred years ago, dance education is often absent from traditional early childhood and elementary programs, relegated to optional after-school programs or to a unit within a larger PE curriculum.

Dance Education, Physical Education or Something Else?

Caregivers and classroom teachers today struggle with the boundaries between dance education and physical education and the degree to which they can justify either in higher-stakes, standardized models of schooling. Caregivers and teachers should be aware, though, of the necessity of physical movement, including dance, to children's ability to learn and retain new information. In early childhood especially, the developing ability to move and coordinate one's own body affects the kinds of learning that can be supported through dance. As such, there is often overlap between what qualifies as physical education and what is more formally dance education.

Understanding the benefits of the two domains, physical education and dance education, can help teachers and caregivers to give appropriate attention to both. This chapter will provide greater detail on the physical, social-emotional, cognitive, and language benefits of creative movement experiences. If teachers must justify this movement as either dance or physical education, they might do so by considering first their learning goals. If the primary learning goal is the artistic process, the conduit for that learning is through the art of dance. Connecting with appropriate dance experts will be useful in making these experiences more authentic for children. If the primary learning goal is physical fitness, dance can be used as a tool in a larger physical education program. If the primary learning goal is other content development, social-emotional development, or language development, dance can be integrated as one of many pedagogical tools.

There is ample evidence to support integrating dance and creative movement across the curriculum. Research suggests that children who receive exemplary dance education in early childhood and elementary programs outperform other learners in reading and math scores. Children who participate in dance exhibit more persistence, especially in problem solving and new challenges, than students with no dance experience. They develop gross motor skills that support engagement in other content, fine motor skills, and specific thinking skills, including pattern recognition, pattern development, increasingly detailed mental representations, symbolic and metaphorical thinking skills, the ability to abstract concepts, and the ability to observe. Teachers describe how integrating dance into their classrooms supported a deeper understanding of individual children as learners, increasing their ability to differentiate for different learning styles and levels. Dance programs support teacher capacity by increasing their receptivity to co-teaching and collaborative models, increasing the authenticity of their instruction, and increasing the transferability of content taught to other areas. Teachers integrating dance reported higher levels of their own engagement, deeper knowledge of concepts from their students, social buy-in for collaborative learning models, intellectual rigor and challenge, and classrooms that reflected higher levels of respect and support between students.

At the same time, dance is the least likely of the arts to warrant its own specialist for instruction in U.S. elementary schools. Only 3% of public schools in the United States offer separate instruction in dance, a number which has declined in the last 15 years. Increasingly, teachers report integrating dance into their own classrooms to make up the difference. In 1999–2000, only 38% of classroom teachers reported integrating dance education. By 2010, that number rose to 57% and continues to increase. As dance is a powerful tool for learning and development, it falls to teachers and caregivers to bridge the gap between children's need for dance and creative movement and school structures that may exclude it.

Social-Emotional Learning and Dance

As adults, many of us experience anxiety or self-consciousness when we're asked to dance. How is it, then, that it may be a source of social-emotional comfort and growth for children? Our hesitation about dance is learned. In early childhood, infants, toddlers, and children will naturally look to movement and dance as a means of strengthening and expressing social bonds. For infants and toddlers, dance provides an opportunity to form secure relationships with caregivers. Infants will naturally move when they hear a steady beat. An adult response that affirms that movement or enters into it allows time for meaningful interaction based on the infant's initiation. Likewise, a crying infant who is soothed by the gentle rocking in his parent's arms is comforted both by the natural rhythm and by the human connection that occurs, connecting gentle movement with a sense of comfort and safety. An infant moving in the arms of a loving, responsive adult learns to associate that movement with nurture and care. A toddler dancing with a peer or adult benefits from the joyful interchange as a means of securing connected relationships with both. The more frequent these interactions, the more likely they are to lead to connected relationships, as infants and toddlers learn that their caregivers are reliable, consistent providers of both nurture and joy.

Likewise, as children become more aware of others around them, dance can provide an important social cohesion. Children who dance together develop their awareness of other people's space and bodies, their ability to regulate their own movements and exuberance, and their sense of themselves as a part of a group. Children who are offered quality music to listen and move to independently build an attunement to their own bodies and to new ways to express emotions they may not otherwise be able to articulate. In organized opportunities to dance together, children develop the ability to contribute to something larger than their own experience, to cooperate and collaborate with others, and to regulate the degree to which their own movements influence the group.

Although dance and movement may be intrinsic to human development, a freedom from the judgment of others is not. Teachers and caregivers should be responsive to the degree to which they affirm children's dance. Sitting down, observing, or encouraging without participating may send the message that dance is something "for children only." Instead, caregivers can and should dance with children, modeling both participation and self-regulation. Especially in times of comfort and nurture, adults should provide the emotional closeness of intimate physical space by holding, rocking, and soothing children through movement.

Physical Development and Dance

Of all the arts, the benefits for physical development may be most easily observed through dance. For infants and toddlers, dance offers an early opportunity to begin to coordinate their bodies, to manage the large muscles of their torso, arms and legs, and the small muscles of their feet and hands. As children grow, creative movement and dance supports the development of balance and coordination, as well as important self-regulation skills. Children become aware of how quickly they're moving, how to stop their bodies, and how to change direction. They become more aware of spatial relationships to manage their own personal space and the space of others.

Remember that children's physical development will progress from large muscle groups to small, from gross motor to fine motor control. Younger children, then, will dance using their entire bodies. Infants lying on their backs will respond to music with their arms, legs and torsos, wiggling their entire bodies at once. Toddlers may dance by squatting and rocking, with the prominent movement coming from their torsos, hips, and shoulders on the firm foundation of their legs. In early childhood, children will develop the ability to move their hands and feet independently, tapping one foot on one leg independently or moving their bodies with asymmetrical control.

For toddlers and children in early childhood, caregivers should model a range of diverse movements: marching, walking, tiptoeing, jumping, skipping, hopping, spinning, and galloping. Caregivers can provide models for moving through space in unusual ways, slithering, crawling, or rolling in addition to upright movements. Caregivers may offer open-ended time during which children can move their bodies as they choose to different music styles. Formal dance lessons are also appropriate, to allow practice in isolating muscle groups and developing skill. Group dances, especially simple ones with a few rules and a common dance for all participants, offer opportunities for children to listen to each other and to the music while they execute different actions. Through these organized experiences, children will strengthen their coordination, stamina, and strength. Because dance is naturally engaging, requires no special equipment, and can be easily integrated into a classroom setting, it offers a playful means of physical activity to support children's healthfulness and activity and an authentic opportunity for groups of children to connect to each other and have fun.

Cognitive Development and Dance

Children are active learners who need to move to learn. Movement improves alertness, motivation and the ability to attend to new concepts. It prepares nerve cells to bind with each other and it initiates the development of new nerve cells in the hippocampus. Facilitating and incorporating children's natural tendency to move, then, helps support cognitive development from early infancy. Children in the first 5 years of life enjoy a distinct window for motor development, when movement is uniquely linked to early brain development.

For young infants, provide slowly moving mobiles to support the initial coordination of their eyes from one side of their field of vision to another. As infants grow, they will move their heads to attend to different colors or shifts in lighting, toward people's voices and toward toys that make noise. Allow for this without interruption. The ability to coordinate their own heads and eyes requires practice; support it without rushing by giving infants time to find objects in their field of vision. In later infancy, children will be able to copy the expressions and movements of caregivers. Support this by offering ample "face time," maintaining eye contact with infants, and exploring expressions and simple hand movements. Allow time for infants to reach for objects and hold objects still within reach as infants develop the ability to coordinate those efforts.

As infants develop their locomotor skills, sitting, crawling, standing, and walking, new cognitive growth simultaneously unfolds. These early movements experiences develop the parts of the brain needed for regulating behavior and emotion. Children who engage in active play throughout the day present lower levels of cortisol, a hormone known to damage neurons in the frontal lobe. Active play allows not only for the development of physical skills, it supports neural connectivity and protects the brain.

The noticeable physical growth during preschool is matched by equal change in the development of children's brains. Physical movement begins to be connected to specific intent, and learning happens concurrently to movement, happens more easily, and is retained more easily. Children who engage in purposeful movement also demonstrate consistent advancement in the development of executive functioning. Creative movement and dance boosts the levels of brain-derived neurotrophic factor, a protein necessary for the growth of brain cells and stimulates neurogenesis, the development of new neurons. It is linked to enhanced brain plasticity, improved reaction time, and improved accuracy on tasks that require concentration and attention. Children who engage in active physical movement regularly, including dance, show improvements in working memory, in cognitive flexibility, in math skills, and in attention.

Language Development and Dance

Movement is as essential to our social worlds as language, offering learners an alternative mode of communication that spans the limits of specific languages. Research suggests that, in addition to the norms of body language, ideas and concepts expressed in words actually begin in movement, in a physical response within the body. For infants and toddlers, caregivers can narrate children's movement, naming for the child what she is doing. "You are stretching your arms toward that mobile," or "Your legs bounce up and down!" For older toddlers, caregivers can begin to link children's language and creative movement through games that engage the child's imagination. "Walk like an elephant," or "Let's slither like snakes," are easy, playful ways to connect with children, to support them in practicing the coordination of their bodies, and to expand their vocabulary through innovative contexts.

Children who are attuned to rhythm and movement can build upon that attunement to include the rhythm of speech and language. Consider the pace and rhythm of well-crafted children's books; children attend to these changes in rhythm with their entire bodies. Sequencing activity, like the sequences that support creative movement and dance, is a precursor to the ability to link words into sentences and sentences into paragraph. Both require children to select parts that flow together toward a coherent whole—to begin, change, and end. Learning to sequence movements additionally is linked with the ability to access other modalities for learning:

visual learning, auditory learning, tactile learning, vocal learning, kinesthetic learning, creative learning, and long- and short-term mnemonic learning.

As a tool to support language development, children prefer active, creative movement and retain learning best when it's linked with creative movement. Consider the specifics of language learning. Prepositions (over, under, near, beside) are essentially movement terms—language used to describe physical relationships in space, relationships best retained when children are able to experience them with their own bodies. Children's spatial awareness is essential for identifying letters and orienting symbols on a page. When children speak to each other and listen to each other in engaged games, they practice vocabulary and communication skills in an authentic, engaged way. Active group games often lead to new rules, to the development of further communication skills and to practice with the ones children may already know. Children can practice complex language structures, like adverbs and unusual vocabulary, by enacting it with their bodies through dance and creative movement. Games that ask children to move like a dinosaur or dance like a butterfly, to pounce or slither or squirm, to hop quickly or walk tenderly, practice complicated understanding of symbolic thinking, supporting children's language development, and expanding vocabulary. In enacting language prompts in their own bodies, children internalize new vocabulary and relationships with greater retention and understanding.

As children practice these creative movements, they will expand their retention of the vocabulary that accompanies them. The National Dance Educators Organization publishes a comprehensive glossary of dance terms for early childhood dance programs, including distinct vocabulary like: alignment, agility, axial movement, beat, choreography, cross-lateral movement, dynamic, force, form, improvise, kinetic, locomotor, musicality, proprioception, rhythm, transition, and unison. Introducing unusual dance terms in context will enhance children's understanding of those terms and increase retention and generalization to other settings.

Language development can also be supported through group dances that require children to listen to the dance "call," process the direction and the visual cues they see from other dancers and execute the dance. Simple square dances and folk dances are easy to integrate into classroom settings, supporting the interconnectedness of the group while building new vocabulary and linguistic processing skills for the dancing children. Children can also take the lead in calling dances for each other, creating their own language prompts for other children.

Dance for Skill-building

In language development, physical development, and cognitive development, dance offers aligned supports for the development of specific skills. Because dance requires careful coordination of physical sequences, caregivers should prepare to explore the components of those sequences in isolation. A folk dance, for example, that requires children to move in and out of a circle, to link arms, to grapevine over their ankles or to do-si-do a partner may seem like easy, fun activities, but can be frustrating for children who have not mastered first the ability to coordinate those components individually.

Consider ways in which creative movements can be isolated and integrated into other classroom or environmental experiences. Moving between activities, for example, provides an opportunity to practice grapevining your legs. Wait time, like the time before children are dismissed or when waiting for friends to all arrive at a circle time, offers time to practice skills like tapping one foot at a time or reaching in and out of a circle. Because children are active learners, the more often caregivers can integrate movement into the day, the lower the behavioral challenges that come with intellectual boredom will arise. Dance is an effective classroom management tool, giving children a common goal to which to attend, and offsetting some of the required functions of school settings with engaging activities. Walking through the hallway "like egrets," or swaying one's torso "like a willow tree" while waiting on the line engages children's minds and bodies. Even fine motor skills can be approximated through dance games. Dancing "with your fingertips" provides children necessary practice in isolating the muscles of the hand and fingers without tedious pincer grip drills.

Dance for Social Cohesion

Dancing as a group requires children to listen to each other, to agree to collaborate for the benefit of the group, to regulate their own impulses to keep the group on task and to rely on each other to do the same. As such, dance is a unique tool for building social cohesion in a classroom setting. In the early weeks of a new classroom, dance can be used to teach children each other's names, to familiarize each other with personal space and to share the common experiences that help to build a classroom identity. Throughout the year, dance can be used to remind children of the rules and norms of respectful touch, to allow children to problem-solve together and to practice leadership and participation in the group.

At special benchmarks, dance can be used to celebrate together, to share joys or express common emotions. While there are ample examples of folk dances that are appropriate to use with children toward these efforts of social cohesion, class dances can also be choreographed by the children themselves.

Because dance also provides authentic access to folk stories and cultural narratives, dance is an effective tool for affirming the goals of a democratic education. Dance allows children to contribute to a project in which each member's contribution is invaluable, to take responsibility for their individual contribution as a part of a larger social goal. Dance can be used to convey the traditions and norms of distinct cultures and to learn how those norms are different or the same from ones with which the children are more familiar. Many folk dances, for example, include similar components (dancing in a circle, holding hands, moving in one direction together). Dance can be used to contrast cultures and to identify that which is universal, offering personally relevant connections for children to distinct cultural traditions.

Dance to Support Other Content

Dance also serves as a useful support to other curricular goals, especially in early childhood and elementary classrooms. In language arts, dance can be used to enact vocabulary, to demonstrate awareness of grammatical relationships, to tell stories, and to demonstrate listening skills. It can be used to demonstrate reading and listening comprehension and as an organizer for writing or composition skills. In math, dance can be used to demonstrate relationships of numbers, fractions, even distribution, geometric relationships, and logical thinking skills. Social studies is a natural match for dance, as dance can be used to make more immediate comparative cultural norms through folk dance or sequences and progressions through timelines. Studying and enacting dances from across eras is an immediate and personal way to understand differing social norms and values. Even science skills can be supported through dance. Relationships in space, scientific phenomena, changes in states of matter: if a concept has an example in our universe, it's likely that children can demonstrate their understanding of that concept by enacting it with their bodies.

Imagine, for example, the complicated and abstract concept of time. For early childhood learners, time is a phenomenon difficult to internalize, and yet clearly prioritized by society around them. A child's birthday may be a ripe opportunity to make concrete this abstract concept, through dance. Ask the children to sit in a circle. Place a candle or lantern in the middle of the circle to represent the Sun. Hand the birthday child a small globe and guide the child to carry the globe around the Sun as many times as the Earth has orbited the Sun since the child's birth. Children who are older will need to walk for longer. Children who are younger may make only three or four revolutions around the Sun. Enrich each orbit by describing the skills or experiences the child had during the respective year. For older children, choose another child to carry a mirror to represent the Moon and instruct that child to orbit the child with the globe twelve times for each revolution the globe makes around the Sun. Here, a complicated scientific principle, the orbit of the Moon around the Earth and the Earth around the Sun, is made concrete and physical by the choreography of the dance. A complicated cognitive principle, that of the passage of time, is made equally concrete, and the children's understanding of the relationship of both is enhanced.

Learning Standards for Dance in Early Childhood

Dance allows children to express themselves and their knowledge through movement, to internalize and enact understanding, to compose, interpret and present that understanding in a way that others will understand as well. In early childhood settings, dance can be studied as its own art form or as a means of supporting other development. Many states, then, publish dance education standards both for dance as a discipline and dance as physical fitness, and dance standards in early childhood are included in the 21st Century Skills and Readiness. For example, standards in movement, technique, and performance anticipate that children should be able to practice how to move with action vocabulary, how to use simple non-locomotor body actions (like bend, twist, stretch, and shake) and how to use simple locomotor actions (like jump, run, hop, and roll). Children should be able to explore movement in their own bodies and space and to make changes to that movement based on common descriptors, like size, shape, level, direction, and stillness. Children should be able to perform simple phrases of movement as they experience sequence, rhythm, and spatial relationships. For standards in composition and choreography, children should be able to translate simple ideas and stories into movement, exploring with movement different feelings, shapes, sizes, levels, and directions. They should be able to make patterns in space and time, to select some movements from larger groups and sequences and to use sensorial stimuli and real-life situations to create original dances. In anticipating children's experience of dance for historical and cultural context, standards expect that children will be able to recognize dances from around the world, to explore the country of origin, to explore dance as a means of cultural expression, and to understand how people in different cultures move in similar and different ways. Children should be able to explore dance as a means of celebration in different cultures and to describe the dances they observe. Finally, for standards in reflection, connection and response through dance, children should be able to observe and identify different dance genres, to experience observing and responding to dance in a joyful way, to demonstrate movement as a means of expressing emotion, and to be able to translate what they've seen in other ways, by speaking or drawing, for example. They should be able to observe dance with attention and appreciation and to demonstrate their observation through thinking skills including describing, analyzing, interpreting, evaluating, and discussing what they've seen.

Benchmarks for Physical Development and Creative Movement

Remember that movement and learning are deeply entwined in early childhood. Teachers and caregivers should prepare opportunities to expand children's natural movement but should be cognizant of the developmental norms for most children's development.

Between birth and three months, most infants will

- demonstrate rooting, sucking and grasping reflexes
- raise their heads slightly when placed on their stomachs
- hold their heads upright for a few seconds without support
- clench fists tightly
- discover their own hands, tugging and pulling on their own hands and fingers
- repeat movement

At this time, the environment is best prepared with gentle, nurturing movement from caregivers. Children have not yet begun to coordinate their movements independently but will be more responsive to gentle rhythms that mirror regular heartbeats, swaying and rocking in a caregiver's arms. Avoid electronic bouncers, which are unresponsive to child-initiated movements, and instead consider infant seats which respond to an infant's real movement.

Between three and six months, most infants will

+ roll from their stomachs to their backs and back again
+ pull their bodies forward using their shoulders or forearms
+ use their torsos to move forward when sitting upright
+ pull themselves up on the sides of a crib or while holding an adult's hands
+ reach for and hold objects
+ bring objects to their mouths (and their mouths to objects!)
+ shake and play with objects in their hands

At this time, infants benefit from time on their stomachs and the gentle modeling of adult caregivers. Spend time on the floor with infants, rolling and rocking from side to side, or on your stomach lifting your own head to model looking at the infant. Infants will begin to coordinate the movements of their torsos, making this an appropriate time to introduce higher-paced music to dance to while the infant is in his or her caregiver's arms. Infants will respond eagerly to music at this stage, kicking their legs and spreading their arms in response.

Between six and nine months, most infants will

+ scoot
+ crawl
+ reach, grasp, and pull objects to their chests
+ transfer objects from one hand to the other

At this time, infants will demonstrate more coordinated movements of their arms, legs, and torsos, encouraging more active caregiver-infant dancing. Look for infants to begin responding to music while they're on their stomachs, shifting the weight in their hips with more coordination and "dancing" with their whole bodies.

Between nine and twelve months, most infants will

+ stand with assistance
+ sit up unassisted
+ walk with assistance or without
+ throw objects
+ roll balls

+ use their thumb and forefinger or middle finger to pick up objects

Children will enjoy standing up to dance, holding on to a rail or a caregiver's fingers while they squat, wiggle, and move to music. Allow ample time for this, and for the predictable falls as infants learn to coordinate eager movement while on their feet. Avoid "container seats," that hold children in one place and don't allow them to control where they move their bodies. Instead, prepare environments that are safe for children to move through and explore, including mirrors hung low to the floor so children can observe themselves as they shimmy, scoot, and crawl.

Between one and two years, most toddlers will

+ pick things up while standing
+ walk backwards
+ walk up and down stairs while holding a rail, wall, or adult's hand
+ move and rock to music
+ turn knobs and handles

Dancing abounds! Offer a variety of music to dance to, including softer music and more high-energy melodies. While younger children will enjoy music with distinctive tones, children at this age have developed sufficient auditory discrimination to enjoy more complicated music. Consider parent-child dance programs to dance together but be cognizant of the ample opportunities for dance and movement throughout the day.

Between two and three years, most older toddlers will:

+ run forward
+ jump in one place
+ kick a ball without aiming
+ stand for a moment on one foot

Children at this age have developed sufficient gross-motor control for formal dance programs. Those programs should focus on isolating movements, for example, tapping toes in rhythm, extending the limbs and moving forward, backwards, or to the side with coordination. Healthy dance programs for children this age will be responsive to children's short attention span, will be emotionally positive and encouraging and will allow for and affirm unpredictable movements as children learn to coordinate their own movements with the movements of a larger group. At home and in care settings, provide opportunities for children to dance to a wide variety of musical styles and model dancing with children.

Between three and four years, most children will

+ manage a tricycle or ride-on toy
+ throw and catch balls
+ pull and steer toys
+ walk in a straight line
+ walk toe to heel
+ tap toes forward
+ tap toes back

Children are ready now to observe and enjoy longer dances, to visit dance performances designed for children (like children's ballets), and to learn about different cultural dances. Look for opportunities to expand children's understanding of the types and styles of dance, including live folk dances, Native American dances, classical dance performance, and street dance. Help children to understand what they observe by narrating dances you watch together and by identifying movements or short sequences of movement that you can try on your own.

Between four and five years, most children will

+ jump on one foot
+ walk backwards with ease
+ roll somersaults
+ move one leg at a time forward, out, back, and in
+ learn and retain choreography for simple dances
+ do-si-do

Highly social, children at this age can engage in short choreographed dances in a group, can dance with each other, and often enjoy dancing for an audience. Children will look to each other to model dance moves and benefit from teachers and caregivers who engage in dancing with them or who serve as eager audiences to their self-choreographed dances. This is a ripe time to encourage children to dance through familiar stories, to dance along to books read aloud, or to demonstrate their understanding of different characters by showing how each would dance.

Teacher Guidance and Feedback

Early childhood classrooms should offer a balance of high energy, fully engaged creative movement and dance experiences, and smaller, repeated movement and patterns that include opportunities for stillness. Consider ways to support social development through dance, by asking children to enact their understanding of imagery, sounds, vocabulary, and contexts, to make connections to other learners and to develop an appreciation for their own agency. Look for specific basic dance skills to emphasize in isolation: jumping, hopping, pointing and flexing, bending, and stretching. Look, too, for qualities of dance that can apply to other content: imagery, textural qualities of movement, spatial relationships, etc. Because young children benefit from clear, concise instruction, dance experiences can be focused on a few skills in isolation and build over time to become more complicated sequences of movements. Think about ways to integrate body development, like balance, strength, ranges of motion, coordination, and breath through intentional learning experiences. Likewise, notice when those qualities enhance other learning experiences and make them explicit for children.

Elements of dance can and should be integrated into other content area, in addition to opportunities to explore dance as its own discipline. Consider common elements that are appropriate for young children:

+ Space: What direction will you travel? What path will you take to get there? At what level or levels will you keep your body? What shapes can you make with your body while moving? What shapes can you make with the path you take? How will you move in relationship to other learners? How will you move in relationship to the larger space of the classroom?
+ Energy: How will your movement be defined? Will you move with high energy or low energy? When will you move and when will you be still?
+ Performance: What are the qualities of the environment of which you need to be aware to perform here? What needs rehearsal and repetition? What parts of the movement allow opportunity for reflection? For refinement?
+ Emotion: How will you express emotion through your dance? What are common ways of conveying complicated emotions with our bodies? What are examples of universal body language?

+ Choreography: Will your dance have a beginning, middle, and end? Will you invoice axial movement? Locomotor movement? A combination? What patterns will you include?
+ Feedback: How can we talk about dance? How was your intent aligned with what your audience observed? How did a dance you observed reflect different states of emotion? Of narrative? Of relationship? Of conflict or of resolution?

Consider what you intend to teach by the integration of dance, and how you will know whether learners have learned what you intended. Remember that, while children are active learners and sensorimotor exploration is essential to learning in early childhood, children are this age are also especially sensitive to teacher feedback and criticism. Children in older early childhood may also demonstrate a strong sense of fairness and equity. As such, this will be a time when children are able both to engage in dance with some enthusiasm and to begin to reflect on that engagement, especially how they respond to the feedback of their peers. As such, teachers and caregivers should model enthusiastic engagement in dance. It is easy to cast ourselves in the role of choreographer, instructing children to dance without becoming involved in the dance ourselves. To do so, however, misses a critical learning opportunity. Children will adopt the effect of their teachers and caregivers toward new experiences, including dance. If, then, dance is presented as something for children to do separate from their caregivers or teachers, children may be more hesitant than if dancing is something the entire class, including teachers, does together.

Dance is a natural, instinctual tendency for humans, evident from our births and visible even in the toe-tapping of those of us who, as adults, have come to believe that we can't dance. It provides an opportunity to practice the coordination of muscle groups children need for independent learning and living. It offers authentic opportunities for nurture and collaboration between caregivers and children. It mirrors the values and norms of different cultures and maintains universal components that span time and heritage. It conveys emotion and meaning without verbal language. It precedes the internalization of concepts learned in other modalities and it supports a social cohesion between learners. It offers an alternative to waiting, to boredom, and to disengagement. It's free. It's both pedestrian and high-culture. It offers its own vocabulary, supports the adoption of new vocabulary, and offers children a way to demonstrate what they understand before their language skills catch up. Although it is increasingly absent from school settings, it is no less essential to learning and to the quality of this human existence. As such, it falls to teachers and caregivers to protect, to preserve, and to promote children's opportunity to learn, express, reflect, and grow through dance.

Discuss

As adults, we may have come to conclude that we are not good dancers. How do you identify as a dancer? How does your sense of your own dance ability influence the choices you hope to make with children? Consider formal and informal dance experiences you may have had as a child. What did you learn from those experiences about the nature of dance, its cultural importance, or your ability to participate?

View Sir Ken Robinson's lecture entitled, "Do Schools Kill Creativity?" at https://www.ted.com/talks/ken_robinson_says_schools_ kill_creativity?language=en. What message does Sir Robinson intend to convey? How does this message resonate with your beliefs about children's learning, attention, and movement in the classroom? If you agree with Sir Robinson's perspective, how would you enact that belief in your own classroom? How would you defend it to parents? If you disagree, what counterargument would you make? How would you defend your position to dance and movement advocates?

In the early 20th century, dance education was a regular part of the school setting, made popular by the inclusion of gymnasiums and open-air settings in Europe. National dances were taught in school, and thinkers including John Dewey advocated dance education as a support for learning about democracy. By the turn of the 20th century, dance education had been replaced with fitness and physical education. What do you view as the appropriate role of dance education in school settings?

Collaborate

With a partner, identify a science standard for a grade level you intend to teach. How might you introduce this concept through dance? How might you use dance to support children learning about the concept after it's been introduced? How might you structure a dance as an assessment of learning? For each benchmark of learning, specify what language you would use to introduce the dance experience, what model you would provide for children, and what kinds of enactments you would expect from children to know they had learned what you intended them to learn.

With a partner, investigate after school or enrichment dance programs in your area. Look at the language the programs use to describe their philosophy and teaching. See if you can identify dance programs that are developmentally driven and dance programs that focus on talent-development. How do the expectations of children differ between programs? How do they reflect our current understanding of developmentally appropriate practice? What guidance would you give to a parent in choosing between programs? What more would you need to know to be able to discern?

With a partner, choose a work of children's literature appropriate for the age of the child you intend to teach. Choreograph a ballet to express an important scene or plot line in the book. Consider how different characters might move. Consider what kind of music would accompany your ballet. Teach your ballet to another group of teachers in your setting and allow them to perform it for your group.

Create

Consider your daily schedule for the age class you intend to teach. Presume you teach in a school with no formal dance education time allotted. Chart the times during your schedule when you could integrate dance or creative movement. Consider what qualities of dance (space, energy, emotion, performance, choreography, and feedback) you might include and what choices you would make within each. Can you imagine a daily schedule that regularly integrates dance as a support to other content? Can you imagine a daily schedule that regularly integrates dance as its own discipline? How would these perspectives change how you would manage your classroom or your distribution of time?

Consider a piece of children's literature that can be enjoyed across a range of childhood development, like *Charlotte's Web* or *James and the Giant Peach*. Choreograph a dance to accompany a major scene in the book that would be appropriate for preschoolers. Choreograph a dance to accompany the same scene that would be appropriate for early elementary learners. How do the themes you emphasize in each influence your choices for dance? How does your knowledge of children's physical capacity change what you can include in your choreography?

Investigate a folk dance reflective of your family's heritage. Design a lesson plan in which you introduce this dance to children. What information would you share about your family's heritage to engage learners? What changes might you make to the dance to make it appropriate for children in your classroom? How might you encourage children to share folk dances from their own heritage? Prepare guidelines to send home to parents to invite them to share a folk dance with your class. How would you explain your learning intent? What would you want parents to know about how to teach a dance from their own culture in your classroom?

For Further Reading

Andress, B. (1991). Research in Review. From research to practice: Preschool children and their movement responses to music. *Young Children, 47*(1), 22–27.

Arts Education Partnership. (2002). Critical links: Learning in the arts and student academic and social development. Washington, DC: Author. Online: www.aep-arts.org/cllinkspage.htm.

Before and after school … Creative experiences. (1993). Video. Child Care Collection. Muncie, IN: Ball State University.

Blumenfeld-Jones, D. 2009. Bodily Kinesthetic Intelligence and Dance Education. *The Journal for Aesthetic Education, 43*(1), 59–75.

Bruner, J. (1996). *The culture of education.* Cambridge, MA: Harvard University Press.

Bucek, L. (1992). Constructing a child-centered dance curriculum. *JOPHERD,* Nov/Dec.

Chen, J-Q., ed. 1998. Project Spectrum: Early learning activities. Vol. 2 of Project Spectrum: Frameworks for early childhood education, eds. H. Gardner, D.H. Feldman, & M. Krechevsky. New York: Teachers College Press.

Cherry, C., & Nielsen, D. M. (2001). *Creative movement for the developing child: An early childhood handbook for non-musicians* (3rd ed.) Torrance, CA: Fearon Teacher Aids.

Cline, D., & D. Ingerson. (1996). The mystery of Humpty's fall: Primary school children as playmakers. *Young Children, 51* (6), 4–10.

Crawford, L. (2004). *Lively learning: Using the arts to teach the K–8 curriculum.* Greenfield, MA: Responsive Classroom, Northeast Foundation for Children.

Davies, M. (2003). *Movement and dance in early childhood.* London: Paul Chapman Pub.

Forman, G., & Kuschner, D. (1983). *The child's construction of knowledge: Piaget for teaching children.* Washington, DC: NAEYC.

Fraser, D.L. (2000). *Danceplay: Creative movement for very young children.* Lincoln, NE: Authors Choice Press.

Gardner, H. (1993). *Frames of mind: The theory of multiple intelligences* (10th anniv. ed.). New York: Basic.

Goldhawk, Sara. (1998). Young children and the arts: Making creative connections. A report of the Task Force on Children's Learning and the Arts: Birth to age eight. Washington, DC: Arts Education Partnership. Online: http://aep-arts.org/PDF%20Files/Young%20Children.pdf.

Head Start Bureau. (2000). A creative adventure: Supporting development and learning through art, music, movement, and dialogue. Creative adventure media kit includes guide for parents and professionals, videotape, and poster. Washington, D.C.

Isenberg, J. P., & Jalongo, M. R. (2001). *Creative expression and play in early childhood* (3rd ed.). Upper Saddle River, NJ: Merrill/Prentice Hall.

Isenberg, J. P., & Quisenberry, N. (2002). Play: Essential for all children. *Childhood Education, 79*, 33–39.

Joyce, M. (1994). *First steps in teaching creative dance to children.* Mountain View, CA: Mayfield.

Levin-Gelb Communications. (2002). Getting in tune: The powerful influence of music on young children's development. Brochure. Washington, DC: Zero to Three.

Mayesky, M. (2003). *How to foster creativity in all children.* Albany, NY: Delmar.

Moore, T. (2002). If you teach children, you can sing. *Young Children, 57*(4), 84–85.

Moravcik, E. 2000. Music all the livelong day. *Young Children, 55*(4), 27–29.

National Dance Association. (1994). *National standards for dance education: What every young American should know and be able to do in dance.* Hightstown, NJ: Princeton Book Company.

National Dance Education Organization (NDEO). (2002). Standards for dance in early childhood. Draft. Ed. R. Faber. Bethesda, MD.

Organizati, N. D. (2001). The child's bill of rights in dance. *Journal of Dance Education, 1*(1), 34. doi:10.1080/15290824.2001.10387171

Oussoren-Voors, R. (2010). *Write dance in the early years.* Los Angeles: SAGE.

Papatheodorou, T. (2012). *Debates on early childhood policies and practices: Global snapshots of pedagogical thinking and encounters.* London: Routledge.

Paley, V. G. (1992). *You can't say you can't play.* Cambridge, MA: Harvard University Press.

Palmer, H. (2001). The music, movement, and learning connection. *Young Children, 56*(5), 13–17.

Pica, R. (2000). *Experiences in movement with music, activities, and theory.* Albany, NY: Delmar Thomson Learning.

Riley, D. A. (2008). *Social & emotional development: Connecting science and practice in early childhood settings.* St. Paul, MN: Redleaf Press.

Sansom, A. N. (1999). The meaning of dance in early childhood.

Saracho, O. N. (2012). *Contemporary perspectives on research in creativity in early childhood education.* Charlotte, NC: Information Age Pub.

Smith, K. L. (2002). Dancing in the forest: Narrative writing through dance. *Young Children, 57*(2), 90–94.

Standards for dance in early childhood. (2005). Bethesda, MD: National Dance Education Organization.

Thraves, B., & Williamson, D. (1994). *Now for a dance: Integrating dance and movement in primary and early childhood learning.* Albert Park, Vic.: Phoenix Education.

Weikart, P.S. 1997. *Movement plus rhymes, songs, and singing games.* 2nd ed. Recordings on CD available. Ypsilanti, MI: High/Scope Press.

Weikart, P.S. 1998. *Teaching movement and dance.* 4th ed. Ypsilanti, MI: High/Scope Press.

Williams, C. 1986. How do children learn by handling objects? *Young Children*, 42(1), 23–26.

Chapter 6

Integrating Music

"I would teach children music, physics, and philosophy; but most importantly music, for the patterns in music and all the arts are the keys to learning."

—Plato

Music Development and Methods

With "charms to soothe a savage breast, to soften rocks, or bend a knotted oak," music may be the most ubiquitous of the arts, present in our homes, in our cars, in the background at a coffee shop or grocery store (Congreve, 1753). We define cultures through their music, from the orchestrations of national anthems at state events to the underground independent music teens share between themselves. We play music to babies in utero and pick grandma's favorite hymns to accompany memorials. Indeed, music is a lifelong accompaniment to our societies, helping to deepen relationships, to expand on our understanding of the human experience, to provide comfort, to inspire, to enrich.

And while we can strengthen our understanding of music as its own medium, we also know that the connection to music is innate in human development. Infants can distinguish sound from about 16-weeks gestation. Within the noisy environment of the womb, infants begin to distinguish between the constant sounds of their mothers' heartbeats and the unique sounds of human voices and music. Especially in the last 10 weeks of pregnancy, infants in utero respond to music just as they respond to the human voice as their physical development refines their ability to process and understand noises. In this window, critical connections develop between the cochlea and the brain. As the cochlea, which receives sounds, begins to communicate with the auditory centers of the brain that distinguish and recognize those sounds, infants will begin associating those sounds with the human engagements that accompany them. Within hours of an infant's birth, he will be able to distinguish his mother's voice and his native language. Familiar music will offer comfort. Infants prefer happy voices over angrier tones, slower tempos to faster ones, and higher pitches to lower pitches. Infants instinctively prefer consonant tones played together and their attention to changes in music is surprisingly nuanced. Research demonstrates that infants notice differences in tempo, even when the same musical composition is played at different rates. They notice when patterns in music change and when a wrong note is played. They distinguish between major and minor chords, and are often more accurate than adults in distinguishing notes that are played wrong but are within the same key.

Children's ability to receive, distinguish, and prefer some music to others seems to appear with birth. There are clear musical abilities that are natural to human development. Likewise, learned abilities for musical discernment develop quickly within the first year. Infants begin to connect emotion to types of music and to link music to particular relationships and engagements. They begin to incorporate and prefer the typical tones and patterns of the music of their own culture. They make connections to particular kinds of music and to the behaviors they evoke, from excitement at faster paced music to calm for more soothing melodies.

Children's development in and through music is a complex unfolding of their physical, emotional, cognitive and language development. It's important to remember, though, that while a child's exposure to music may enhance her receptiveness to other learning, music doesn't "make us smarter." Instead, experiences with music are often tied to experiences with parents and caregivers. Music becomes a conduit for communication, of emotion, of connection, of support and nurture. A music-rich environment supports the kinds of experiences which support infant and early childhood learning; they do not substitute for them.

Trends in Music Education

Music education has long been a part of the American culture, with the first formal "singing school" founded in 1717 in Boston to support learning to sing and read music in church services. This model of singing education spread throughout the colonies, with more than 375 books published by

1820 to instruct parishioners in reading music. Boston remained a leader in both music education and education in general. In 1832, the Boston Academy of Music opened under the direction of Lowell Mason and George Webb, designed to teach singing, musical theory, and music education methods. Building from the methods theories of Pestalozzi, Mason and Webb influenced local education in Boston. In 1838, the Boston School Committee approved the first formal music education curriculum in the United States, with Lowell Mason appointed as the first "supervisor of music education." As music education was included as a foundational skill for teachers in the first normal school, formal music education, under the direction of a specially trained teacher, became the standard for public education across the country. By the beginning of the 20th century, music education was near universal in the four-year teaching degree programs developed out of the normal school model. The Music Supervisors National Conference (now the National Association for Music Education) was founded in 1907. In the first quarter of the 20th century, formal music education expanded to include school band, orchestra, and expansive record libraries developed for school use.

By the mid-20th century, music education was established as a regular component of most public schools. Band directors organized within a national movement by 1953 and choral directors followed suit within the decade. But the firm footing of music education, like education in other arts, was threatened with the national response to the launch of Sputnik, when school reformers focused their efforts on science, math and technology at the expense of the arts. Music educators responded with well-organized counter arguments. The Contemporary Music Project in 1959 sought to increase the relevance of music education in schools by introducing composers and performers to schools directly. The Juilliard Project in 1964 developed a comprehensive catalogue of musical works to be used in elementary and secondary schools. In 1965, the National Endowment for the Arts secured federal financial support for music education. In 1967, the first Tanglewood conference of music educators articulated national goals for music education, with a challenge to schools to integrate wider varieties of musical experiences and teaching methods. By 1969, the first set of national standards for music education were presented by the Music Educators National Conference.

Music education at the end of the 20th century mirrored the larger debates about the relationship of content-based learning to the education of the whole child. By 1978, music education research began to emphasize the benefits of music education to children's cognitive development, memory processing, motivation, affect and motor development. Symposia offered presentations on the importance of music learning to the development of cultural understanding and as a support to learning in other content areas. By 1994, national standards for music education were adopted or developed in most states across the country.

Enjoying strong public support and a well-connected advocacy network, music education remains a regular theme in the national conversation around children's development and school reform. That is not to say that music education is well-funded or consistently-implemented. Indeed, music education seems to be constantly bobbing and dodging budget cuts in favor of activities perceived to be more academically focused. So, while near 95% of Americans believe that music is an essential component of children's development and education, only 25% of eighth graders report being asked to sing or play music at lease once a week.

Music education, while often vulnerable to other priorities, is consistently linked with higher performance across a number of factors. The College Entrance Examination Board, which coordinates the SAT, reports that students involved in public school music programs score over a hundred points higher on the SAT than their peers in schools without school-based music. Data from the U.S. Department of Education suggests that students who are engaged regularly in instrumental music education through their middle and high school years also demonstrate higher math proficiency in grade 12. Early music training is linked to higher abstract reasoning skills, with specific improvements in math, chess, science, and engineering. Likewise, research suggests that students involved in school-based music programs also enjoy stronger social climates at school, enjoy being at school more, and experience less stress than their peers without that involvement.

In response to the generational struggle between the documented benefits of music education and the changing context of public schools, the 2007 Tanglewood II conference revisited the recommendations made some 40 years earlier to publish its declaration for the future of music education for the next 40 years. Tanglewood II articulated a path for music education and a call for new practices and innovations in music education. In some ways, the declaration encourages more humane, child-centered approaches to music education, naming the inherent relationship of music development and human development, the powerful capacity of music to communicate new ideas and strengthen both local and global communities, and the potential for music education to serve as a leveling tool to the disparity of experiences between student backgrounds and to increase both equity and access to education for all students. Simultaneously, Tanglewood II set a high standard for the policymakers, teachers, and other stakeholders who might implement these goals, calling for innovation in curricula to represent more diverse cultural experiences, closer links between research and practice and more research around the role of music in other development, professional norms for music faculty in higher education and increased expectations for admissions and graduation in higher education for music education experiences.

Today, music education remains an important, if often misunderstood or erratically implemented, tool for schools and teachers. A long history of music specialists may support traditional classroom teachers' fears that music is something for other people to teach. Likewise, challenges for limited school resources may threaten reliable funding for practitioners with expertise in music education. Understanding the relationship of music to human development, then, may help teachers and caregivers to identify, protect and expand on music experiences available to children inside and outside of school settings.

Social Emotional Learning and Music

Music supports children's development across multiple domains, but perhaps none more so than in the social and emotional experiences children enjoy through music. Research suggests that music experiences build children's emotional maturity, their ability to regulate their behavior, to share work with others, and to express their own thoughts clearly. Music reflects varied emotional states with some safe distance. Listening to music together, then, gives children an opportunity to talk with their parents and caregivers about their own emotions and the emotions of others. These experiences, too, offer a shared interaction around symbolic representations and the opportunity to discuss individual perceptions, understanding, and feelings. Because we tend to share emotional responses to particular types of music, music can be used to calm and relax multiple learners, decreasing tension in classroom settings or, conversely, to demonstrate complex emotions that may be too difficult to convey in words. Research suggests, too, that the process of making music, even in open improvisation, relaxes the learner.

Music supports social and emotional development through self-awareness and management, an awareness of social relationships and self regulation. Multiple studies suggest a strong link between social skills and music-based experiences. Mothers who engaged with their infants for music education programs are more likely to report high quality attachment to their babies, even when compared with mothers who engage in other, nonmusical play. Toddlers who participated in scheduled music education programs demonstrate higher levels of social cooperation, independence and interaction when they enter school. Parents who report singing with their children regularly also report stronger social skills for their children. Infants who experience active music programs demonstrate stronger emotional regulation behaviors than infants who in passive programs, and music-based experiences are associated with more varied use of expressive emotion. Music experiences that are active, that support social experiences, and especially those with warm, nurturing interactions with parents and caregivers, are associated with stronger social emotional development for infants, regardless of gender, race, or socioeconomic background. In addition to the benefits for social and emotional learning for typically developing children, music experiences offer strong therapeutic supports for children with atypical development, especially for children with disorders that impair social skills and communication. Multiple studies suggest that music therapy strengthens the social and emotional development of children with autism in particular, with planned music experiences offering greater gains than other social play.

Physical Development and Music

Children's physical development is supported and strengthened through music-based experiences. Consider the infant who is rocked in her caregiver's arms. That steady rhythm soothes the child, comforted in a nurturing embrace. Even before she can sit up unassisted, the infant will wiggle and move to music she hears, practicing the coordination of the large muscles of her body. The toddler who is able to pull herself up to a standing position will strengthen her legs and hips as she bounces and moves to music she hears. Dancing, both fast and slow, to music will support even the youngest children in the natural coordination of their bodies.

Likewise, as children begin to coordinate the smaller muscles of their hands, fingers, and faces, they can joyfully practice that coordination through finger plays and expressive singalongs. Incorporating sticks for drumming, hand bells, and shakers, the natural propensity to make and engage in music can support young children's developing ability to control and regulate their own movements.

The developing ability to coordinate their bodies will increase children's ability to engage in their world independently. But it is also an important precursor for the development of their brains. Learning to balance, as children are able to practice through moving to music, requires children to shift their weight from one side to the other, to coordinate messages across their bodies. Watching, mirroring, and exploring movements that are demonstrated for them, like group music games such as "The Hokey Pokey" or "Head, Shoulders, Knees and Toes," gives children the opportunity to interpret what they've observed and enact that interpretation in their own bodies. Practicing movements that cross the midline, like playing a piano keyboard or xylophones or engaging in twisting, more complex dances, contributes to bilateral development across the two hemispheres of the brain. Other common musical experiences for young children, like playing a drum with both hands, patting out rhythms on their knees, transferring bells from one hand to the other, or playing a triangle also support children in exploring and practicing this essential skill.

For children's physical health, music is an engaging way to encourage physical activity. Large, active group games allow the enthusiastic participation of children, even in classroom settings that may be more traditionally sedentary. For schools with limited physical education or outdoor time, incorporating music into the classroom and allowing children to move and dance to the music may be the only physical exercise children enjoy each day. Both gross and fine motor development benefit from music experiences: While exuberant group games exercise children's large muscle groups, controlled experiences like finger dances or dancing with scarves that require grasping and releasing are equally supportive to children's fine motor skills.

Cognitive Development and Music

While there has been some debate in the research around whether music influences cognitive development or cognitive qualities increase a learner's propensity for music, recent studies suggest that music training leads to other precursor skills and cognitive change. Children with musical training demonstrate stronger skills in the areas linked to music, fine motor skills, rhythm discernment, and auditory discrimination among them. These skills, too, seem to transfer to other areas, building executive functioning and nonverbal reasoning in particular.

When these changes can be observed in children's brains, they are more significant for children whose musical training has been active and when those music experiences have aligned with sensitive periods in children's cognitive development. The influence of sensitive periods (when the impact of a particular kind of experience is particularly high on the brain) and critical periods (specific windows during which particular development must happen or it cannot later) determines the degree to which music experiences impact individual learners. For example, the auditory cortex (that part of the brain that is linked to discrimination of sound) does not complete its myelination until almost 5 years old. Music experiences within this range, then, should hold the potential for significant influence to later cognitive growth.

And recent research supports that: with 14 months of early childhood musical training, children demonstrated stronger growth in both brain activity and behavioral expressions than their nonmusical peers. Likewise, the kind of music experiences in which learners engage will be reflected in the development of the related areas of the brain. Children with keyboard training tend to demonstrate development in the area of the brain linked to motor and the hands. Children who receive musical training in keys and harmonics of Western music demonstrate more nuanced ability to discriminate pitch differences. The auditory perceptive abilities of children to distinguish harmony, pitch, volume, voice onset, and duration increase for children who have training in those areas. Listening skills, sound discrimination, processing speech separately from other noises, developing rhythm, and maintaining attention are all enhanced by early musical training.

Finally, children who experience musical training in early childhood demonstrate stronger development in executive functioning, including attention and self restraint, working memory, and task switching. These cognitive functions and flexibilities, essential in learning to play an instrument or to control one's own voice in complex singing, transfer to other learning experiences. While there is limited research to suggest that children's intelligence is increased by musical training, the conduits to learning represented by the development of their brains are stronger for children with musical training. That is to say, while musical training may not make you smarter, it does make learning easier.

Language Development and Music

Although speech and music are different phenomena, they share common processes in the auditory system and research suggests that the benefits of music training transfer to linguistic skills. For example, the ability to discriminate between particular sounds, to distinguish subtle changes in the qualities of sound, can be developed through musical training and is essential to learning to speak and read. The mechanisms of the brain that are developed in musical training are shared in language development.

Language and music share common auditory networks in the brain, so development in one area may transfer to development in the other. A learner's ability to discern tone, for example, may transfer to her ability to distinguish between similar sounding letters. In addition, music experiences often have high emotional reinforcement. When children love what they're doing, when their learning is engaged with other positive emotional experiences, that learning is more distinct. For music experiences, that leads to increased stimulation in the auditory networks of the brain and, as a result, stronger networks. When those networks are exploited for language development, the pathways are already functioning and active.

Research links these experiences to increased verbal abilities, like verbal fluency, memory, second language development, reading abilities and vocabulary abilities. Children with musical training perform better on vocabulary assessments and on assessments of reading speed and fluency. Children with musical training demonstrate stronger receptive and expressive language in second language acquisition and more attuned pronunciation in the second language. Research also links musical training and phonological skills, including visual mapping, sound categorization, and decoding. Children with a stronger sense of pitch tend to also have stronger reading skills and fluency. Research also suggests a link between language skills and the ability to distinguish and recreate rhythm, an ability that is also linked to higher executive functioning, working memory, and reasoning skills. Because linguistic development and musical development use similar neural pathways, development in one supports development in the other. Again, music instruction may not make you smarter, but it may give learners the skills they need to develop linguistically, serving as a conduit for other learning.

Music for Social Cohesion

In addition to the cognitive, linguistic, physical, personal, social, and emotional benefits connected to music education, music experiences offer children authentic, relevant opportunities to connect with each other, to build communities, and to contribute to them in meaningful ways. Consider the side-effects of making music together: children learn to cooperate with each other, to coordinate their choices with the choices of their peers, to communicate both verbally and nonverbally. They build an interconnectedness and cohesion within the group, agreeing to "play their part" because the alternative affects the group. Research indicates these social benefits. Children who develop the ability to act in synchrony with each other, that is, to do what their peers are doing with their bodies and voices, also demonstrate stronger prosocial behaviors and commitments. They trust their peers more and demonstrate increased compassion to others. This, in turn, increases the emotional reward of the musical experience. By contributing to a song together, or drumming in synchronicity, or playing an instrument along the same melody as one's peers, children experience an emotional satisfaction as a result of that cooperation, which, in turn, increases their openness to cooperation in other settings. Simultaneously, learning to play music independently offers children a unique creative outlet, distinct to their own abilities and identities. It relaxes children as it develops learning skills transferrable to other settings. It allows children to be both distinct in their individualism and contributing members to a larger social group. The complex interaction of children's brain development, their physical development, and their emotional development that underly synchronized music-making is unique among other group activities and unique within the arts. As a result, music education, especially in early childhood, leads to other advantages throughout the child's life.

Music to Support Other Content

We've discussed the ways in which musical experiences can be used to support children's linguistic development. Music also offers aligned supports to learning in other content areas.

For example, basic and instinctual music responses, like demonstrating steady beat, rhythm, and melody, share common mathematical concepts. Developing these areas in early childhood gives children concrete experience with concepts they will express more abstractly in later school. For example, steady beat represents a child's understanding of one-to-one correspondence, being able to match one thing to another. Comparative language, like less and more, faster and slower, louder and softer, can be demonstrated through children's ability to clap out a beat earlier than they may have the verbal ability to express the same understanding. Experiences with rhythm in early childhood support children's ability to identify and represent patterns in later experiences. Matching melodies also supports pattern perception for young children.

Older children can represent mathematical relationships through music, demonstrating in sound mathematical operations, fractional relationships, and proportions. When children learn to read music, they can transfer the annotations of music to other symbolic annotations, like writing out number sentences and more complex equations.

Enacting music with their bodies also supports children in understanding spatial relationships, geometric relationships, and spatial-temporal reasoning skills. They can demonstrate patterns by composing their own musical phrases or by translating songs into new keys. They can practice number sense through engaging songs, supporting their ability to count and sequence.

Learning content through song has long been praised for its mnemonic benefits. Think about the ABC song or the United States song, through which even very young children can memorize and recall extended lists of information. Children retain their memorized facts better when they've had the opportunity to sing them. But recent research also suggests that some content, including scientific concepts, are actually better understood when children absorb them through music. When, for example, children watch videos describing complex scientific concepts, they retain what they've learned in those videos longer and with greater detail when the videos included a musical accompaniment. Learners can easily learn lists of facts, like the elements on the periodic table or the order of the planets in our solar system, by memorizing songs that include those facts. More importantly, though, when learning new information that requires deeper understanding, research suggests that learning *to* music is more effective than the same experiences without music.

Finally, music offers an easy and authentic opportunity for children to learn about other cultures and time periods. Social studies content, from learning about their own home communities to learning about what they have in common with children around the world, is easily supported by sharing, comparing and contrasting musical traditions. Folk songs and dances reflect their home communities distinctly, but they also offer certain commonalities shared across the human experience. As such, they bring to life the study of social groups and social relationships, by allowing children to enact and internalize them through music and song.

Learning Standards for Music in Early Childhood

For over 40 years, the National Association for Music Education (NAME, 2014) has promoted standards for music education in school settings and beyond. Most states include state standards for school-age children that align with the NAME standards, although some states have developed their own standards.

In general, though, music standards nationwide share some common values. They recognize that music is an essential part of children's development from infancy onward and they acknowledge the positive influence quality music experiences have on children across their development. They prioritize the role of music in developing emotional and intellectual connections and the benefits of integrating music across children's environments and routines so that it is a regular part of children's lives.

Further, music education standards emphasize that children's exposure and education to and through music should be developmentally appropriate: individually appropriate, age appropriate, and culturally appropriate. National standards affirm that there is no one "right" kind of music to use with children, but that music should reflect diverse cultural backgrounds, various eras, and multiple genres. They encourage music both as its own content for study and as a complement to other content, with standards specific to musical skills and abilities and with standards that allow music to be used to meet other content goals.

In early childhood, national standards encourage music as a play-based, integrated experience, with opportunities for individual and group experiences, cross-cultural and cross-curricular exposure, and with the modeling of both music specialists and "regular" teachers and caregivers. They recognize that caregivers across children's lives can model and guide musical experiences.

Music education in early childhood, then, should include varied experiences across multiple modalities: singing, playing instruments, movement, and dance and listening, as well as content-specific vocabulary and themes of music as a content domain. Musical works should be of high quality and matched to the learning goals appropriate for each child, including folk songs, classical music, contemporary music, music from diverse contexts and cultures, and traditional children's songs.

NAME also publishes a list of "Beliefs about Young Children" to help guide educators and caregivers in incorporating music in service to children. These beliefs form the skeleton upon which high-quality musical experiences can be constructed and allow for flexibility within classrooms and care settings and national norms for how children's learning and development are best supported through music education.

For example, NAME (2018) asserts that "all children have musical potential." While, as adults, we may not consider ourselves to be musical, or we may have begun classifying "musicians" as people with special musical skills and training, that is, people not like us, all young children have the capacity for profound relationships with music. This is not to suggest that every child has the capacity to be a virtuoso, but that a positive relationship with music is constructed over time and through experience. Children benefit from regular engagement with diverse music and ample opportunities to participate in meaningful ways in and through music. NAME also reminds caregivers that, while the capacity for a positive relationship with music is innate in all children, children offer their own interests and tastes and appreciation for music. A child's individual preferences can help to direct their learning, especially in early childhood, and will influence their developing awareness as music as something that propels and supports them in part as a result of the agency they are allowed in engaging with it. Because children's interests in music vary, the learning environment should offer diverse choices for how children engage with music.

NAME (2018) further articulates the capacity of young children to develop advanced thinking skills through music, and that the development of those skills through active, engaged activities should help drive music education. Children should be exposed to high-quality music and related activities and should be supported in learning about and through music without high-stakes performance demands. Because music informs children's social and emotional development, their thinking skills, their language skills, and their physical development, caregivers should assure quality musical experiences that are focused on the experience itself and the child's ability to make meaning through that experience, rather than on recitals or performances for adults' benefit.

Children's development, as defined in these standards, reflects their diverse experiences, home lives, and cultures. The music offered to them in care settings, then, should be equally diverse, offered in a warm and responsive environment, and with the support of nurturing adults. Quality music learning environments will include play, individual and group games, dialogue between children and teachers, opportunities to imagine and represent concepts, narratives and stories, common experiences of relationships and cultures, and personal involvement in both individual and socially-driven experiences. They will shy away from rote, drill-and-kill experiences, and incorporate, instead, active, hands-on, creative spaces in both regularly scheduled opportunities and in open-ended free-choice play spaces in the classroom.

Finally, NAME challenges caregivers to embrace a role of engagement and modeling in incorporating music in learning environments. Recognizing that children will bring as wide a range of natural dispositions toward music education as we hold as adults, caregivers will model open-ness and authentic engagement, participating with children in musical experiences. Simultaneously, caregivers should acknowledge that the wide range of children's propensities toward music education will include children who are comfortable observing music-based play, but not par-ticipating actively in it. Caregivers are encouraged to be observant to the ways in which music may still be enacted as an important resource, even to children who are more hesitant about engaging with it in public spaces. Caregivers, then, model healthy comfort with singing aloud, trying new musical instruments, struggling with music, and joyfully engaging with it. While NAME encourages teachers and caregivers to engage professionally prepared music educators in developing music experiences for the children in their care, they prioritize the effects of music appreciation over musical skill in defining what all teachers and caregivers should model, regardless of their own musical abilities. Teachers and caregivers, NAME asserts, should be first and foremost loving advocates for young children. They should value music in their own lives and as an important experience in the lives of young children. They should model interest and receptivity to new musical experiences and to the incorporation of music across their days, and, most importantly, they should model confidence when engaging with music, even if they don't identify themselves as a proper musician. Teachers and caregivers, at least while they are caring for the development of young learners, should model active engagement with multiple domains of musical experiences and with multiple means through which learners can participate and contribute. They should be playful and open in their affect toward music, and able to seek out assistance from other resources to identify quality musical resources and developmentally appropriate musi-cal practices.

Music Developmental Benchmarks

Although there are wide variations in learners' ability to recreate and create music, and distinctions for natural talents in some learners, most typically developing children will progress through predictable benchmarks for mu-sic development. For example, infants almost universally demonstrate an innate ability to process some complexities of music, and those complexities are reflected in the universal properties of lullabies and soothing melodies across cultures. In general, infants show a sensitivity to relational qualities of music, preferring them to absolute qualities, an awareness of unequal or unpredictable step structures in scales, a preference for consonant tones over dissonant ones and a sensitivity to the typical musical structures of their home cultures.

Although infants will be "singing" early in their development, children do not master the rules of music until about 6 years old. In those first 6 years, significant changes take place. Newborn cries, for example, have a wide range of pitches (as most parents can describe!) but there is little evidence to suggest that these are musical in nature. It is not until the infant is 3–6 months old that he can match single pitches modeled for him, and only after the end of the first year of life that infants can he match sets of two notes at a time. In those 6–12 months, infants will babble, singing a continuous pitch on a single breath or varying between pitches with no apparent relationship. While infants can match pitch, they cannot match rhythm. They may bang on objects, but it's generally after the first birthday before infants can maintain a rhythm.

At around 18 months, young toddlers are able to mirror discrete pitches and intervals, although they don't use adults' pitches or scales. They may move in and out of tune or between keys in the songs they invent or mirror. Children tend not to sing the songs they've heard as often as they invent their own melodies at this age. As they approach 2 years old, they begin to establish the structures of their home cultural music, including tonal organization and pitch. Children are able to vocalize across a wider and more fluid range than most adults, and tend to sing comfortably at higher pitches than adults. They begin to sing the songs of their own cultures, to reproduce songs they hear and to invent songs which reflect structures of others to which they've been exposed. Children will incorporate predictable lyrics before they establish predictable melodies, and will cement their understanding of rhythm last, although they will be able to match rhythm earlier than they can reproduce exact pitch. Around age 2–3, children can reproduce general melodies. By age 4, they can maintain mirrored intervals. By age 5 or 6, they can maintain a key.

Children's musical development will often be predictable and sequenced. For example:

+ Between birth and 3 months, children's emotional state will respond to music, becoming alert and calm with soothing music, or jarred with louder music. They will prefer infant-directed music, that is, music which is largely monotonal, including soft, higher-pitched tones in a sing-song pattern and directed specifically to the infant.
+ Between 3 and 6 months, infants will experiment with babbling. They will turn their faces toward the music they hear and begin

to move their bodies predictably in response. They will still prefer higher pitched voices.

+ Between 6 and 9 months, infants will match a single pitch and respond to familiar tunes. Their own singing will tend to swoop down the scale and they will attend to swooping tones from caregivers.

+ Between 9 and 12 months, infants will sing, especially when they hear familiar songs (although their songs will consist largely of sustained coos and other noises).

+ Between 12 and 18 months, infants will attend closely to lyrics and notice when lyrics change. They will be able to sing short excerpts from longer songs, to match multiple pitches and sets of tone and to begin to align their body movements to music.

+ Between 18 months and 2 years, toddlers will seek out partners to enjoy music with them, spinning and wiggling with dance partners. They will march to music they hear and be able to match songs with a predictable rhythm. Although they won't often match pitch, they will remember and reproduce lyrics to familiar tunes.

+ Between 2 and 3 years, older toddlers will distinguish between their singing and speaking voices. They'll transpose songs into various keys, match pitch reliably and may be able to identify differences between instruments they hear.

+ Between 3 and 4 years old, children will more easily distinguish differences between common musical instruments. They will use rhythm sticks to accompany their own invented songs or reproduced songs. They will match melodies and enjoy making up songs of their own, often as an accompaniment to other activities.

+ Between 4 and 5 years old, children will develop their own invented songs, with more complex melodies, emotions and lyrics. They will be able to distinguish melodies to familiar songs when the lyrics are missing and will be able to add their own invented lyrics to familiar melodies. They will be able to both maintain a steady beat and to match changes in beats from others.

+ Between 5 and 6 years old, children will be able to maintain a steady beat while moving on their feet. They will be able to sing on pitch, play simple melodies on accessible instruments and remember songs they've learned.

+ Between 6 and 7, children will establish their tonal center, maintaining the same key while they sing for extended melodies. They will begin to harmonize and will be able to maintain their own pitch-appropriate tunes even in the company of other singers, even singing in rounds.

- Between 7 and 9 years old, children will expand the vocal range around which they can sing and maintain pitch comfortable. They will be able to incorporate more complex musical structures in their own singing and will demonstrate a preference for some music over others.

For caregivers and teachers, then, understanding typical development in music will allow us to provide music-rich environments that integrate music into children's lives. Offer children a wide variety of music from infancy. Because different music offers different tempos, tonal relationships, rhythms, and structures, children benefit from hearing multiple modalities, including those less familiar to their home culture.

Be careful not to use music constantly, though. Just as children benefit from a wide variety of musical exposure, they also need time without music and time with limited other sounds. Although pure silence may be impossible to provide, balance when you offer music in your environment to match particular routines, to complement other learning, or to learn about music as its own content, including times when you do not play music at all. Link children's musical experiences with the behaviors and emotion you hope to evoke, and include musical styles and genres beyond what is typically considered "children's music." Classical music, jazz, Americana, bluegrass, country, pop, independent music, reggae, rap and others all have potential use for early childhood environments, and can be used when the behaviors they evoke match your goals for your classroom.

Although many caregivers may avoid describing themselves as musicians or, indeed, may say, "I *can't* sing," it's important to sing with children anyway. Use musical instruments and recorded music, but also use your own voice. Incorporate finger plays and rhythmic poetry. Use music to support transitions for children between activities, to complement classroom climates, and as the focus of activities itself.

Allow for both independent experimentation with musical instruments and structured opportunities to learn specific instrument-based skills. Invite musicians to your classroom and welcome parents who can play or sing to join your classroom to share their skills. Model listening skills for children, asking probing questions about what qualities of music children have heard and times when you are listening intentionally to music with children.

Remember, too, to offer resources for children to learn about the content of music as its own field. Look for high-quality picture books about music to include in your classroom library. While there are great examples of books that illustrate classical music, like Jack Prelutsky's *The Carnival of the Animals* or Suzie Templeton's *Peter and the Wolf*, look for illustrated books for contemporary music as well. Wynton Marsalis offers *Squeak, Rumble, Whomp! Whomp! Whomp!* as an introduction to jazz percussion. Ziggy Marley's *I Love You Too* is a playful retelling of his music, while *Outlaw Pete* introduces children to Bruce Springsteen.

Other children's books address how children might experience music. *I See a Song* by Eric Carle connects melodies and imagination. *The Girl Who Heard Colors* introduces children to the phenomena of synesthesia. *Ruby Sings the Blues* tells the story of a girl with a loud voice who loves to sing despite her parents' and teacher's requests to tone it down. *The Bat Boy and His Violin* and *The Django* emphasize how music enriches our lives. Great illustration books are available to teach children about the history of musical genres and artists, various musical instruments, and the influence and impact of music on social events and on our individual lives. A musically rich environment will offer diverse music, matched to children's interests and development, for personal exploration and group activities, as a support to other content and as content in its own right.

Discuss

+ Although we are all born with innate musical capacity, many of us learn that we are "not good at music," through our school and family experiences. As teachers and caregivers, we are challenged to preserve children's innate musical openness while supporting the natural skills of children with particular propensities for music. Discuss how you would differentiate in your classroom for a wide variety of children's musical talents and skills without discouraging some children from maintaining a powerful connection to music in their lives.
+ What are the ways in which music holds purpose for you as an adult? How is music's influence similar or different from the ways in which it will hold meaning for the children for whom you care? Discuss the challenges of modeling engaged appreciation for music with children when you have your own preferences for genre, artist or style.
+ How do you distinguish "good" music? Discuss what resources you would consult to identify "good" music across multiple styles: Classi-

cal, Jazz, Americana, Folk, Funk, Latin, Reggaue, R&B, Progressive and Soul. What qualities would you look for in music that is designed for children? What qualities might be universal across music that is not specifically designed for children, but still classroom-appropriate?

+ The children's music industry is currently in what's been described as a "golden age," with the number and quality of children's music performers growing as rapidly as the audience of parents and children. At the same time, marketers design music programs for infants and young children that promise the "Mozart effect," the ability to increase children's intelligence through passive exposure to particular types of music. Investigate "the Mozart effect." What does the research suggest about this phenomenon? How does that research differ from the promises made by these products? As a teacher or caregiver, how would you respond to a parent seeking your advice on whether to use videos or music at home in order to increase his or her child's intelligence?

Collaborate

+ A common kindergarten standard for social studies expects kindergarteners to be able to identify major national holidays, including their purpose and people or events celebrated. With a partner, prepare a lesson appropriate for kindergarteners linking a national holiday to music. Select from Labor Day, Columbus Day, Veterans Day, Thanksgiving Day, Martin Luther King Jr. Day, Presidents' Day, Memorial Day, Flag Day or Independence Day. In designing your lesson, avoid experiences which emphasize the performance of a song or rote memorization. Instead, consider how you can use music associated with your holiday to introduce, expand or enrich children's understanding of relevant themes or concepts.

+ With a partner, prepare a timeline of children's development through music that includes children's physical, cognitive, linguistic, and social and emotional development. Consider your timeline in relationship to how you envision a classroom setting for each relative age or span of development. Identify qualities of your imagined or real classroom that you would include to support and facilitate children's engagement with music in the environment. Prepare a sample daily schedule that identifies classroom activities, including opportunities for individual and group, exploratory and structured music education.

- Prepare a song to teach to a small group of colleagues. Consider how you will introduce your song, what hand motions or dance movements may accompany it, and whether you will use only your voice or other instruments. Prepare as though you are teaching a group of children. Teach your colleagues your song (and allow your colleagues to teach you the ones they've prepared!) Afterwards, discuss your emotions in preparing your song and presenting it to your peers. What parts of the experience were stressful? What parts were comfortable? What elements can you identify that you can incorporate into your own classroom to increase your comfort with singing aloud with children?

Create

- Music is often used to convey understanding or to support children's meaning-making of complicated abstract concepts. Prepare a song list of songs that describe your development as a teacher. Include at least nine songs. Annotate your list to detail how each song's lyrics represent your experiences becoming a teacher. How is your ability to describe your progress as a teacher different by the use of music to detail it?
- Integrating music in your classroom should include inviting musicians into your classroom community and visiting music venues appropriate for children. Prepare a resource directory of music venues and visiting experts to which you can refer in your own classroom. Investigate feedback from other teachers about the developmental appropriateness of different venues that market to children and schools. If you were to choose to take your class to visit one of these venues or invite a musician in, what potential topics would you consider? What preparation would your class require before your visit? What sense-making might you help to facilitate afterward? Organize your resources into a flexible, editable document that you can share with other teachers and add to as your experience and knowledge of community resources expands.
- While teachers have long known the benefits of singing and making music together for classroom cohesion and social norms, research increasingly points to the importance of social and emotional learning as an intentional domain in early childhood classrooms. Consider

common categories of prosocial behaviors: sharing behaviors, helping behaviors, and cooperation behaviors. Identify music you might use in your classroom to support children's understanding of each of these categories. Then, consider common examples of prosocial behaviors: sympathy, kindness, helping, sharing, concern, cooperation, demonstrating positive physical contact, demonstrating positive verbal contact, and taking the perspective of another. Describe what routines or norms you can establish during structured group music experiences that would provide children with authentic opportunities to practice these kinds of behaviors. How would you introduce them? What language or interventions would you use to support children who have not yet internalized them?

For Further Reading

Batcheller, J. M. (1975). *Music in early childhood.* New York: Center for Applied Research in Education.

Burton, S. L., & Taggart, C. C. (2011). *Learning from young children: Research in early childhood music.* Lanham, MD: Rowman & Littlefield Education.

Congreve, W. (1753). *The Mourning Bride: A Tragedy.* Dublin: J. and R. Tonson and S. Draper in the Strand.

Delavenne, A., Gratier, M., & Devouche, E. (2013). Expressive timing in infant-directed singing between 3 and 6 months. *Infant Behavior and Development, 36*(1), 1–13. doi:10.1016/j.infbeh.2012.10.004

Greata, J. (2006). *An introduction to music in early childhood education.* Clifton Park, NY: Thomson Delmar Learning.

Greenberg, M. (1974). The development and evaluation of a preschool music curriculum for preschool and head-start children. *Psychology of Music, 2*(1), 34–38, doi:10.1177/030573567421004

Gudmundsdottir, H. R., & Gudmundsdottir, D. G. (2010). Parent–infant music courses in Iceland: Perceived benefits and mental well-being of mothers. *Music Education Research, 12*(3), 299–309. doi:10.1080/14613808.2010.505644

Loth, H. (2013). Review of the book *Music therapy and parent–infant bonding,* by Jane Edwards (Ed.). *British Journal of Music Education, 30*(01), 152–154. doi:10.1017/s0265051712000538

L'Etoile, S. K. (2006). Infant behavioral responses to infant-directed singing and other maternal interactions. *Infant Behavior and Development, 29*(3), 456–470. doi:10.1016/j.infbeh.2006.03.002

May, B. N. (2013). Public school early childhood music education: Challenges and solutions. *General Music Today, 27*(1), 40–44. doi:10.1177/1048371313494783

MENC, the National Association for Music Education (U.S.). (2000). *Spotlight on early childhood music education.* (2000). Reston, VA: MENC, The National Association for Music Education.

Metz, E., & Andress, B. (1988). Using tactile modeling to increase musical perception in the preschool. *General Music Today, 1*(2), 8. doi:10.1177/104837138700100205

Metz, E. (1989). Movement as a musical response among preschool children. *Journal of Research in Music Education, 37*(1), 48. doi:10.2307/3344952

Music, G. (2004). Review of the book *The cradle of thought: Exploring the origins of thinking,* by Peter Hobson. *Infant Observation, 7*(2–3), 125–128. doi:10.1080/13698030408405048

Music. (n.d.). NAEYC.

Nardo, R. (2008). Music technology in the preschool? Absolutely! *General Music Today, 22*(1), 38–39. doi:10.1177/1048371308323272

National Association for Music Education (NAME). (2014). 2014 Music Standards. Retrieved from https://nafme.org/my-classroom/standards/core-music-standards/.

National Association for Music Education (NAME). (2018). Early Childhood Music Education: A position statement of the National Association for Music Education. Retrieved from https://nafme.org/about/position-statements/early-childhood-music-education/.

O'Gorman, S. (2006). The infant's mother: Facilitating an experience of infant-directed singing with the mother in mind. *British Journal of Music Therapy, 20*(1), 22–30. doi:10.1177/135945750602000105

Pratt, R. R. (1990). Music in special education, music therapy and music medicine. *International Journal of Music Education, 16*(1), 56–57. doi:10.1177/025576149001600111

Sams, R. W. (1989). Preschool music education: Where do we begin? *General Music Today, 2*(2), 9–12. doi:10.1177/104837138800200204

Sims, W. (1991). Early childhood music education. *International Journal of Music Education, 17*(1), 71–73. doi:10.1177/025576149101700116

Smithrim, K., & Upitis, R. B. (2007). *Listen to their voices: Research and practice in early childhood music.* Toronto: Canadian Music Educators' Association.

Snyder, S. (1996). Early childhood music lessons from "Mr. Holland's Opus." *Early Childhood Education Journal, 24*(2), 103–105. doi:10.1007/bf02353289

Street, A. (2010). Infant musicality: New research for educators and parents. *Music Education Research, 12*(4), 447–449. doi:10.1080/14613808.2010.520499

Trainor, L. J. (2010). Perceptual development: Infant music perception. In E. B. Goldstein (Ed.), *Encyclopedia of Perception.* doi:10.4135/9781412972000.n241

Trainor, L. J., Clark, E. D., Huntley, A., & Adams, B. A. (1997). The acoustic basis of preferences for infant-directed singing. *Infant Behavior and Development, 20*(3), 383–396. doi:10.1016/s0163-6383(97)90009-6

Trainor, L. J., & Zacharias, C. A. (1998). Infants prefer higher-pitched singing. *Infant Behavior and Development, 21*(4), 799–805. doi:10.1016/s0163-6383(98)90047-9

Wheeler, B. L., & Stultz, S. (2007). Using typical infant development to inform music therapy with children with disabilities. *Early Childhood Education Journal, 35*(6), 585–591. doi:10.1007/s10643-007-0224-1

Witt, A. E., & Steele, A. L. (1984). Music therapy for infant and parent: A case example. *Music Therapy Perspectives, 1*(4), 17–19. doi:10.1093/mtp/1.4.17

Woodward, S. (2009). Critical matters in early childhood music education. In D. J. Elliot (Ed.), *Praxial Music Education* (pp. 249–266). doi:10.1093/acprof:oso/9780195385076.003.13

Young, S. (2016). Early childhood music education research: An overview. *Research Studies in Music Education, 38*(1), 9–21. doi:10.1177/1321103x16640106

Chapter 7

Aesthetics and Criticism

"Any great art work ... revives and readapts time and space, and the measure of its success is the extent to which it makes you an inhabitant of that world—the extent to which it invites you in and lets you breathe its strange, special air."

—Leonard Bernstein

What is Aesthetic Education?

Aesthetics is that branch of philosophy that seeks to define the nature of beauty. In education, it encompasses the perspectives and practices that evoke children's understanding of beauty through hands-on experiences and opportunities to discuss and question, to reflect, and to create art. Aesthetic education offers a model for learning how to question new content and how to experience familiar content in new ways. Learners are challenged, in this lens, to consider new "ways of knowing," with the belief that interacting with traditional disciplines expands our understanding of the limits and connections between them.

When we teach children to explore multiple ways of seeing and knowing, we offer them tools to discover qualities within disciplinary knowledge that we have not predetermined. We teach them, through an aesthetic education, how to question and how to learn, skills far more valuable in the life of a learner than any specific content test may provide. By prioritizing aesthetics in our approach to teaching, we help to establish the habits of mind for learners that will propel them beyond our classrooms.

The influence of aesthetic education has contributed to educational theories for as long as we've considered education something about which to theorize. Before traditional school structures or curricula developed, before we regulated teacher education or established licensing standards, before we debated the specific content that should be taught in fourth grade, before we had a "fourth grade," we asked the underlying questions that drive aesthetic education. "What is important? What is essential? What is beautiful? What is valuable?" When Plato proposed that the physical world is a decaying copy of its original, essential and perfect design, he was asking aesthetic questions. When Dewey argued that "works of art are the most intimate and energetic means of aiding individuals to share in the arts of living. Civilization is uncivil because human beings are divided into non-communicating sects, races, nations, classes and cliques,"[1] he advocated for an aesthetic approach to education. Likewise, when contemporary theorists seek to balance the content-driven rigor of a high-stakes testing climate in American schools, they are arguing for a consideration of the aesthetic development of the child.

The aesthetic includes a vast range of applications, from understanding nature to unpacking social constructs. Art offers an easy access to these conversations, by identifying the ways in which we represent human experience, including visual symbolism, movement and dance, sound, noise and voice, perspective, positioning, and verbal and written expression. Emphasizing art aesthetics includes a focus on the analysis and translation, that is, the meaning-making of the art experience, for both artist and audience, rather than the technical skills involved.

The goals of aesthetic education, then, include:

+ developing a sense of what is beautiful
+ developing a sense of proportion and perception
+ offering experiences to process, create, critique and represent what is beautiful
+ integrating a disposition toward beauty in the personal life of the learner and in the interactions between learners

An aesthetic model offers these experiences as specific learning goals for children and does so in environments that by design reflect particular understandings of beauty. There won't be a class period, for example,

---

1 Dewey, J. *Art as Experience*, http://www.comp.dit.ie/dgordon/Courses/ILT/ILT0003/ TheReflexArcConceptIinPsychology.pdf

scheduled for "Aesthetic Education." Instead, the intent to seek, identify, define, and experience beauty will be an undercurrent throughout the lived experiences of the school. Some general qualities will emerge in common: experiences that increase perception, experiences that allow authentic emotional connections, experiences that encourage creation, and experiences that support discernment and critique.

Experiences that increase perception challenge teachers and learners alike to notice what is beautiful in the worlds around them. Most of us become comfortable with the environments around us. Aesthetic education asks learners to observe even the familiar for qualities of beauty. To do so, learners need experience observing, language for describing what we see, to name shapes, colors, and qualities. They need opportunities to observe without specific outcomes, to notice things they may otherwise overlook, to compare what is familiar to what is new. Learners need open-ended experiences noticing qualities of beauty in their every day lives, and time for experiences noticing and naming the same in Art.

Experiences that allow authentic emotional connections require time, trust, and access. Beautiful things inspire us to feel joy, to be hopeful, to be inspired. Remember: aesthetics draws its name from the Greek, *aesthetis*, to experience, to feel. It is the opposite of "anaesthesia," which allows you not to feel. In order to connect with beauty, children need opportunities to experience beauty, to be emotionally connected to what is beautiful.

Experiences that encourage creation engage learners in opportunities to affect their classrooms, their homes, and their worlds by increasing the beauty they find there. These are not technique-driven experiences that build the muscles of a dancer's legs and ankles. Instead, these are the open-ended opportunities to dance. Aesthetic education presumes that children will be given more opportunities to refine their own creativity within an environment that encourages aesthetic noticing and authentic emotional connections to beauty.

Experiences that support discernment and critique are equally important, developing in the learner a common language to describe beauty and proportion in an effort to define its essence. Learners need experiences with differing criteria for judging beauty, experiences in dialogue that allow the articulation of personal definitions of beauty and compare them to outside criteria, and which allow both the individual's definition of beauty to become more refined and to place that definition within a larger context of human experience. Is the Mona Lisa beautiful? Is the Eiffel Tower? By talking with children about how we have defined beauty throughout history, we support their ability to critique beauty themselves.

To support the development of an aesthetic awareness, teachers need to encourage learners to observe, to notice, and to be moved by what they see, to create and to acknowledge what is beautiful in their environments and in their relationships with others, to express their own experience of beauty, and to be able to define and describe what is beautiful around them. To begin here elevates the work of classrooms, from places in which students learn particular, predetermine sets of content, to places that help to construct contributors to a greater community.

Aesthetic Development in Young Children

Children's aesthetic development will follow their sensorial development, as children learn to discern elements of color, texture, form, and structure essential to aesthetic awareness. Between birth and 2, infants and toddlers build the capacity to control their motor reflexes, reaching for objects, controlling their hands and legs, coordinating their bodies in time and space. They begin to react to distinct characteristics of objects and show special attention to color and form. Between birth and 6 months, children prefer visual patterns and children as young as 6 weeks can distinguish visual form. Research suggests they use these preferences to link familiar faces. By identifying the welcoming face of a caregiver, for example, infants may be able to contribute to stronger emotional bonds with those individuals.

Between the ages of 2 and 7, children move through two important periods of development influential to their aesthetic awareness. In the younger range for this spectrum, typically between 2 and 4, children may be able to classify by a single factor but may be challenged to classify by multiple factors. So, for example, they may be able to sort objects which are rough from those which are smooth, but they may have a harder time distinguishing between smooth small stones and rough large stones. Within this range, children learn to name and distinguish color, to match colors, and to sort into color palettes from lightest to darkest. Between roughly the ages of 4 and 7, children are able to distinguish more complex relationships, to classify by multiple factors, and to classify the same original group of objects into multiple categories. The child may be able to sort building blocks into sets of red, blue, and green blocks, to sort them into sets of 4×4, 4×2, or 2×6 blocks, and to sort them into sets of red 4×4, red 4×2, red 2×6, blue 4×4, blue 4×2, blue 2×6, and so on. At around age 5, children can distinguish forms of objects based on their orientation in space. A prism on its side may appear as a rectangle, but on its end may appear as a triangle. Children begin to internalize concepts related to shape, like roundness, squareness, etc. They develop more complex schema to describe the world around them, to make sense of what they experience and to control that sense-making by naming it and classifying it.

Children absorb the qualities and values of the environments around them, and come to understand the norms of their lived environments as a reflection of what has value and what does not. Often, though, environments prepared for children are designed to be primarily safe and washable, rather than beautiful and evocative. Shelves are cluttered or overstuffed. Materials that hold academic importance (like literacy and math manipulatives) are in abundance, so much so that no one material stands out as particularly important or valuable and, instead, the tools for learning become fungible and disposable. Children's appreciation of beauty is challenged to find support in classrooms overflowing with uncapped markers and broken crayons.

While teachers and caregivers may be primarily concerned with the durability of their classroom environments, child development challenges us to foreground beauty in the environment, to assure that it is safe, no doubt, but not to ignore the critical influence an aesthetically prepared environment has on children's development. We understand that children are drawn to beautiful things. They observe nature thoughtfully and for longer than we may understand as adults. Imagine the toddler who stops repeatedly on a family walk to notice a pebble on the sidewalk, or the infant whose attention is fixed on the light through branches above her stroller. Consider the preschooler who has a distinct preference for one illustrator's work over another's, or the 4-year-old who becomes fascinated with the way particular words string together, repeating them to himself as if he's lost in the music of the language. As teachers and caregivers, these moments are not to be rushed along. They reflect the child's natural interest in aesthetics and his developing sense of beauty.

It stands to reason that a child's ability to feel, her aesthetic awareness, will be tied to her sensorial development. Infants sense with their entire bodies. They experience sensations across their bodies without distinguishing them as separate from themselves. Rather, they offer strong, emotional feedback about their preferences, long before they may be able to communicate those preferences complexly. An infant prefers the smell of one blanket to another. He finds the texture of his mother's hair fascinating, stroking it and watching his own fingers move. She attends thoughtfully to one colorful wooden toy but shows no interest in another.

As children grow, they experience a wider range of sensorial stimuli and, as a result, develop more classifications within which they define what is "good" or "beautiful." They may organize their food by tastes, preferring the order of some tastes over others. They may insist on particular types of clothing, describing the qualities of fabrics by touch or smell. While their evolving preferences may be disregarded by caregivers as "picky" or "stubborn," children in toddlerhood and early childhood are developing the ability to classify and categorize stimuli by their sensorial experience. With time, these classifications will inform their aesthetic awareness.

Theorists have debated how caregivers and teachers should respond to this developing aesthetic awareness. In one model, theorists argue that an aesthetic awareness will develop in children at each child's own pace, evolving through open-ended experiences with a wide variety of art media and when those experiences are not stifled by adults. From this perspective, children should be offered time and encouragement to explore creative materials, to engage with art materials and to create independently of critical feedback. Proponents argue that adult definitions of beauty should be held back from children's self-directed choices, with a belief that the child's artistic abilities can be squelched otherwise.

Alternatively, Elliot Eisner (2002) and others emphasize the potential influence fine arts have to supporting children's developing aesthetic sense, arguing that in order to appreciate great art, one must be exposed to great art. Children's aesthetic awareness, from this viewpoint, is developed as a response to what they have seen, felt, experienced, and been exposed to. This lens presents art history and criticism as its own discipline for early exposure and encourages teachers to help evoke connections and responses from children to great works of art.

Both models influence early childhood education today, and they are not mutually exclusive. Children's open-ended art experiences can include exposure to great artists as well. Visiting museums, displaying prints of art in the environment, visiting performances of live artists, dancers and actors, offer children authentic lived experience with beauty. These experiences should not be offered to children as the single expression of beauty, but can be used to spark conversations, to describe what qualities evoked an emotional response and which did not, to introduce the language of color, line, proportion, movement, etc. and to support meaningful connections between the child and beautiful things. Likewise, that language can be used when talking with children about their own creations and processes. While children may not have the technical skill to create a professional work of art, they can be supported in discussing their artistic intent, their work process, and their own meaning-making within the vocabulary of aesthetics. Research suggests that when children are exposed to high-quality art, their own artistic expressions become more detailed and developed. Children can benefit from being exposed to a wide variety of artistic styles and media, through conversations about the nature of the kind of art that withstands time and evokes emotion. When those conversations are focused on the meaning-making, on the experience of the viewer and the shared experience of teacher and learner, children may not experience the same performance-standard as if those great works of art were presented as models to be copied.

Indeed, children seem to have, by nature, a different aesthetic preference than adults. Young children in particular prefer contrasting colors, objects that are familiar and comforting to them, clear relationships in space, and simple compositions. Their receptivity to complex compositions increases over time, while their preference for representations that reflect real relationships stays firm through early childhood. The most important influence on children's aesthetic preferences seems to be how they feel about the art, rather than specific subjects or qualities. Because developing vocabulary restricts children's ability to convey complicated understandings, it may be harder to measure how complex children's aesthetic awareness is. Research suggests that, when teachers provide accurate vocabulary to discuss the process of creating art, children demonstrated a greater interest in discussing that process, creating more complex works, and were able to persist in more complicated discussions about their own art and the art of others than when teachers did not offer specific, discipline-based vocabulary. Conversation during and around the art materials should be rich in describing the experience and processes involved rather than focused on tidying up.

Balancing the influence of the adult with the individual aesthetic of the child is important to the child's growing ability to notice, to be emotionally affected, to create independently, and to critique beauty. In many classrooms, however, the teachers' guidance encourages children to reproduce predetermined crafts rather than to create personally relevant work. To support children's aesthetic awareness, the experiences of the classroom need to be focused on children's self-expression rather than prepared models. Children need regular, open access to media in good condition and of high quality. In guiding children, teachers' language should focus on evoking children's thinking about their intent and their plan for executing, clarifying through conversation what the child wants to produce rather than directing children toward particular outcomes. When teachers limit access to media or limit the ways in which varying media can be used, or provide prepared models of how the art should look when the child is finished, the child learns to match his or her own work to the intentions of the adult. It may be easier to clean up, but it does little to propel a child's internalized sense of beauty or her ability to contribute to creating it in the world.

The Indoor Environment

Remember that all the experiences children have will inform their aesthetic awareness—not just the ones that include art materials! Children learn to discern beauty when it is offered to them throughout their environments, and they learn to value their own contribution to it when those contributions are meaningful and authentic. While you may not be able to control the aesthetic of many places learners experience, you can influence the prepared environment of your classroom or home space.

Many environments designed for children are visually overwhelming, cluttered, or chaotic. We know children's natural preferences are for spaces that are warm and inviting, for simple compositions, and realistic representations. How often, though, do we offer them, instead, spaces that are loud, with multiple complicated combinations of shapes and color, disproportionate furnishings, and unrealistic characters and stimuli? Classroom settings should be durable and tidy. They should be accessible to children and safe for their open-ended exploration. But that does not mean they have to also be made entirely of plastic or disposable materials.

Consider first the color scheme of the indoor environment. Color is a powerful and evocative tool. It can create a climate of cheerfulness or calm. It can help learners to concentrate or it can distract them from other tasks. Because the colors you choose for your environment include both the materials you offer and the walls, floors and ceilings against which they are viewed, it's important to consider the color of the entire space as well as the colors of individual experiences.

For example, if your classroom includes a large, brightly colored mural of animated characters painted on the wall, children will be drawn to attend to the mural. If you have special materials or presentations on the shelves or tables around the room, children will see those with the constant visual influence of the mural in the background. Consider the child's visual scope, the area the child can see and make sense of at any given time. To support the child's developing attention, the field should be one that encourages her to attend to the materials that have been provided for learning and acting upon, rather than the background color of the walls. Choose soft colors for the walls and floors, and avoid large scale installations that distract from the materials children with which children can engage.

Hang artwork low to the floor, at the child's eye level rather than the adult's, and choose artwork with some meaning for the children in the environment. Look for relevant themes to children's lives. Claude Monet's *Woman with a Parasol—Madame Monet and Her Son* and Keith Haring's *Mother and Baby* both depict mothers and children, but in very different styles. Klimt's *Mother with Children* can be presented with Bonnat's *An Egyptian Peasant Woman and Her Child*. Remember that everything in the environment will teach the children there something. Choose artwork because it offers an opportunity to draw children's attention to particular qualities in the art rather than as background filler. Avoid displaying children's artwork haphazardly or presenting some children's artwork as worthy of display while others' may not be.

Consider the color of the shelves, trays, and baskets when you design your classroom space. When you scan your environment, are your eyes naturally drawn to the materials with which you want the children to engage, or do you find yourself distracted by colors across the classroom? If you cannot change the color of your walls or shelves, consider draping them with neutral colored cloths or wall-hangings against which your intended activities will stand out.

Include attention for the floor. While early childhood classroom spaces should be easily mopped and cleaned, children will walk, sit, and lie down on the floor as well. Soften these spaces with area rugs to create visually smaller spaces. If installing tile or flooring, choose neutral tones and simple designs rather than vivid checkerboxes. The floor is a part of the visual field in your classroom. Avoid drawing attention to it, but instead use it to define particular spaces and to encourage attention.

Look up! Although you may rarely look at the ceiling, children often do, as a backdrop when they're gazing up at someone taller than they are, or while lying down on the floor or just looking around their space. Make sure your ceiling is tidy and neutral. For infants and toddlers, lower the ceiling if possible to create a visually smaller space. Hang soft neutral drapes across the ceiling to create a softer effect. Repair or replace water stains. For infants and toddler spaces, hang simple mobiles that represent realistic objects, like butterflies or bird. Use plant hooks to hang plants lower to the floor so they can be enjoyed by the children, rather than hanging them from the ceiling, where the children may only be able to see the undersides of their pots.

Introduce well-maintained and beautiful examples of nature in your classroom. Small plants in simple pots will draw children's attention. Include simple animal habitats, like a clean fishbowl for a small fish or an ant farm that can be viewed from all sides. Remember to include only those plants and animals for which you can regularly care. Neglected habitats teach children that their animal companions and their spaces can be overlooked. Your classroom design will be better served by one beta fish in a sparkling clear fish bowl than a large aquarium with dirty glass walls.

On your art shelves, offer children materials that are in good working condition and of good quality. Remove baskets that are broken or flimsy. Remove markers that are dried out. Sort crayons by color to create an attractive display. Make sure your art materials are available and accessible to children, that the art shelf is clean and tidy before the children arrive, and that the materials you choose allow children to create their own work rather than copy a model.

Think of each of the materials on the shelf as teaching children about proportion and beauty. Sort small objects and figures into their own containers rather than piling them all in one large bin. Use quality containers, wooden baskets, boxes and trays, and sturdy glass jars that offer different textures for children's hands and encourage care for the materials they contain. Make sure puzzles have all their pieces and are displayed in an attractive way. Curate your classroom shelves to put like activities together and to display them on the shelf in an orderly and visually appealing way. When children are presented with materials that have been cared for, their instinct to care for them as well will improve. If everything that's available to a child is fungible, the child has no reason to learn to take care with certain objects. Create a space which is beautiful, knowing that children will be motivated to keep it that way and that the physical environment will become a part of how they appreciate order and beauty around them.

Remember the unusual spaces: cloak rooms, bathrooms, hallways, etc. While these may not be the places we think of first in designing classroom environments, they are important parts of the children's experience and space within which the children may spend quite a bit of time!

Prepare the classroom space as though it was a well-designed home environment. Balance the harsh light of overhead fluorescent lights with lamps using full spectrum lightbulbs. Present learning materials to act upon, like manipulatives, puzzles, art media, blocks and books, and materials to observe, like small wooden sculptures, figures, natural shells, stones, etc. Think of each of the child's senses and consider the classroom from that perspective. How does the classroom appear from the height of a child? Is it visually orderly or overwhelming? Can you notice small details when you're observing things, or are you distracted by other colors or backgrounds? How does the classroom smell? Are there interesting scents naturally occurring in some areas, like flowering plants or baked muffins? How does the space feel to your skin? Is the temperature comfortable? Are there interesting things to touch and feel? Is there variety in how things feel in your hand? In their weight and proportion? Are there curious things to taste at snack time? Are there interesting sounds, gentle tones, bells, and quiet areas, or is the classroom consistently loud and cacophonous? In addressing the aesthetics of the space, consider all the ways a child can feel the space sensorially.

Finally, provide ample areas from which to observe and classroom structures that allow for observation. A tall director's chair is a safe perch from which children can watch the activities of open play in their classroom. A cozy loft, which serves as a safe place for retreat from the noise of the room, is also an unusual angle from which to watch the classroom. A rocking chair set near a window gives children a space to observe, rest, and reflect on their experiences. Remember that children need time both to observe what is beautiful and to reflect upon it. Offer space for those experiences by providing areas for individual children or pairs of two children to sit together quietly in observation. Respect children's need for reflection and quiet and preserve both time and space in the classroom for retreat when individual children need. Remember that children will absorb the norms of the environment. If a classroom space is designed in a cluttered or sensorially overwhelming way, children will have a harder time being at ease in that space. If a classroom is designed to draw children's attention to beautiful things and to allow them to sustain that attention without interruption, children will build the capacity to notice, define, reflect, and create beauty in their world.

The Outdoor Environment

The child's conceptualization of beauty is built over time and through multiple experiences that help to inform his understanding of the world. It is affected by any environment within which the child learns and grows and is not limited to a particular time of day or classroom space. Likewise, facilitating the development of an aesthetic awareness in children can't be parceled out to the art teacher or to specific times of day. Teachers and caregivers should plan, whenever and wherever possible, intentional, child-centered experiences with beauty in all its forms. This includes during outdoor play.

Many early childhood outdoor environments are designed to allow for open play, with an emphasis on gross motor development through climbers, swings, and riding toys. Children are encouraged to "go play," and teachers often play purely supervisory roles. Remember, though, that children don't turn off their construction of the world. The outdoor environment offers rich opportunity for children to observe and notice beauty in ways that cannot be replicated indoors. Teachers and caregivers should give careful attention to facilitating these opportunities, both by intentional design of outdoor spaces before the children arrive and by responsive practices when children are present.

Remember: the development of an aesthetic sense requires experiences that increase perception, experiences that allow authentic emotional connections, experiences that encourage creation, and experiences that support discernment and critique. Consider how each of these may be included into the intentional design of outdoor spaces.

Experiences that increase perception: Prepare the outdoor space with various areas that work together visually, that offer opportunities for distinct smells and touch, that introduce interesting sounds and even allow for tasting. Think about how your outdoor environment will be experienced from ground level, from the height of any seating areas, or from the top of the climber. Imagine your outdoor space as a carefully constructed garden, with distinct areas for color and interaction. Include different plants in your garden that flower throughout the year to draw children's attention to the cycles of plantlife. Include plants that feel different to the hand or have different fragrances. Plant edible plants.

Consider the aesthetic opportunities for gross motor activities as well. Provide high quality outdoor blocks for constructing and allow ample time for children to explore relationships of proportion, weight, and scale when building their own projects. Incorporate language that helps to classify experiences while you are talking with children out of doors. Notice out loud the opportunities to see things differently. The slide looks different from the top of the ramp. The soil smells different when it is wet. Draw children's attention to these observations and use rich diverse language to describe them.

Think of the outdoor space as its own canvas. Make it beautiful and inviting.

Experiences that allow authentic emotional connections: Gardening with children is an incomparable opportunity to facilitate authentic emotional connections to learning. Children can be involved in preparing a garden space, turning soil with their hands or shovels, and digging holes for seedlings. They can plant small plants in the garden, and will experience the smell of the soil on their hands as they notice the different temperatures between plant, soil, and root system. They will attend to the small differences that distinguish one kind of seedling from another and will move with care through the land they've helped to plant. Noticing seedlings grow into plants, vines, and fruits is sure to engage children's attention with authentic enthusiasm and joy. Allow time and space in the garden every day, and support children who want to notice and observe changes by providing quiet places from which to watch. Model observing the garden in your own interaction. Draw children's attention to the differences between blossoms on the same plant or the small variations in the standard shape of a plant's leaves.

Experiences that encourage creation: Give careful thought to the opportunities to create new works out of doors. Let children explore with paintbrushes and buckets of water to create evaporating shapes on paths and walls. Hang a common canvas out of doors to encourage children to paint together in the open air. Provide diverse materials for constructions of the children's own design. Offer long strands of well-made ribbon for children to weave through playground fences. Engage children in predicting the balance of colors that will come when their gardens blossom. If you are able to plant a vegetable garden, encourage children to combine tastes in new ways, to explore how herbs taste differently when eaten by the leaf or steeped in water or added to other foods.

Experiences that support discernment and critique: A critical factor to the intentional design of outdoor spaces is the preparation of teacher language and interactions within them. Remember that teachers model behavior for children whether they are indoors or out. While children will certainly find entertaining ways to pass the time outdoors, without the limits imposed to volume or speed that come with their time indoors, teachers shouldn't think of this as break time or time during which their roles change from facilitators of learning to supervisors of safety. Talk with children while they explore the outdoors. Name their experiences with them, using high-quality and accurate language to describe what you observe the children doing and what you are doing together. Learn and use the proper names for the parts of a plant and for the different plants you place in the garden. Model comparisons with children and probe for them their own experiences of space, proportion and beauty outdoors. Offer great works depicting nature and the outdoors for children to consider, including visual art like Monet's *Water Lily Pond* and musical interpretations of relationships in nature, like Vivaldi's "Four Seasons." Introduce types of garden design, from English gardens to hedge mazes, zen gardens, and rock gardens. When given linguistically rich opportunities to discern and compare outdoor design, children can develop a more nuanced understanding, too, of the beauty of nature and the ways in which human interactions can affect that.

When preparing an environment, either indoors or out, keep in mind some common qualities of aesthetic appreciation. Aesthetics encompasses an appreciation of beauty and a sense of wonder, driven in children through their senses and imagination. These are opportunities to enhance the human experience by engaging in activities for pure joy. For children, this includes acting upon their environments, exploring their environments and objects freely and joyfully. Activities and spaces, including conversation with teachers and intentionally designed materials can support children in expressing their own opinions and feelings about beauty. Teachers and caregivers should offer opportunities to reflect on these experiences without judgement from adults or competition with other children, looking instead for activities which stimulate curiosity and attentiveness and wonder. These experiences are not limited to art education, but, especially in early childhood, can be integrated across content areas, discovering the way new sounds work together or the interactions of scientific phenomena, creating geometric shapes from combinations of triangles or exploring the ways families are represented across the world. Slow down your teaching and allow time for wonder, for the appreciation of nature and its rhythms, for a fascination with poetry and music, dance or the solar system.

Picture Books and Aesthetic Awareness

As children develop the perception and discernment necessary for aesthetic appreciation, teachers and caregivers can propel that awareness through great conversations that allow children to reflect and critique the nature of beauty, art and the human experience. This may seem advanced for children's early development, but remember: it is within the first six years of life that children learn how the world works, whether they are safe in it, whether their perceptions can be trusted. In this critical window, children, whether we discuss it explicitly or not, are struggling to discern whether the world is an essentially good or bad place, whether they can influence it, and whether their influence in the world will be meaningful. Those judgements can be supported through learning activities that evoke conversation about abstract ideals. Picture books are a great place to start.

Not all picture books will lead to interesting conversations about the essence of beauty and humanity. Indeed, most won't. But many will. Most picture books combine written word and visual imagery, challenging children to look closely at illustrations, at the layout on the page, the relationship of written language to illustration ... even the differences between what is printed on the book sleeve and what is printed on the cover itself can draw children's attention to different possible interpretations of the story. As such, they provide rich opportunities to discuss beauty, art, and humanity. Children will often be more attentive to these details than adults are. Allow time for their curiosity to be met. That careful looking evokes new questions about what the story is really about, and new opportunities to discuss how color, line, shape, language, perspective, and proportion influence the meaning readers make.

Consider picture books as intentional aesthetic objects, designed to evoke meaning in the interaction. The size and shape of the book itself leads to particular kinds of engagements. Books which are small allow small hands to handle them easily, to experience privately. Books which are larger are open to a common experience. Horizontal books tend to support landscape illustrations or panoramas that spread across the page. Vertical books invite readers to look more closely, binding the image within a narrower field.

The dust jacket and cover of the book offer other elements that contribute to learners' aesthetic experience. Does the story begin on the cover, or within the book? Does the dust jacket copy the image on the cover, or does it tell a different side of the story? Tao Nyeu's *Bunny Days* includes a jacket that, when removed, contributes in an entirely new way to the story. Graeme Base's *The Water Hole* offers a more complicated premise when its jacket is removed. Sendak's classic *Where the Wild Things Are* challenges viewers with an image that spans from the front cover to the rear, inviting us to see exactly how wide Max's imagination becomes.

The endpapers, too, represent intentional aesthetic choices in well-designed books. Eleanor Levenson's *What I Think About When I Think About Swimming* includes endpapers overflowing with the narrator fish wobbling through different positions. Viewers have an immediate sense of the zen-like state of the fish's thinking. Margaret Chodos-Irvine's *Best Best Friends*, which begins at the beginning of the school day and follows children throughout the day, presents endpapers that contribute to the passing of time. At the beginning of the book, the cubbies illustrated in the endpaper are full. At the end, they are empty, but for a few lost items left behind. Endpapers can offer commentary on the story itself, a sort of visual aside to the reader, like in Chris Raschka and Vladimir Radunsky's *Table Manners*. They may even stand alone as their own artistic interpretation, like in Peter Sis's extraordinary *The Tree of Life*, where the endpapers tell their own beautiful, ordered, and visually balanced story.

The paper on which a picture book is printed offers another aesthetic choice, evoking particular experiences in the reader. Glossy papers add shimmer to the visual field, but they detract from attending to any one part of the illustration. Matte or heavier stock paper feels different in the hand, inviting readers to stay with each page longer and feel the weight of the story in their fingers. Chris Van Allsburg's *Jumanji* allows for the texture depicted in his detailed illustrations to stand out. Ted Dewan's illustrations for *The Divide Trilogy* are printed on embossed paper, creating a mythic quality to the experience of holding the book. Speciality presentations, like Benjamin Lacombe's enchanting pop-up book *Once Upon a Time*, break through the dimensions of the page.

Within the illustrations, picture books offer opportunities to introduce elements of design, color, line, shape, texture, and value. Drawing children's attention to these qualities is a chance to describe, with appropriate vocabulary, how particular combinations come to evoke common experiences. Bryan Collier's *Trombone Shorty* uses vibrant colors and line to create movement and strength in the story of Trombone Shorty. His use of collage complements the historical story, while his perspective invites the reader to feel as though she is the single audience of the tale. Alternatively, Kevin Henkes's *Waiting* uses soft pastels and a neutral palette to welcome the reader to enjoy the story slowly, just as the characters themselves are patiently anticipating the everyday beauty around them. Illustrations like Christian Robinson's in *Last Stop on Market Street* pay homage to Ezra Keats and the aesthetic of earlier illustrators, placing the story in a long history of art representations and a shared experience for the reader. Illustrators with unique artistic styles can both place their work within a larger body of genre, like Dennis Nolan's use of pointillism in *The Castle Builder*, and invoke the tone of other forms of art, like Paul Zelinksy does in *Swamp Angel*, creating a uniquely Americana feel by creating his illustrations on painted wood. Peter Spier's *Noah's Ark* juxtaposes close details which draw the reader into the uncountable challenges for Noah and his family with sweeping horizons to emphasize the vastness of the ark and the surrounding flood. Finally, the artist's choice of medium influences the tone and feel of the story. Eric Carle's vibrantly painted paper cuts convey an energetic and playful spirit, while Alan Say's realistic watercolors temper the reader to engage the story slowly and methodically. Slowing down to experience a picture book for its use of color, shape, texture, line and value offers children the chance to practice describing aesthetic choices, to reflect and judge the complete text with the companionship of an interested teacher.

Finally, the narrative story of picture books can be used to help draw children's attention to abstract ideals of beauty, goodness and the human experience. In Peter Reynolds's *Ish,* an enthusiastic young boy is discouraged from drawing by his older brother's insensitive criticism, realizing only after seeing his drawings through his younger sister's eyes that his artwork can still be beautiful. Reynolds introduces the ideal of perfection. In Ramon's efforts to make his drawings look "right," was he striving for perfection or for approval from his brother? Teachers can discuss with children what it means to "look right," whether art needs to be realistic to be "good art," and whose judgment gets to determine its rightness. *Ish* presents perspectives on motivation, emotion and creativity, inspiring conversations about how other people's judgments may influence one's own motivation, how negative responses influence our emotional openness, and whether the idea of art looking right, can limit the kinds of art experiences one is willing to explore.

Bob Munsch's *The Paper Bag Princess* introduces readers to Elizabeth, a determined princess who outsmarts the dragon who has devoured her kingdom and kidnapped her boyfriend. Elizabeth challenges traditional roles for women and especially princesses, just as Prince Ronald falls short of the traditional heroic prince. *The Paper Bag Princess* invites conversation about social roles and norms even in storytelling. Does Elizabeth act like a princess should? Does Ronald behave like a prince? What do those labels mean and how have we come to decide? When Elizabeth saves Ronald, only to be chided by her prince for looking like she's just followed a dragon into battle, she chooses a different kind of happy ending for herself. The reader wonders whether happiness, as an ideal, can be predetermined. Does getting everything you want make you happy? If not, how do we define what happiness is?

Older children may be engaged by the philosophical questions raised in *Something Beautiful* by Sharon Dennis Wyeth, in which a girl in an urban neighborhood ventures out to try to find something beautiful in her environment. *Something Beautiful* is a powerful introduction to conversations around aesthetics. Does beauty have to reflect positive things, or can sadness be beautiful? Can something be beautiful even if it is not everyone finds it beautiful? Does your personal definition of beauty carry weight? Can something be beautiful just because you say it is? What does the experience of beauty evoke in us?

Mem Fox's *Wilfrid Gordon McDonald Partridge* allows children to compare their own understanding of abstract ideals with ones held by adults. When Wilfrid Gordon McDonald Partridge overhears his parents discussing how his neighbor in a nearby retirement home, Miss Nancy, has lost her memory, he decides to find it for her. Asking other residents what a memory is, Wilfrid Gordon McDonald Partridge collects a jumbled assortment of objects that match those definitions in his own experience, evoking deeply personal memories in Miss Nancy when he offers them to her. *Wilfrid Gordon McDonald Partridge* moves between concrete and abstract representations and between the understanding of children and that of adults.

American philosopher Denis Dutton identifies seven universal "signatures" in human aesthetics. Picture books offer powerful entries into each of these modalities, each with related vocabulary and types of questioning for teachers to model.

- Virtuosity: describes the technical expertise of an artist, the degree to which it is evident to an observer, how it is cultivated, and what that expertise evokes in an audience
- Non-utilitarian enjoyment: the degree to which the art is enjoyable, whether or not it is useful. Does it create joy? Does it evoke pleasure? Is it of value as "art for art's sake"?
- Style: the formal and shared qualities of composition that define genre and place the work within a commonly understood set of artistic "rules," the defined place for a piece of art within a larger defined category
- Criticism: whether the work evokes multiple points of view and engages reflection and critique. Is this a work you want to talk about?
- Imitation: how closely the art represents real human experiences, how universal the representation within the art is to what is "real."
- Special focus: whether the work warranted a special place separate from every day life. Can a toaster be elegant? Does the work invite viewers to consider the every day in a new way?
- Imagination: how deeply the work invites the viewer to explore in possible worlds. Can you "go" with the artist in your imagination?

Does the work engage you to image what might be, to be invested in the possibilities it considers?

Facilitating the development of an aesthetic awareness in young children does not happen by chance, nor is it limited to particular times of day or content areas. Because aesthetics considers the big questions, and seeks to understand how symbolic representations of those questions inform our understanding of the answers, it crosses the boundaries of class schedules, environments, and disciplines. Children's development through the arts would be limited to children's technical advancement within the discipline of art were it not for the explicit meaning-making that a consideration of aesthetic allows. Teachers and caregivers should attend to the web of meaning created by multiple interactions across the lived experience of the child. Ideas of what is beautiful, what is important, what is of value may be more easily articulated in later childhood and adolescence, but they are informed by children's early experiences.

Discuss

How do you define beauty? Is beauty really "in the eyes of the beholder," or are there universal definitions of beauty? How does your understanding of beauty influence your idea of a beautiful classroom? Do classrooms need to be beautiful before they are useful or useful before they are beautiful?

Disciplines that require handiwork, like quilting, paper-making and furniture-making, are often considered "crafts," while disciplines that interpret media more openly, like sculpture and painting are often considered "arts." Do particular disciplines align more clearly with what you know about children's physical, emotional, social, and cognitive development? Do you think different criteria should be used for judging crafts from art?

What relationship do you see between children's aesthetic development and their academic development? Is one set of priorities more important than the other? Can you imagine times in your teaching when you may have to choose? If so, how will you articulate your choice to administrators, colleagues or parents?

Collaborate

With a peer or small group of colleagues, explore a shared learning environment, like the classroom in which you teach or one in which you are a student. How would you describe the aesthetic of the environment? Are there spaces that evoke an emotional response? Are there intentional designs to include beauty? Are there areas or opportunities for wonder or reflection? What qualities of the human experience are evoked by the design of the environment?

With a peer, choose a Caldecott-Medal-honored book. Consider it within the qualities described in this chapter, from the presentation of the book itself to the illustrations included within it. Is this a text you could use to discuss aesthetics with children? What ideals or truths are considered in the text? How do the illustrations help to evoke a particular experience of those ideals?

National standards for art in early childhood classrooms are available at https://www.nationalartsstandards.org/. With a peer, review the framework for standards online. How do these standards support children's development of technical skills for art? How do they support children's development of an aesthetic awareness? Look closely at a grade level of your choosing and reclassify the standards by aesthetic and technical qualities.

Create

Design an aesthetically engaging classroom for the age or developmental level of your choosing. Prepare a floor plan of your imagined indoor or outdoor classroom. Include examples of colors, materials you would present, light sources, floor coverings, etc. How would you describe your personal aesthetic as it is represented in your ideal classroom? Present your plan to your peers or colleagues and invite critique.

While many parents appreciate the importance of reading aloud to children, their comfort with how to read a picture book or how to talk with their children about picture books may vary. Develop a plan for a parent evening introducing the aesthetics of picture books. What qualities should parents know to look for in choosing books for their children? What kinds of questions would you recommend parents ask to engage children in close experiences of the books? How would you present what you know to parents?

Independently, identify five children's book titles that could be used to introduce or discuss aesthetic themes. Create a spreadsheet that includes the title of each book, its author and illustrator, major themes addressed, and a brief description of the audience or context within which you think each book is best suited. Share your spreadsheet with peers or colleagues to build a flexible resource database of high quality picture books you might use in your classroom.

For Further Reading

Arnheim, R. (1974). *Art and visual perception: A psychology of the creative eye*. Berkeley and Los Angeles, CA: University of California Press.

Bader, B. (1976). *American picturebooks from Noah's ark to the beast within*. New York: Macmillan.

Bang, M. (1991). *Picture this: Perception and composition*. Boston, MA: Little, Brown.

Beiser, F. C. (2009). Baumgarten's Science of Aesthetics. *Diotima's Children* (pp. 118–155). doi:10.1093/acprof:oso/9780199573011.003.0006

Cech, J. (1983–1984). Remembering Caldecott: The three jovial huntsmen and the art of the picture book. *The Lion and the Unicorn*, 7/8, 110–119.

Cianciolo, P. (1984). Illustrations in children's books. In Z. Sutherland & M. C. Livingston (Eds.), *The Scott, Foresman anthology of children's literature* (pp. 846–884). Glenview, IL: Scott Foresman.

Considine, D. (1987). Visual literacy and the curriculum: More to it than meets the eye. *Language Arts*, 64(6), 634–640.

Dooley, P. (1980). The window in the book: Conventions in the illustration of children's books. *Wilson Library Bulletin* (October), 108–112.

Doonan, J. (1993). *Looking at pictures in picture books*. Stroud, Gloucestershire, United Kingdom: The Thimble Press.

Eisner, E. W. (2002). *The Arts and the Creation of Mind*. New Haven: Yale University Press.

Elkins, J. (2008). *Visual literacy*. New York: Routledge.

Fehr, K. K., & Russ, S. W. (2016). Pretend play and creativity in preschool-age children: Associations and brief intervention. *Psychology of Aesthetics, Creativity, and the Arts*, 10(3). doi:10.1037/aca0000054

Genette, G. (1982). *Palimpsestes*. Paris, France: Seuil.

Golden, J. (1990). *The narrative symbol in children's literature*. New York: Mouton de Gruyter.

Gombrich, E. (1961). *Art and illusion: A study in the psychology of pictorial representation* (2nd ed.). Princeton, NJ: Princeton University Press.

Harms, J., & Lettow, L. (1989). *Book design: Extending verbal and visual literacy*. Journal of Youth Services in Libraries, 2(2), 136–142.

Hearne, B., & Sutton, R. (Eds.). (1993). *Evaluating children's books: A critical look: aesthetic, social, and political aspects of analyzing and using children's books.* Champaign: University of Illinois at Urbana-Champaign.

Hellman, G. (1977). Symbol systems and artistic styles. *Journal of Aesthetics and Art Criticism,* 35(3), 279–292.

Hoffmann, J., & Russ, S. (2012). Pretend play, creativity, and emotion regulation in children. *Psychology of Aesthetics, Creativity, and the Arts,* 6(2), 175–184. doi:10.1037/a0026299

Kiefer, B. (1993). *Visual criticism and children's literature.* In B. Hearne & R. Sutton (Eds.) *Evaluating children's books: A critical look: aesthetic, social, and political aspects of analyzing and using children's books.* Champaign: University of Illinois at Urbana-Champaign.

Kiefer, B. (1995). *The potential of picturebooks: From visual literacy to aesthetic understanding.* Englewood Cliffs, NJ: Prentice Hall.

Landes, S. (1985). Picturebooks as literature. *Children's Literature Association Quarterly,* 10(2), 51–54.

Messaris, P. (1994). *Visual "literacy": Image, mind, and reality.* Boulder: Westview Press.

Mirzoeff, N. (2008). Visual culture, everyday life, difference, and visual literacy. *Visual Culture Studies* (pp. 17–32). doi:10.4135/9781446213957.n2

Moebius, W. (1986). Introduction to picturebook codes. *Word and Image,* 2(2), 141–158.

Neumeyer, P. (1990). How picture books mean: The case of Chris Van Allsburg. *Children's Literature Association Quarterly,* 15(1), 2–8.

Nodelman, P. (1988). *Words about pictures: The narrative art of children's picture books.* Athens, GA: University of Georgia Press.

Parsons, M. J. (1976). A suggestion concerning the development of aesthetic experience in children. *The Journal of Aesthetics and Art Criticism,* 34(3), 305. doi:10.2307/430012

Roxburgh, S. (1983–1984). A picture equals how many words?: Narrative theory and picture books for children. *The Lion and the Unicorn,* 7/8, 20–33.

Simon, R. (1976). Pictorial Styles In The Art Of Children. *The British Journal of Aesthetics,* 16(3), 272–279. doi:10.1093/bjaesthetics/16.3.272

Schwarcz, J. (1982). *Ways of the illustrator: Visual communication in children's literature.* American Library Association.

1
2
3
4
5
6
7

Chapter 8

Art Assessment in Early Childhood

"If you don't know where you are headed, you'll probably end up someplace else."

—Douglas J. Eder

Art Assessment in Early Childhood

Can you remember a time when you received critical feedback that disappointed you? When you had accomplished or completed or created something of which you were proud, only to have someone else's feedback lead you to question your work? Most of us can think of a time when, whether intentional or not, the feedback of someone whose opinion we valued discouraged us from feeling good about our own work. And, for many learners, the strongest memories of these perceived failures are in the arts. Maybe it was when a choir teacher asked you if you'd usher instead of sing. Maybe it was when you didn't get cast in a theatre production at school, or when you compared yourself to other dancers at the school dance. Maybe it was the first time you noticed that another student's artwork looked more realistic than yours.

These experiences, sometimes private and sometimes public, are significant in their singular impact and in the aggregate of lots of times over our lives as learners when we decided whether we were "good" at art. For teachers and caregivers working with young children, we often want to protect children from the same kind of hurtful feedback that discouraged our own artistic risk-taking when we were children. We commend all artistic endeavors, whether or not we're really impressed by them. We offer

207

only praise, and avoid challenging children to revise or revisit their art. In doing so, we offer little substantive support for children's development as artists and children's development through the arts. Instead, we sprinkle praise for all art expression equally and, as a result, children learn not to trust our review.

A number of working presumptions perpetuate this practice in teachers and caregivers and discourage us from thinking about assessment as a formal structure to be applied to the arts equally as to other content. Especially in early childhood, we may view artistic expression as a purely emotional experience, one requiring little thought or intellectual engagement, best used as a break time from the more rigorous demands of school. From that perspective, assessment is unnecessary. Indeed, who would suggest that one's chosen paths to relax and take a break should be measured by anyone but the person needing the break? If you believe that children have little to learn from their engagement in the arts, there is no need to assess them.

On the other hand, if you recognize the profound influence that art has on society and on our own development as individuals, you might also acknowledge the deep thinking that is necessary for the imagination, design, and implementation of great works of art. Consider Dewey's description of the complex understanding of relationships, qualities, symbols, and representations necessary to creating art. "Indeed, since words are easily manipulated in mechanical ways, the production of a work of genuine art probably demands more intelligence than does most of the so-called thinking that goes on among those who pride themselves on being 'intellectuals'."[1]

The presumption that art does not require intellectual rigor is founded on bad science: the idea that affect and cognition are distinct processes that can be parceled out from each other. We view cognition as a cold and mechanical process, and affect as the reflection of a child's sense of self and emotion, never the twain to meet. Quite the opposite, the synthesis of affect and cognition is evident even in infancy, when children establish affective connections to individuals concurrent with the development of object permanence. Once infants understand the individual nature of objects, they begin to assign value to those objects. Continuing, as the child grows in her understanding of the world and her role within through early childhood, she uses cognitive processes, like language and reasoning, to test affective presumptions. She orders and classifies her environment,

1 John Dewey, *Art as Experience*, New York, Capricorn Books, 1939.

incorporating experiences in the outside world into her schema, including beliefs about her own efficacy and value. Throughout learners' lives, our ability to organize through cognitive processes the new experiences we have in the world contributes to our continually developing sense of self. Elliot Eisner argues that this interplay between our cognitive and affective development is innate to the work of creation. If intellectual life, as Eisner argues, is based on the "absence of certainty," and "the inclination to see things from more than one angle,[2]" then the arts are an essential tool for intellectual development. Intellectual development, if it is to be more than the regurgitation of facts, requires an understanding of relationships, an ability to describe that which is difficult to describe, to create meaning in new and thought-provoking ways. Children not only *can* think when they're engaging the arts—they must.

Another pedagogical presumption that interferes with our willingness to assess children's development in the arts is this insistent belief that children's ability to create will necessarily be limited by the interference of adults, no matter how well meaning. In this image, children create art in some emotional abandon, expressing their inexpressible essence through the process of fingerpainting or dance. Indeeed, many early childhood texts discourage teachers from directing children's engagement in the arts at all, encouraging a laissez-faire model in which the involvement of the teacher or caregiver is in providing materials and helping to clean up. Taking this approach, teachers avoid modeling their own engagement in the arts or introducing children to the work of great artists, for fear that it will stifle children's intrinsic creativity. More recent research, and the lived examples of curricula like the Reggio Emilia schools, demonstrate that active engagement with the arts can healthfully include both the teacher as artist and exposure and consideration of other artists, and that these experiences can actually increase children's creative comfort and risk-taking. As with the development of an aesthetic awareness, engaging children in learning to look, at the art of others and at their own art, contributes to the complexity of what they independently try to create. Think of it this way: withholding examples of other artists, including your own art, from children in order to support their artistic development is like asking them to explore the world on bicycle by first reinventing the wheel. Exposure to other artists contributes to children's artistic literacy, to their understanding of symbols and relationships, and to the universal models of expressing and evoking human response.

---

2 Elliot Eisner, *Cognition and Curriculum Reconsidered*, London. Sage Publications Ltd. 1997.

Other teachers may shy away from assessing children's art because of a fear that doing so will muddle children's willingness to take risks with their own work, seeking instead to create art that is "right" rather than art that is personally important. Art becomes the one time of the day when children don't have to know the right answer, when the practice itself reflects a belief that there is no one way to make art, and that to assess children's art erroneously suggests that there is. In this lens, the art experience is open-ended, with teachers offering the same unmitigated praise to all children. When children ask for help, teachers respond, "Make it however you choose," or "Try your hardest," instead of offering specific direction in the processes that will help a child to create what he has in his mind.

This perspective privileges some types of thinking in school settings over others. A child who is struggling with a literacy concept or a math skill isn't encouraged to "make it however you choose." By restraining from offering guidance or feedback to children in the arts, we implicitly suggest that the arts are not as important as other subjects. Yet, visual literacy, or "the ability to recognize and critically appreciate meaning in visual content and to use visual elements to create effective communication,[3]" in addition to being a valuable cognitive process in its own right, is a critical component of scientific and mathematical reasoning. When we offer specific guidance in all content areas except the arts, we teach children that the kinds of thinking that artists do is irrelevant or less valuable to the real work of education.

Finally, many teachers and caregivers shy away from offering critical feedback, preferring instead to abdicate that kind of guidance to art specialists. This may be driven by the same kind of privileging of their teacher education programs that focused on literacy, math, science, and social studies pedagogy over the preparation of art specialists, or it may reflect a fear that they don't know enough about art to be able to assess it beyond their own subjective response. Whatever the cause, limiting feedback to children to particular expert voices relegates the arts to something that only some people can appreciate or understand. A teacher who was "no good at math," couldn't choose not to teach math or to assess children's mathematical development. To do so would suggest that some ephemeral talent is required to learn math. In the same way, avoiding assessment because, "I can't dance," or "I'm not good at art," limits that learning to those students who have exceptional talent. Exceptionally talented students in any domain, linguistic, scientific, mathematical, and, yes, even the arts, can

---

3 EDUCAUSE Learning Initiative https://net.educause.edu/ir/library/pdf/ELI7118.pdf

be supported by discipline-specific experiences that advance and develop their gifts. But that does not mean that the rest of us don't benefit from a common understanding of these same content areas.

These presumptions often influence teachers' willingness to offer critical feedback in the arts, a bias which is mirrored in high-stakes testing environments that require testing of some content areas but pay only lip-service to the importance of art education. For children's development, this becomes an increasingly problematic cycle: the less critical feedback children receive, the less relevant and rigorous their art experiences and artistic development become. The less often we think of the arts as irrelevant and lacking rigor, the less feedback we will give to children to help support their learning in and through the arts. It falls to the courageous classroom teacher to break that cycle, and no better place than early childhood to do so.

Assessment as a Support to Development

In early childhood, children develop an awareness of themselves and others and begin to develop an understanding of the norms of their world, primarily through their sensorial experience of it: sight, smell, taste, touch, sound and movement. Likewise, cognition involves the same processes: processing information and connecting it to our existing understandings, expanding and refining those through the experience. In early childhood, when perception is a stronger influence to cognition than logic, children's understanding of diverse media and their ability to exploit that media provides opportunities for them to develop increasingly abstract and sophisticated conceptual understandings. In other words, understanding the tools of art can propel children's developing ability to make meaning about the world around them. Children experience concepts with their entire bodies: moving, playing, acting upon and enacting, relationships they are motivated to understand more deeply. These personal experiences become expressed through children's growing use of symbol systems and are well promoted through experiences in the arts.

The process, though, should not be haphazard or random. The symbol systems present in the arts include their own rules and grammar, rules which, like symbol systems in math, science or literacy, must be learned to be most effectively used. The symbol system of visual arts relies on an understanding of color, line, image, form, and texture. The symbol system of drama and theatre is enacted through the body, engaging understanding and representation in sound, movement, touch, appearance and language.

The symbol system of dance involves form, shape, and movement. The symbol system of music relies on sound, but includes the effect of that sound on both the musician and the audience. By their nature, these are systems that are enacted through the body, in the same way that children in early childhood develop their cognitive processes through their bodily experiences. Children make sense of their lived experience through their physical exploration, in the same way that the symbol systems of the arts require an embodied representation of ideas. The most refined understandings of those symbol systems, then, will come from children experiencing the systems in reliable, consistent ways.

Assessment, in its most authentic implementation, helps teachers to understand both what children know and how they have come to know it. Artistic assessment in early childhood, then, requires a spectrum of both observed and interpreted artifacts. It is not enough for a teacher to look at a child's finished product to determine what that child understands about a particular enacted concept. Instead, the teacher must also be able to consider the complicated processes at play during the creation of the work. This can be more challenging in an early childhood setting, in which children may lack the ability to describe their thinking and teachers may, then, have to make more subjective interpretations of children's processing. If the arts are limited to short, independent activities, this interpretation is even more difficult.

However, models like the Reggio Emilia schools or project-based schools demonstrate that, with design, teachers can observe children's enacted understanding over long periods of time with the same subject or concepts. Consider, for example, the well-loved Reggio Emilia example of the children's exploration of lions. Children explored different kinds of lions. They attempted to represent what they understood about lions in their visual art. They ventured into the community to visit lions at the zoo. They sketched the statues of lions near to city hall. They created sculptures of lions, paintings of lions, drawings of lions, lion masks, lion figures ... the process took many weeks, but over that time both the children's understanding of lions changed and evolved, becoming more complex with multiple experiences from different perspectives, and the teachers' understanding of the children's thinking became more complex, observing children's efforts to represent the concept of lions, including the editing and revising and reconceptualizing evident in that process. Longer-term assessment models which allow multiple points of observation from multiple perspectives are both better suited to the development of young children and offer more complex information to the teacher forming the assessment.

In early childhood, assessing the child's learning and development also requires evaluation of the degree to which the environment within which that development occurs supports or obstructs it. In order to understand the child, we need to understand the environment around the child.

Assessing the Classroom Design

The first field for evaluation is the classroom space itself. Ask yourself:

+ Is the classroom large enough for the number of children participating there?
+ Does the layout of the furniture allow for unobstructed movement through the space?
+ Does it provide opportunities for different kinds of movement, for children to stand, sit, and lie down, or does it drive children toward particular limits for their bodies by restricting them to a single chair or one square on a checkered carpet?
+ Does the environment provide areas for group activities, small clusters of children, and independent work?
+ Does it provide areas for variations of volume, areas in which the class volume can be loud, and areas for quieter retreat?
+ Does the classroom include diverse media? Can children explore visual media? Can they construct? Are there tactile activities? Can they create and interpret sound? Can they explore scents and tastes?
+ Does the area allow children to display their creations when they choose?
+ Does the area allow for children's private reflection on their artwork, or is all artwork presented publicly?
+ Does the schedule of the classroom allow for time to explore, create, reflect, and assess? Does it allow for the full cycle of activities for full groups, smalll clusters, and individual children?

More difficult to quantify than the physical space is the environmental climate. Ask yourself:

+ Does this environment feel warm and welcoming?
+ Are children encouraged to take risks in their learning and creations?
+ Do children feel emotionally and psychologically safe here?
+ Is mistake-making supported as a part of learning, or is it discouraged?

+ Can children experiment with materials in new ways or are there limited appropriate uses of media?
+ Does the environment invite questioning and conversation?

The classroom space should be a place within which children can explore new experiences with enough time and agency to make them personally relevant, within which multiple dispositions toward discovery are supported and multiple modalities are demonstrated. It should be a place that concretely supports children's enacting new ideas. That is to say, the materials children need to be able to create what they want to try to create should be readily available, accessible, and manageable to the child, and the emotional response to their engagement should support children in constructing new ways of thinking, even if those are unexpected to the teacher. Learning requires risk. Classroom spaces should be places within which children feel safe to venture out intellectually to explore and construct new meaning.

Assessing Teaching and Curricula

Effective teaching in the arts engages children in applying and expanding the physical, emotional, intellectual, and social skills they need to be able to explore and represent new knowledge. The degree to which teaching practices support children's agency and risk taking contributes to the authentic experience of the arts. In assessing teaching, ask yourself:

+ Does the teaching elicit question-asking?
+ Are mistakes valued as an important part of learning?
+ Does the teacher ask open-ended questions or is there a "right" answer most of the time?
+ Does the teacher ask for theories to predict what may happen? Are children encouraged to think critically and proactively about their work?
+ Are all questions answered, or are some left unanswered by intent?
+ Are qualities of artwork discussed in highly value-based language, like "good" and "bad" or "right" and "wrong," or are qualities of artwork discussed in terms of what they evoke, what techniques artists used, and what meaning was suggested?
+ Does the teacher protect time to observe? Does he or she protect time to create? To reflect? To critique?
+ Does the teacher have the answers, or does the teacher serve as a conduit to children discovering answers?

- Are student responses equally validated, or are some "more equal" than others?
- Does the teacher offer objective feedback or merely praise?
- Does the teacher ask students about their processes and artistic choices?
- The materials and activities available for children are equally important. Art education materials need to offer opportunities to build and develop the physical skills necessary to implement a design, including the muscular refinement to use tools appropriately, to move our bodies and control our voices, and the auditory development to discern and create sound clearly. They must also offer opportunities to learn about the discipline of art itself, including symbol systems of visual art, dance, theatre, and music as well as the history and evolution of the field. They must also offer opportunities for meaning-making across other content areas, as new modalities through which concepts in other disciplines can be experienced, understood, and represented. In assessing curricular choices, ask yourself:
- Are materials available and accessible to children that lead to increasing refinement of physical skills?
- Are materials available that offer a wide range of applications for those skills?
- Are materials accessible for each art area and each sensorial domain? Can children explore theatre, dance, visual art, and music through sight, smell, touch, taste, and sound? Can they explore art media with their whole bodies, or are experiences limited to the hands and heads?
- Are there accessible materials to learn about the history of art and artists? Are artists from diverse backgrounds equally represented? Are artists from diverse genres equally represented? Are examples of art of high quality and lasting importance?
- Do children have materials through which they can experience and internalize common symbols in art?
- Are there many different ways to be able to learn similar concepts in math, science, literacy, and social studies? Can children show what they know through multiple modalities or are they limited to to predetermined models?
- Are common themes repeated throughout different content areas? Is there an underlying conceptual framework for how learning happens in this classroom?

Assessing Dispositions toward Thinking

The physical environment, climate, teaching methods, and materials will work together to provide either a seemingly unrelated set of experiences and expectations, or a coherent system through which children can consistently access new knowledge. Particular dispositions toward thinking will be evident in classrooms which integrate the arts in highly effective ways. Look for evidence of these tendencies in teachers, learners and interactions:

+ Learning is adventurous. Do teachers and learners demonstrate open-mindedness? When predicting solutions, do they generate multiple possibilities? Are alternative interpretations considered and critiqued?
+ Language will challenge learners to move beyond simple answers, to ask themselves, "What else might this mean? Are there other ways to think about this? Would someone else experience this differently? What other perspectives might change what we see? How can we be sure what we know?"
+ Learning includes wonder. Do teachers and learners make time to reflect? To investigate deeply? To follow their curiosity? Are there opportunities to observe? Do teachers model observation, reflection and thoughtfuless, including the time it takes to think?
+ Aesthetics elevates learning. Is there a propensity toward beauty in the environment? Do learners and teachers alike notice beauty? Do they protect it in their practices?
+ Learning identifies patterns. Do learners have the opportunity to repeat activities? Does the classroom respond consistently and reliably to repetition? Do classroom experiences lead to the same conclusions about the nature of learning, of agency and community? Are there rules that are not really rules, or does the space lend itself to an intellectual order and predictability?
+ Learning evolves. Does the classroom allow for increasingly complicated understanding? Do teachers probe for deeper understanding? Are learners encouraged to make connections across content areas, to analogize and compare, to describe knowledge in increasingly complex ways?

These questions lead toward an understanding of the environment within which individual children learn. In order to understand with great accuracy what a child knows and how she knows it, it's important to first know deeply the lessons and messages drawn from the environment within which she learns. These assessment guides for classroom, teacher, curriculum, and dispositions come before we assess children's understanding of and through the arts.

Assessing Children's Learning of and through the Arts

Although some of the biases and presumptions discussed earlier make assessing children's learning of and through the arts more challenging, teachers and caregivers need to understand clearly what children know and how that knowledge is represented in order to best prepare environments which align to children's development. It is insufficient to prepare an environment through which you intend children to learn and then never assess what kind of learning actually happened there. As children refine their capacity in the arts, they need also to refine their ability to both create and critique art around them. Building children's artistic literacy allows them to be literate viewers of art, able to interpret and translate it beyond the simple mechanisms of technique. This section will consider both ways in which teachers can assess children's learning in and through the arts and ways in which children can develop critical assessment skills to enact their own artistic literacy.

While most teachers are familiar with formative assessments in other content areas, the idea of a formative assessment in the arts may be new. Because art expression includes wide variation between learners, no single formative assessment will be sufficient to describe what an individual child understands about a particular concept in total. Instead, formative assessments are best constructed from multiple examples in a collection of children's art. Considering a number of samples of a child's art allows the teacher to understand how that child is using particular materials, whether individual preferences for style, color or symbolic representation are emerging, and whether their understanding of concepts is fixed or dyamic. Considering a set of art experiences rather than single art work also allows teachers to audit the alignment between their teaching goals and the prior knowledge of the child. Small collections also allow for conversation with other teachers and caregivers to provide greater detail and a more nuanced understanding of the child's development than could be developed from reviewing a single piece of artwork.

Collecting small sets of visual artwork is relatively easy: in early childhood, children usually leave them behind! It may be more difficult to document children's dance, singing, or theatre performance, since the camera itself may be a distraction to the child. The more often cameras are present in the classroom, however, the less novel they become to the children and the more likely you are to capture children's spontaneous performance.

Teachers can also use the strategies for documenting children's behavior in the classroom to document children's initial understanding of the concepts addressed through art. Running records, anecdotal records, and checklists of common benchmarks are efficient tools to contribute to a formative assessment. This kind of data can also be used to help develop new materials, by documenting children's interests and curiosities to inform later lesson planning.

Finally, teachers can enrich their understanding of children's understanding of the arts by asking for feedback from parents and other stakeholders about children's exposure, dispositions, and engagement with the arts outside of the school setting. Simple surveys about children's open-ended play, their participation in extracurricular art programs, their independent art choices at home, and their disposition toward visual art, theatre, dance, and music, will help the teacher to better understand each child and help parents to recognize that art education is equally valued as both content and a conduit to other learning.

During intentional art experiences, teachers can look to evidence of sensory engagement and meaning-making within children. Experiences with the arts offer unique opportunities for teachers to observe children's learning in action. Research suggests that physically and sensorially interactive experiences like art interactions lead to lasting, complicated, and nuanced memories in the learner. Meanwhile, children learn about their cultures and their roles within them through the kind of interpretive meaning-making of quality art experiences. Teachers might observe learners' efforts to place their experiences within a larger context of art, listening for the types of memories and understandings that are referenced as children describe their art making and looking for patterns within which the child approaches art engagements. As teachers reliably offer guidance and feedback, children grow in their ability to describe, analyze and interpret their own meaning-making to make their thinking evident and public. During intentional art experiences, teachers and caregivers should probe children's ability to articulate their process, to discuss their own curiosity, their intent in both the enacted message of their artwork and in their intended message. Learners develop the ability to articulate their learning by looking, inquiring, and talking about their art. Likewise, that practice informs their oral, visual, and written literacy which, in turn, makes it easier for them to continue to talk about their art. Communication becomes the primary means of assessing children's understanding during the process of creating.

For many teachers, though, the question is how? We may be comfortable asking simple questions about children's art, but we may be less comfortable probing for more complex ideas. Some of this is a factor of time and expectation. When art experiences can be completed in a single sitting, or require little thought or interpretation from the child, it should be no surprise that they also fail to evoke deep thinking or offer opportunities for meaningful conversations about the learner's intent and understanding. If, though, teachers offer multistep art experiences with rich connections to other content that last over time and include relevant connections to the child's lived experience, children's art and their ability to talk about their art will be more complex. Leinhardt and Knutson (2004) propose that talking with children about their artwork drives them to look in new ways, to explore more deeply, to examine more closely, to attempt to survey and generalize ideas, to measure with specificity, to interpret and translate new ideas, and to synthesize them with existing schema. Prompts from curious teachers emphasize the process-centered value of art experiences and allows children to practice describing that process in interesting ways. David Bell classifies these prompts into seven broad categories: looking questions, describing questions, analytical questions, storytelling questions, contextual questions, doing questions, and evaluative questions.

Looking questions engage learners in detailed examination of particular works of art. Imagine, for example, considering Eugene Martin's *The Nervous Reindeer* with a small group of first graders. A simple prompt can lead to a number of different responses. "What is this a painting of?" "How can you tell?" "What do you see in the painting?" "What is the animal doing?" Looking questions engage children in initial interpretation of a work of art, in visual art, theatre, dance or music. Listen to the *Danse Macabre*. Ask "What do you think is happening in this song?" "Are there people there?" "What are the people (or dancers, or musicians) doing?" "What do you hear that makes you think that?" Looking questions provide a foundational and shared understanding between the teacher and learner.

Describing questions ask children to give summary details about what they notice in a work of art. Consider Wayne Thiebaud's *Three Meringues*. Ask "What is going on here? Describe what you see." A child might respond, "There are three cakes and they've just been iced. The colors are bright and the icing looks tasty and cool. I think there will be a party soon." Children might also enact their answers to describing questions. Listen together to *Peter and the Wolf* Ask "Can you show me which animals are coming now?" Children can "describe" what they hear by enacting it with their bodies. Describing questions allow children to begin interpreting what they've seen when they were looking, to be able to articulate it for someone else. They will use language that's not in the original piece, either oral or written language, like "iced" and "bright" and "tasty" and "cool" or visual language, like holding their arms close to their sides to represent the small wings of a bird on a branch. When children describe what they see, teachers are able to begin to assess their aesthetic understanding. What do they notice? How do they evaluate what's important to include in their description?

Analytical questions evoke more expansive descriptions from children about the symbol systems at play in the art work. Observe *Two Girls Reading* by Picasso. Analytical questions ask the child to describe color, texture, movement, space, depth and other visual features. "What colors stand out to you the most?" "What lines are thickest? Which are thinnest?" "How does the artist draw your attention to the relationship between the two girls?" "How can you tell that Picasso intended this painting to look this way?" Analytical questions engage the child in thinking about the artist's process and intent, drawing attention to the ways in which artists use media create certain effects. In unpacking the artist's process, the child is challenged to think through more than just what he can see in the image, but the steps taken to create that image.

Storytelling questions engage children in open, narrative dialogue through which they can bring to life ideas evoked by the art. Look at Salvador Dali's *The Elephants.* Ask, "Can you tell me what's happening in this painting?" The child may answer, "There are elephants with very long legs and they've going across the desert. Their legs work like spider legs. When they meet in the middle of the desert, they will lie down together and put down the families they are carrying." Storytelling questions ask children to ascribe their own imagined narratives to the work, and in doing so, offer a glimpse for teachers into how learners organize information, what qualities they are drawn most to, and how they make sense of a curious image. Teachers can notice what kinds of relationships and associations are made when the child tries to tell the story of a work of art. In the telling, teachers can ask for more details, "Who lives in those houses? What does it feel like to ride on the back of one of those elephants? How does this elephant feel about the family he's carrying?"

Storytelling questions also allow teachers to notice when children make connections not substantiated by the artwork, when their interpretations of a piece of art are not held up by the art itself. These still help teachers to understand the initial ways in which children make sense of what they see, but they lead, naturally to *contextual questions*—questions which help to link the learner back to the factual context within which a work was constructed. "When was this art made?" "What do we know about the time period when it was made that helps us understand it?" Look together at Warhol's *Campbell's Soup*. "What was it about this time that made this painting so provocative?" Look at van Dyck's *Charles I at the Hunt*. "Who is this depicted?" (He is a king.) "What's he doing?" (Resting during a hunt.) "What choices has the artist made that reflect what was going on at the time?" (Charles is depicted with great confidence, although he's casually dressed. He seems totally at home. The painting labels him as "King of Great Britain," even though the empire of Great Britain was relatively young.) Children may be invited to find out the answers to these questions on their own, or the teacher may be prepared to answer them to expand children's knowledge of the artwork. By taking the time to understand the context of a piece of art's creation, teachers can help to support children's knowledge about how to look at art and how to make sense of what they see.

Great conversations can be had as teachers probe for children's understanding and sense-making, but they should also allow for children to demonstrate what they know without formal language. *Doing questions* engage children by asking them to enact their understanding. Re-presenting what they understand about a work of art through their bodies, through new visual works, through sound, dance or theatre allows children to internalize their learning more authentically. Listen to *L'Enfant et les Sortileges*. With a small group of friends, can you act or dance what you hear in the opera? Can you paint a portrait of l'enfant? Doing questions offer children multiple languages through which to express their understanding of the concepts involved in a work of art. Children need to look closely, to translate and to imagine new qualities not present in the original work to be able to re-present that work in a new way. Doing questions often involve small groups of children working together, negotiating how to represent meaning, and collaborating on the symbols they'll use. Because they ask the child to take on some quality of the original art, they develop empathy and give children an opportunity to practice new roles and explore new identities. Ask children to create new dramatic retellings of an original artwork, to choreograph a dance or sketch a picture, to portray what happens next or what has happened before the moment captured in the art you're considering. Experiences like these allow children to interact with the artwork in personally relevant ways, to test their understanding against the interpretations of others and to re-present that understanding in a new language another audience can understand. And, because these experiences involve multiple senses, they are more likely to engage children and more likely to be memorable afterwards.

Teachers can also assess children's understanding during an artistic experience by asking them *evaluative questions*, questions which require the child to critique the work and to respond to the critiques of others. Questions that begin with, "How well did ..." or "What do you think of ..." invite children to judge the artist's effectiveness in conveying her intended meaning. Teachers can draw attention to the elements of art that are likely to evoke particular outcomes, the use of color and proportion, positioning, movement, space, and form, and the style of art as a match to the message of the artist. Modeling careful listening and response, teachers can challenge children to think about their own response and to consider how their response may differ from others'. Evaluative questioning also leads naturally into conversations about aesthetics, the nature of beauty and art, and children's appreciation of those qualities.

This series of questions progresses from simple observations to more critical judgments, and can be implemented by teachers as part of a structured assessment of children's artistic understanding. But it is important to note that the conversations will only be as meaningful as the children in the classroom are authentically engaged in the work. Children need first to feel safe and supported in the learning, an outcome of intentional design of the classroom space, the teacher interactions and the materials prepared long before any single art lesson. Children need to be at ease in the process of conversation, which requires regular, low-stakes modeling to instill in children dialogic norms. Children need time, too, with the art itself, exploring it over time and re-presenting it in different ways as a deep understanding evolves.

Assessing in situ, that is, while children's understanding is in process, presumes that rich language is already present for children to adopt. The vocabulary of art critique, then, should be incorporated throughout classroom life, describing illustrations in children's books by their techniques, drawing children's attention to the lines of architecture in school buildings when playing outdoors, describing children's movements in every day life as one would describe movements in art or dance. Teachers need a working knowledge of this vocabulary, the same way they need to understand the proper names for geometric solids they may find in their classrooms or how to distinguish a noun from a verb. When art is included as an equal content to other ways of learning, the habits of mind of artists must be integrated in the same way that teachers regularly model the habits of mind of scientists or mathematicians.

Teachers should also regularly consider summative assessments of children's learning in and through the arts. These can be designed for evaluation after a particular unit of study, across some window of children's development or even across an entire year's growth. Working first from the information gathered in formative assessments, teachers might look to portfolios of children's work over time, for evidence of increasing complexity, detail, and incorporation of symbol systems. They may record children's descriptions of their own meaning-making to assess for the complexity, contextual awareness, use of artistic language, and critical judgments evident in the articulation.

Summative evaluations demand an ability to place a single child's development within an understanding of the typical sequence of development across multiple domains. Because artistic expression will reflect social, emotional, physical and cognitive development, teachers must be well versed in each discrete area in order to understand how they collectively influence a child's ability to understand or create works of art. Summative evaluations are more likely to be descriptive than quantitative, although they may include a basic assessment of children's physical capacity to manage and control relevant tools. And, just as teachers need to understand the conceptual intent of literacy lessons or lessons in science in order to develop appropriately aligned assessments, they should have clear goals for what children are likely to learn from individual art experiences and across the span of art experiences in the classroom, with defined articulations for what evidence of that learning might look like.

Planning with Assessment in Mind

Grant Wiggins and Jay McTighe's *Understanding by Design* model argues that the role of curriculum is to meet a desired outcome. That is, the intended learning should be paramount in planning for teaching. A backwards design model for artistic assessment begins by defining the specific learning goal for the art experience. While a teacher may have a specific content goal in mind for an art experience (for example, to understand how life is different in cities or rural areas,) there are also some common artistic outcomes that may help to define how those experiences are assessed.

- If the goal of the experience to support open-ended exploration, evidence of open exploration may include the ways in which children may discover multiple uses of materials or articulate previously unacknowledged relationships between concepts. A teacher might look for evidence of new questions generated by the children or alternative outcomes proposed. Children might ask questions about why experiences work they way they do.

- If the goal of the experience is to develop skillfulness of tools, teachers will look for evidence of gross and fine motor coordination, accurate use of materials, choice of techniques to affect outcomes with media, attention to the demands of the particular media or domain, and an aesthetic awareness.

- If the goal of the experience is to strengthen a sense of self, teachers will see evidence of initiative, agency, and self-reliance in the planning and implementation of the work. They may look for children's active expression of new learning and resilience to frustration. They may notice children's comfort joining and remaining in group experiences, making their ideas known to a group, and responding openly to criticism or feedback from peers. They may seek evidence of prosocial behaviors, empathy, cooperation, and positive negotiations with peers.

- If the goal of the experience is to support habits of mind, teachers might look for evidence of initiative, the degree to which children enter easily into art activities. They may document the specific ideas generated by the learner, their time on task, and attentiveness to their own personal goals in the process. Teachers might look for evidence of creative problem-solving; the ability to plan, enact, and reflect on an artistic process; diligence and resilience against frustration; and the emergence of a distinct "voice" in the art of each child.

- If the goal of the experience is to strengthen discernment, teachers may look for evidence of an evolving sensorial discrimination, of the degree to which children can distinguish between sensory qualities. They may look for the level of detail children enact in their own work or describe in responding to the work of others. They may assess the care with which children use materials toward a desired end. Teachers might look for evidence of abstraction, of children thinking and imagining before they begin to create, or of their ability to place their own choices and the choices of other artists within categories of genre, era, and context.

- If the goal of the experience is to strengthen children's ability to communicate, teachers can look to see whether children intend to use materials in a particular way or if they are exploring at random. They may document use of symbols to express ideas or understanding. They may ask children to provide or dictate captions to their artwork.
- If the goal of the experience is to develop innovative thinking, teachers may look for evidence of cognitive flexibility, risk-taking, and inventiveness. They may look for examples of children adopting new perspectives or challenging limits within and among art domains. They will be attentive to surprising use of media.
- If the goal of the experience is to develop the capacity to interpret and analyze, teachers will look for how children articulate what they've experienced, whether they are able to consider what came before, is evident within or is likely to have come after the moment captured in the art work. They will notice use of terms of art and explicit connections to other content or previous experiences.
- If the goal of the experience is to learn to judge artistic outcomes, teachers will be aware of the ways in which children describe their own work and the work of others, the detail and complexity of what they notice, and the connections they make to context. They will look for evidence that children have accepted other's feedback and for the appropriateness of the feedback they offer others. They will notice what children have noticed, and look for evidence that children's own creations have been influenced by reflection and feedback.
- Children may also be assessed on the degree to which they understand the discipline of art, including the specific vocabulary within each domain of dance, theatre, visual art, and music. Teachers may look for evidence of children's awareness and intentional use of these concepts as well.
- In musical performance or analysis, do children understand elements of music, including beat, rhythm, meter, pitch, harmony, melody, timbre, tone, and dynamics. Do they enact appropriate behaviors in listening to music, singing with others, or playing an instrument? Do they demonstrate an age-appropriate understanding of how music is organized and created? Do they interpret universal symbols conveyed in music?
- In dance performance or analysis, do children understand elements of movement, time, and space? Do they represent or understand symbolic movement? Can they describe movement using age-appropriate terms and details? Do they understand that dance is choreographed?

Can they discuss or enact movement that evokes particular emotion or conveys particular meaning?

+ In visual art creation or analysis, do children understand elements of color, line, shape, texture, form, and space? Are they aware of patterns, visual movement, balance, and proportion in a work? Can they articulate intent? Are they aware of common symbols in use in the art work?

+ In theatre performance or analysis, do children understand elements of drama? Can they describe how language, silence, light, relationships, character, and mood were conveyed? Can they classify theatre performance into common forms (dramatic play, mask drama, puppetry, readers', theatre, etc.)? Do they use age-appropriate terms of art to describe theater spaces and theatrical processes?

Within those broad categories, teachers can look to the details of their local and state standards to understand the specific skills and dispositions to be supported at each grade and developmental level. Authentic art experiences will begin with those assessments in mind. By naming the more complicated, cognitive, affective, or skill-reflective outcomes that a teacher intends, she can more acutely design learning experiences that are likely to promote them in children. Remember, because art experiences reflect learning across multiple domains of child development and multiple academic disciplines, authentic assessment of children's development in and through the arts includes a candid evaluation of classroom design, teacher interaction, and the materials available for children. Children's learning in and through the arts not only requires assessment, its best design begins with assessment.

Discuss

What presumptions have you made about the relationship of assessment to children's art? Are you comfortable providing critical feedback to children about their artwork in the same way that you would provide feedback related to another content area? How can the ways in which you provide feedback in the arts influence the kinds of feedback you offer in other disciplines?

How important is it to you that art experiences in your classroom strengthen children's understanding of other disciplines or content areas? What is the role of "art for art's sake" in school settings? How would you balance your perspective within or against testing demands on teachers that emphasize some content knowledge over others?

What is the ideal relationship between art specialists and classroom teachers, in your understanding? Describe what knowledge you think teachers and art specialists should share? What knowledge is distinct to one role or the other? How would you structure experiences between your classroom and art specialists to construct the relationship you think will best meet the learning needs of your children?

Collaborate

With a peer, design an observation checklist you could use in your classroom to assess children's understanding during an art experience. Choose an art domain (theatre, visual art, music, or dance) and be specific in your checklist for the kinds of behaviors you expect to see to assess children's development.

With a small group of colleagues, assign a different great artist to each group member. Have each group member present an example of one artist's work and practice leading the group in conversation that reflects the goals represented in this chapter. Possible artists that with child-appropriate work include Andy Warhol, Georgia O'Keefe, Wassily Kandinsky, Vincent Van Gogh, Piet Mondrian, Leonardo da Vinci and Pablo Picasso. Afterwards, debrief on the ways in which particular types of artists evoked different kinds of questions.

With a partner, role-play a parent-teacher conference in which a parent informs you that she or he is concerned by her child's hesitation to engage in the arts. The parent describes for you her doubts that she is offering sufficient feedback or guidance to her child. How will you support the parent in responding to her child's artistic development? Afterwards, change roles with your partner. Role-play a parent-teacher conference in which a parent complains about the amount of time his or her child "wastes on art," and asks you to prohibit the child from choosing art experiences during free time at school. How will you respond to this parent?

Create

Spend some time reflecting on *Poet on a Mountaintop*, the Ming dynasty Chinese brush painting by Shen Zhou. Imagine you are on that mountaintop. What do you see, smell, hear? What does the air feel like? How might you return to your everyday life after visiting this space? When you've considered the work, design a station or center for your classroom that supports introspective reflection. Imagine how you might create a space for individual responses to the arts.

Choose a selection from the list of Caldecott Medal and Honor recipients. Write a simple script appropriate for use with young children to translate your selected book into a dramatic performance. Articulate your learning goals for children in participating in this dramatic retelling. What elements of the story will you design and what elements will you allow children to create? What kinds of enactments, behaviors or evidence will you look for to decide whether children have learned what you intended from the experience?

With one or two peers, choose one of the works listed below. Translate what you understand of this work into a new domain. You might create a dramatic representation of it, write a piece of poetry or spoken word, translate it into song or build a playlist of appropriate music to match it, choreograph a dance or choose some other enactment. Be aware of practices that engage each member of your group equally and notice how you may need to negotiate within each other's personal reactions or interpretations of the art to create a new, unified re-presentation. Choose from: *Young Girl in Pursuit* (Marc Chagall, ca. 1927–28), *Persistence of Memory* (Salvador Dali, 1931), *The Two Fridas* (Frida Kahlo, 1939), *Separation* (Edvard Munch, 1896), *Girl before a Mirror* (Pablo Picasso, 1932), *Don't Let That Shadow Touch Them* (Lawrence Beall Smith, 1942), *The Subway* (George Tooker, 1950).

For Further Reading

Alkema, C. (1971). *Art for the exceptional*. Boulder, CO: Pruett.

Anderson, F. (1978). *Art for all the children: A creative sourcebook for the impaired child*. Springfield, IL: Charles C. Thomas.

Barden, M. (1993). A backward look: From Reggio Emilia to progressive education. In C. Edwards, L. Gandini, & G. Forman (Eds.), *The hundred languages of children: The Reggio Emilia approach to early childhood education* (1st ed., pp. 283–295). Norwood, NJ: Ablex.

Baxandall, M. (1985), *Patterns of Intention*, New Haven and London: Yale University Press.

Beattie, D. K. (1997). *Assessment in art education*. Worcester, MA: Davis Publications.

Bell, D. (2011). Seven ways to talk about art: One conversation and seven questions for talking about art in early childhood settings. *International Journal of Education, 7(1)*, 41–54.

Berk, L. E., & Winsler, A. (1995). *Scaffolding children's learning: Vygotsky and early childhood education*. Washington, DC: National Association for the Education of Young Children.

Bodrova, E., & Leong, D. J. (1996). *Tools of the mind: The Vygotskian approach to early childhood education*. Englewood Cliffs, NJ: Prentice-Hall.

Brookhart, S. M. (1999). *The art and science of classroom assessment: The missing part of pedagogy*. Washington, DC: George Washington University, Graduate School of Education and Human Development.

Bredekamp, S., & Copple, C. (Eds.). (1997). *Developmentally appropriate practice in early childhood programs* (2nd ed.). Washington, DC: National Association for the Education of Young Children [NAEYC].

Bruner, J. (1966). *Studies in cognitive growth: A collaboration at the Center for Cognitive Studies*. NY: Wiley.

Burton, J. (1980a). Beginnings of artistic language. *School Arts, 80*(1), 6–12.

Burton, J. (1980b). The first visual symbols. *School Arts, 80*(2), 60–65.

Burgess, L., & Addison, N. (2007). Conditions for learning: partnerships for engaging secondary pupils with contemporary art, *Journal of Art and Design Education, 26*(2), 185–198.

Cadwell, L. (1997). *Bringing Reggio Emilia home: An innovative approach to early childhood education*. New York: Teachers College Press.

Cohen, D., Stern, K., & Balaban, N. (1997). *Observing and recording the behavior of young children* (4th ed.). New York: Teachers College Press.

Colbert, C., & Taunton, M. (1992). *Developmentally appropriate practices for the visual arts education of young children*. Reston, VA: National Art Education Association [NAEA].

Cromer, J. (1975). The influence of verbal language on aesthetic performance. *Art Education, 28*(2), 14–17.

Davidson, B., Heald, C., & Hein, G. (2001). Increased exhibit accessibility through multisensory interaction. In E. Hooper-Greenhill (Ed.) *The educational role of the museum* (pp. 223–238). London and New York: Routledge.

Davis, J., & Gardner, H. (2001). Open Windows, Open Doors. In E. Hooper-Greenhill (Ed.) *The Educational Role of the Museum* (pp. 99–104). London and New York: Routledge.

Dorn, C. M. (2002). The teacher as stakeholder in student art assessment and art program evaluation. *Art Education, 55*(4), 40. doi:10.2307/3193967

Eckhoff, A. (2008). The importance of art viewing experiences in early childhood visual arts: The exploration of a master art teacher's strategies for meaningful early arts experiences, *Early Childhood Education Journal, 35*: 5, 463–472.

Edwards, C., Gandini, L., & Forman, G. (1998). *The hundred languages of children: the Reggio Emilia approach—advanced reflections*. Greenwich, Connecticut and London: Ablex Publishing Corporation.

Engle, B. (1995). *Considering children's art: Why and how to value their works*. Washington, DC: National Association for the Education of Young Children.

Forman, G. (1994). *Different media, different languages*. Paper presented at the study seminar on the experience of the municipal infant-toddler centers and preprimary schools of Reggio Emilia (Reggio Emilia, Italy, May 30–June 10, 1994). (Report No. PS 022 558). Washington, DC: U.S. Department of Education, Office of Educational Resources Information Center. (ERIC Document Reproduction Service No. ED 375 932)

Falk, J. and Dierking, L. (2000). *Learning from museums: Visitor experiences and the making of meaning.* Walnut Creek, Lanham, New York, Oxford: AltaMira Press.

Fox, J., & Diffily, D. (2000). Integrating the visual arts—Building young children's knowledge, skills, and confidence. *Dimensions of Early Childhood, 29*(1), 3–10.

Gardner, H. (1990). *Art education and human development.* Los Angeles: Getty Center for Education in the Arts.

Gilroy, A., Tipple, R., & Brown, C. (2012). *Assessment in art therapy.* London: Routledge.

Goldberg, M. (1997). *Arts and learning: An integrated approach to teaching and learning in multicultural and multilingual settings.* New York: Longman.

Hamblen, K. (1984). Don't you think some bright colors would improve your painting? *Art Education, 37*(1), 12–14.

Harris, D. (1963). *Children's drawings as a measure of intellectual maturity.* New York: Harcourt, Brace & World.

Helm, J., Beneke, S., & Steinheimer, K. (1998). *Windows on learning: Documenting young children's work.* New York: Teachers College Press.

Hendrick, J. (1997). *First steps toward teaching the Reggio way.* Upper Saddle River, NJ: Merrill.

Katz, L., & Chard, S. (2000). *Engaging children's minds: The project approach* (2nd ed.). Stamford, CT: Ablex.

Leinhardt, G., & Knutson, K. (2004), *Listening in on museum conversations.* Walnut Creek, Lanham, New York, Toronto, Oxford: AltaMira Press.

Lloyd, H. (2009). Provoking critical thought in the gallery context. *Scope: Contemporary Research Topics, 4,* 126–134.

Lowenfeld, V. (1958). Current research on creativity. *NEA Journal, 47,* 538–540.

MacGregor, R. N. (1990). Reflections on Art Assessment Practices. *Journal of Art & Design Education, 9*(3), 315–327. doi:10.1111/j.1476-8070.1990.tb00483.

MacRae, Christina (2007). Using sense to make sense of art: young children in art galleries. *Early Years: Journal of International Research and Development,* 27: 2, pp. 159–170. -

National Art Education Association [NAEA]. (1995). National visual arts standards. Reston, VA: Author.

Piscitelli, B. (2009). Children, art and museums. *Scope: Contemporary Research Topics, 4,* 120–125.

Pringle, E. (2006). *Learning in the gallery: Context, process, outcomes.* London: Engage and Arts Council England.

Rand, J. (2001). The 227-Mile Museum, or a Visitors' Bill of Rights, *Curator: The Museum Journal, 44*(1), 7–14.

Schirrmacher, R. (1997). *Art and creative development for young children* (3rd ed.). Albany, NY: Delmar.

Seefeldt, C. (1995). Art: A serious work. *Young Children, 50*(3), 33–38.

Suina, J. (2001). Museum multicultural education for young learners. In E. Hooper-Greenhill (Ed.) *The Educational Role of the Museum* (pp. 105–109). London and New York: Routledge.

Talboys, G. (2005). *Museum Educators Handbook,* Aldershot, England: Ashgate Publishing Ltd.

Wright, S. (1997). Learning how to learn: The arts as core in an emergent curriculum. *Childhood Education, 73*(6), 361–366.

Appendix

Caldecott Award and Honor Books

2015 Winner—*The Adventures of Beekle* by Santat

2015 Honor—*Nana in the City* by Castillo

2015 Honor—*The Noisy Paint Box* by Rosenstock

2015 Honor—*Sam and Dave Dig a Hole* by Barnett

2015 Honor—*Viva Frida* by Morales

2015 Honor—*The Right Word: Roget and his Thesaurus* by Bryant

2015 Honor—*This One Summer* by Tamaki

2014 Winner—*Locomotive* by Floca

2014 Honor—*Journey* by Becker

2014 Honor—*Flora and the Flamingo* by Idle

2014 Honor—*Mr. Wuffles!* by Wiesner

2013 Winner—*This is Not My Hat* by Klassen

2013 Honor—*Creepy Carrots!* by Reynolds

2013 Honor—*Extra Yarn* by Barnett

2013 Honor—*Green* by Seeger

2013 Honor—*One Cool Friend* by Buzzeo

2013 Honor—*Sleep Like a Tiger* by Logue

2012 Winner—*A Ball for Daisy* by Raschka

2012 Honor—*Me ... Jane* by McDonnell

2012 Honor—*Blackout* by Rocco

2012 Honor—*Grandpa Green* by Smith

2011 Winner—*A Sick Day for Amos McGee* by Stead

2011 Honor—*Dave the Potter* by Hill

2011 Honor—*Interrupting Chicken* by Stein

2010 Winner—*The Lion & the Mouse* by Pinkney

2010 Honor—*All the World* by Scanlon

2010 Honor—*Red Sings from Treetops* by Sidman

2009 Winner—*The House in the Night* by Swanson

2009 Honor—*How I Learned Geography* by Shulevitz

2009 Honor—*A River of Words* by Bryant

2009 Honor—*A Couple of Boys Have the Best Week Ever* by Scanlon

2008 Winner—*The Invention of Hugo Cabret* by Selznick

2008 Honor—*Henry's Freedom Box* by Levine

2008 Honor—*First the Egg* by Seeger

2008 Honor—*Knuffle Bunny Too* by Willems

2008 Honor—*The Wall: Growing Up Behind the Iron Curtain* by Sís

2007 Winner—*Flotsam* by Wiesner

2007 Honor—*Gone Wild* by McLimans

2007 Honor—*Moses: When Harriet Tubman Led Her People to Freedom* by Weatherford

2006 Winner—*The Hello, Goodbye Window* by Juster

2006 Honor—*Rosa* by Giovanni

2006 Honor—*Zen Shorts* by Muth

2006 Honor—*Song of the Water Boatman* by Sidman

2006 Honor—*Hot Air: The (Mostly) True Story of the First Hot Air Balloon Ride* by Priceman

2005 Winner—*Kitten's First Full Moon* by Henkes

2005 Honor—*The Red Book* by Lehman

2005 Honor—*Coming on Home Soon* by Woodson

2005 Honor—*Knuffle Bunny: A Cautionary Tale* by Willems

2004 Winner—*The Man Who Walked Between the Towers* by Gerstein

2004 Honor—*Ella Sarah Gets Dressed* by Chodos-Irvine

2004 Honor—*Don't Let the Pigeon Drive the Bus!* by Willems

2004 Honor—*What Do You Do with a Tail Like This?* by Jenkins

2003 Winner—*My Friend Rabbit* by Rohmann

2003 Honor—*The Spider and the Fly* by Howitt

2003 Honor—*Hondo & Fabian* by McCarty

2003 Honor—*Noah's Ark* by Pinkney

2002 Winner—*The Three Pigs* by Wiesner

2002 Honor—*Martin's Big Words: The Life of Dr. Martin Luther King, Jr.* by Rappaport

2002 Honor—*The Stray Dog* by Simont

2002 Honor—*The Dinosaurs of Waterhouse Hawkins* by Kerley

2001 Winner—*So You Want to Be President?* by St. George

2001 Honor—*Casey at the Bat* by Thayer, ill. by Bing

2001 Honor—*Olivia* by Falconer

2001 Honor—*Click, Clack, Moo: Cows that Type* by Cronin

2000 Winner—*Joseph Had a Little Overcoat* by Taback

2000 Honor—*A Child's Calendar* by Updike

2000 Honor—*Sector 7* by Wiesner

2000 Honor—*The Ugly Duckling* by Pinkney

2000 Honor—*When Sophie Gets Angry—Really, Really Angry* by Bang

1999 Winner—*Snowflake Bentley* by Martin

1999 Honor—*No, David!* by Shannon

1999 Honor—*Snow* by Shulevitz

1999 Honor—*Tibet Through the Red Box* by Sís

1999 Honor—*Duke Ellington: The Piano Prince and His Orchestra* by Pinkney

1998 Winner—*Rapunzel* by Zelinsky

1998 Honor—*The Gardener* by Stewart

1998 Honor—*Harlem* by Myers

1998 Honor—*There Was an Old Lady Who Swallowed a Fly* by Taback

1997 Winner—*Golem* by Wisniewski

1997 Honor—*Hush!* A Thai Lullaby by Ho

1997 Honor—*The Graphic Alphabet* by Pelletier

1997 Honor—*The Paperboy* by Pilkey

1997 Honor—*Starry Messenger* by Sís

1996 Winner—*Officer Buckle and Gloria* by Rathmann

1996 Honor—*Alphabet City* by Johnson

1996 Honor—*Zin! Zin! Zin! A Violin* by Moss

1996 Honor—*The Faithful Friend* by San Souci

1996 Honor—*Tops & Bottoms* by Stevens

1995 Winner—*Smoky Night* by Bunting

1995 Honor—*John Henry* by Lester

1995 Honor—*Swamp Angel* by Isaacs

1995 Honor—*Time Flies* by Rohmann

1994 Winner—*Grandfather's Journey* by Say

1994 Honor—*Peppe the Lamplighter* by Bartone

1994 Honor—*In the Small, Small Pond* by Fleming

1994 Honor—*Owen* by Henkes

1994 Honor—*Yo! Yes?* by Raschka

1994 Honor—*Raven: A Trickster Tale from the Pacific Northwest* by McDermott

1993 Winner—*Mirette on the High Wire* by McCully

1993 Honor—*Seven Blind Mice* by Young

1993 Honor—*Working Cotton* by Williams

1993 Honor—*The Stinky Cheese Man and Other Fairly Stupid Tales* by Scieszka

1992 Winner—*Tuesday* by Wiesner

1992 Honor—*Tar Beach* by Ringgold

1991 Winner—*Black and White* by Macaulay

1991 Honor—*Puss in Boots* by Perrault, ill. By Marcellino

1991 Honor—*"More More More," Said the Baby* by Williams

1990 Winner—*Lon Po Po* by Young

1990 Honor—*Bill Peet: An Autobiography* by Peet

1990 Honor—*Color Zoo* by Ehlert

1990 Honor—*The Talking Eggs* by San Souci

1990 Honor—*Hershel and the Hanukkah Goblins* by Kimmel

1989 Winner—*Song and Dance Man* by Ackerman

1989 Honor—*The Boy of the Three-Year Nap* by Snyder

1989 Honor—*Free Fall* by Wiesner

1989 Honor—*Goldilocks and the Three Bears* by Marshall

1989 Honor—*Mirandy and Brother Wind* by McKissack

1988 Winner—*Owl Moon* by Yolen

1988 Honor—*Mufaro's Beautiful Daughters* by Steptoe

1987 Winner—*Hey, Al* by Yorinks

1987 Honor—*Alphabatics* by MacDonald

1987 Honor—*Rumpelstiltskin* by Zelinsky

1987 Honor—*The Village of Round and Square Houses* by Grifalconi

1986 Winner—*The Polar Express* by Van Allsburg

1986 Honor—*The Relatives Came* by Rylant

1986 Honor—*King Bidgood's in the Bathtub* by Wood

1985 Winner—*Saint George and the Dragon* by Hodges

1985 Honor—*Hansel and Gretel* by Lesser

1985 Honor—*Have You Seen My Duckling?* by Tafuri

1985 Honor—*The Story of Jumping Mouse* by Steptoe

1984 Winner—*The Glorious Flight* by Provensen

1984 Honor—*Little Red Riding Hood* by Hyman

1984 Honor—*Ten, Nine, Eight* by Bang

1983 Winner—*Shadow* by Cendrars

1983 Honor—*A Chair for My Mother* by Williams

1983 Honor—*When I Was Young in the Mountains* by Rylant

1982 Winner—*Jumanji* by Van Allsburg

1982 Honor—*Where the Buffaloes Begin* by Baker

1982 Honor—*On Market Street* by Lobel

1982 Honor—*Outside Over There* by Sendak

1982 Honor—*A Visit to William Blake's Inn* by Willard

1981 Winner—*Fables* by Lobel

1981 Honor—*The Bremen-Town Musicians* by Plume

1981 Honor—*Mice Twice* by Low

1981 Honor—*Truck* by Crews

1981 Honor—*The Grey Lady and the Strawberry Snatcher* by Bang

1980 Winner—*Ox-Cart Man* by Hall

1980 Honor—*Ben's Trumpet* by Isadora

1980 Honor—*The Garden of Abdul Gasazi* by Van Allsburg

1980 Honor—*The Treasure* by Shulevitz

1979 Winner—*The Girl Who Loved Wild Horses* by Goble

1979 Honor—*Freight Train* by Crews

1979 Honor—*The Way to Start a Day* by Baylor

1978 Winner—*Noah's Ark* by Spier

1978 Honor—*Castle* by Macaulay

1978 Honor—*It Could Always Be Worse* by Zemach

1977 Winner—*Ashanti to Zulu* by Musgrove

1977 Honor—*The Amazing Bone* by Steig

1977 Honor—*The Contest* by Hogrogian

1977 Honor—*Fish for Supper* by Goffstein

1977 Honor—*The Golem: A Jewish Legend* by McDermott

1977 Honor—*Hawk, I'm Your Brother* by Baylor

1976 Winner—*Why Mosquitoes Buzz in People's Ears* by Aardema

1976 Honor—*The Desert is Theirs* by Baylor

1976 Honor—*Strega Nona* by dePaola

1975 Winner—*Arrow to the Sun: A Pueblo Indian Tale* by McDermott

1975 Honor—*Jambo Means Hello: Swahili Alphabet Book* by Feelings

1974 Winner—*Duffy and the Devil* by Zemach

1974 Honor—*Three Jovial Huntsmen* by Jeffers

1974 Honor—*Cathedral* by Macaulay

1973 Winner—*The Funny Little Woman* by Mosel

1973 Honor—*Anansi the Spider* by McDermott

1973 Honor—*Hosie's Alphabet* by Baskin

1973 Honor—*When Clay Sings* by Baylor

1973 Honor—*Snow-White and the Seven Dwarfs* by Grimm, ill. by Burkert

1972 Winner—*One Fine Day* by Hogrogian

1972 Honor—*Hildilid's Night* by Ryan

1972 Honor—*If All the Seas Were One Sea* by Domanska

1972 Honor—*Moja Means One: Swahili Counting Book* by Feelings

1971 Winner—*A Story, A Story* by Haley

1971 Honor—*The Angry Moon* by Sleator

1971 Honor—*Frog and Toad are Friends* by Lobel

1971 Honor—*In the Night Kitchen* by Sendak

1970 Winner—*Sylvester and the Magic Pebble* by Steig

1970 Honor—*Goggles!* by Keats

1970 Honor—*Alexander and the Wind-Up Mouse* by Lionni

1970 Honor—*Pop Corn & Ma Goodness* by Preston

1970 Honor—*Thy Friend, Obadiah* by Turkle

1970 Honor—*The Judge: An Untrue Tale* by Zemach

1969 Winner—*The Fool of the World and the Flying Ship* by Ransome

1969 Honor—*Why the Sun and the Moon Live in the Sky* by Dayrell

1968 Winner—*Drummer Hoff* by Emberley

1968 Honor—*Frederick* by Lionni

1968 Honor—*Seashore Story* by Yashima

1968 Honor—*The Emperor and the Kite* by Yolen

1967 Winner—*Sam, Bangs & Moonshine* by Ness

1967 Honor—*One Wide River to Cross* by Emberley

1966 Winner—*Always Room for One More* by Leodhas

1966 Honor—*Hide and Seek Fog* by Tresselt

1966 Honor—*Just Me* by Ets

1966 Honor—*Tom Tit Tot* by Ness

1965 Winner—*May I Bring a Friend* by de Regniers

1965 Honor—*Rain Makes Applesauce* by Scheer

1965 Honor—*The Wave* by Hodges

1965 Honor—*A Pocketful of Cricket* by Caudill

1964 Winner—*Where the Wild Things Are* by Sendak

1964 Honor—*Swimmy* by Lionni

1964 Honor—*All in the Morning Early* by Leodhas

1964 Honor—*Mother Goose and Nursery Rhymes* by Reed

1963 Winner—*The Snowy Day* by Keats

1963 Honor—*The Sun is a Golden Earring* by Belting

1963 Honor—*Mr. Rabbit and the Lovely Present* by Zolotow

1962 Winner—*Once a Mouse* by Brown

1962 Honor—*Fox Went Out on a Chilly Night* by Spier

1962 Honor—*Little Bear's Visit* by Minarik

1962 Honor—*The Day We Saw the Sun Come Up* by Goudey

1961 Winner—*Baboushka and the Three Kings* by Robbins

1961 Honor—*Inch by Inch* by Lionni

1960 Winner—*Nine Days to Christmas* by Ets

1960 Honor—*Houses from the Sea* by Goudey

1960 Honor—*The Moon Jumpers* by Udry

1959 Winner—*Chanticleer and the Fox* by Cooney

1959 Honor—*What Do You Say, Dear?* by Joslin

1959 Honor—*Umbrella* by Yashima

1959 Honor—*The House that Jack Built: La Maison Que Jacques A Batie* by Frasconi

1958 Winner—*Time of Wonder* by McCloskey

1958 Honor—*Fly High, Fly Low* by Freeman

1958 Honor—*Anatole and the Cat* by Titus

1957 Winner—*A Tree is Nice* by Udry

1957 Honor—*Mr. Penny's Race Horse* by Ets

1957 Honor—*1 is One* by Tudor

1957 Honor—*Anatole* by Titus

1957 Honor—*Gillespie and the Guards* by Elkin

1957 Honor—*Lion* by Du Bois

1956 Winner—*Frog Went A-Courtin'* by Langstaff

1956 Honor—*Play With Me* by Ets

1956 Honor—*Crow Boy* by Yashima

1955 Winner—*Cinderella* by Perrault, ill. by Brown

1955 Honor—*Wheel on the Chimney* by Brown

1955 Honor—*Book of Nursery and Mother Goose Rhymes* by De Angeli

1955 Honor—*The Thanksgiving Story* by Dalgliesh

1954 Winner—*Madeline's Rescue* by Bemelmans

1954 Honor—*Journey Cake, Ho!* by Sawyer

1954 Honor—*When Will the World Be Mine?* by Schlein

1954 Honor—*A Very Special House* by Krauss

1954 Honor—*Green Eyes* by Birnbaum

1954 Honor—*The Steadfast Tin Soldier* by Andersen, ill. by Brown

1953 Winner—*The Biggest Bear* by Ward

1953 Honor—*Puss in Boots* by Perrault, ill. by Brown

1953 Honor—*One Morning in Maine* by McCloskey

1953 Honor—*Ape in a Cape: An Alphabet of Odd Animals* by Eichenberg

1953 Honor—*The Storm Book* by Zolotow

1953 Honor—*Five Little Monkeys* by Kepes

1952 Winner—*Finders Keepers* by Will & Nicolas

1952 Honor—*Mr. T. W. Anthony Woo* by Ets

1952 Honor—*Skipper John's Cook* by Brown

1952 Honor—*All Falling Down* by Zion

1952 Honor—*Bear Party* by Du Bois

1952 Honor—*Feather Mountain* by Olds

1951 Winner—*The Egg Tree* by Milhous

1951 Honor—*Dick Whittington and His Cat* by Brown

1951 Honor—*The Two Reds* by Will & Nicolas

1951 Honor—*If I Ran the Zoo* by Dr. Seuss

1951 Honor—*T-Bone, the Baby Sitter* by Newberry

1951 Honor—*The Most Wonderful Doll in the World* by McGinley

1950 Winner—*Song of the Swallows* by Politi

1950 Honor—*America's Ethan Allen* by Holbrook

1950 Honor—*The Wild Birthday Cake* by Davis

1950 Honor—*The Happy Day* by Krauss

1950 Honor—*Bartholomew and the Oobleck* by Dr. Seuss

1950 Honor—*Henry Fisherman* by Brown

1949 Winner—*The Big Snow* by Hader

1949 Honor—*Blueberries for Sal* by McCloskey

1949 Honor—*All Around Town* by McGinley

1949 Honor—*Juanita* by Politi

1949 Honor—*Fish in the Air* by Wiese

1948 Winner—*White Snow, Bright Snow* by Tresselt

1948 Honor—*Stone Soup* by Brown

1948 Honor—*McElligot's Pool* by Dr. Seuss

1948 Honor—*Bambino the Clown* by Schreiber

1948 Honor—*Roger and the Fox* by Davis

1948 Honor—*Song of Robin Hood* by Malcolmson

1947 Winner—*The Little Island* by Brown

1947 Honor—*Rain Drop Splash* by Tresselt

1947 Honor—*Boats on the River* by Flack

1947 Honor—*Timothy Turtle* by Graham

1947 Honor—*Pedro, the Angel* of Olvera Street by Politi

1947 Honor—*Sing in Praise* ill. by Torrey

1946 Winner—*The Rooster Crows* by Petersham

1946 Honor—*Little Lost Lamb* by MacDonald

1946 Honor—*Sing Mother Goose* ill. by Torrey

1946 Honor—*You Can Write Chinese* by Wiese

1946 Honor—*My Mother is the Most Beautiful Woman in the World* by Reyher

1945 Winner—*Prayer for a Child* by Field

1945 Honor—*Mother Goose* by Tudor

1945 Honor—*In the Forest* by Ets

1945 Honor—*Yonie Wondernose* by De Angeli

1945 Honor—*The Christmas Anna Angel* by Sawyer

1944 Winner—*Many Moons* by Thurber, ill. by Slobodkin

1944 Honor—*Small Rain: Verses from the Bible* by Jones

1944 Honor—*Pierre Pidgeon* by Kingman

1944 Honor—*The Mighty Hunter* by Hader

1944 Honor—*A Child's Good Night Book* by Brown

1944 Honor—*Good-Luck Horse* by Chih-Yi Chan

1943 Winner—*The Little House* by Burton

1943 Honor—*Dash and Dart* by Buff

1943 Honor—*Marshmallow* by Newberry

1942 Winner—*Make Way for Ducklings* by McCloskey

1942 Honor—*An American ABC* by Petersham

1942 Honor—*In My Mother's House* by Clark

1942 Honor—*Paddle-To-The-Sea* by Holling

1942 Honor—*Nothing At All* by Gag

1941 Winner—*They Were Strong and Good* by Lawson

1941 Honor—*April's Kittens* by Newberry

1940 Winner—*Abraham Lincoln* by d'Aulaire

1940 Honor—*Cock-a-Doodle Doo* by Hader

1940 Honor—*Madeline* by Bemelmans

1940 Honor—*The Ageless Story* by Ford

1939 Winner—*Mei Li* by Handforth

1939 Honor—*Andy and the Lion* by Daugherty

1939 Honor—*Barkis* by Newberry

1939 Honor—*The Forest Pool* by Armer

1939 Honor—*Snow White and the Seven Dwarfs* by Gag

1939 Honor—*Wee Gillis* by Leaf

1938 Winner—*Animals of the Bible* ill. by Lathrop

1938 Honor—*Four and Twenty Blackbirds* ill. by Lawson

1938 Honor—*Seven Simeons* by Artzybasheff

Recommended Picture Books: Music

1, 2, Buckle My Shoe by Anna Grossnickle Hines

The 39 Apartments of Ludwig Van Beethoven by Jonah Winter and illustrated by Barry Blitt

All of You Was Singing by Richard Lewis

A Band of Angels: A Story Inspired by the Jubilee Singers by Deborah Hopkinson and illustrated by Raúl Colón

Banjo Granny by Sarah Martin Busse and Jacqueline Briggs Martin and illustrated by Barry Root

The Banza by Diane Wolkstein and illustrated by Marc Brown, ISBN 0140546057

The Bat Boy and His Violin by Gavin Curtis and illustrated by E.B. Lewis, 0689841159

The Bear: An American Folk Song by Kenneth Spengler, ISBN 1590341902

Carnival of the Animals by John Lithgow and illustrated by Boris Kulikov, ISBN 0689873433 Carnival of the Animals by Barrie Carson Turner, ISBN 0805061800

Crash! Bang! Boom! by Peter Spier, ISBN 0385067801

Dancing Drum: A Cherokee Legend by Terri Cohlene and illustrated by Charles Reasoner, ISBN 0816723621

Dreamsong by Alice McLerran and illustrated by Valery Vasiliev, ISBN 0831743573

Duke Ellington by Andrea Davis Pinkney and illustrated by Brian Pinkney, ISBN 0786821507

Earthsong by Sally Rodgers, ISBN 0525458735

The Eensy-Weensy Spider by Mary Ann Hoberman and illustrated by Nadine Bernard Westcott, ISBN 0316363308

Ella Fitzgerald: The Tale of a Vocal Virtuosa by Andrea Pinkney and illustrated by Brian Pinkney, ISBN 0786805686

Ernie Dances to the Didgeridoo by Alison Lester, ISBN 0618104429

The First Song Ever Sung by Laura Krauss Melmed, ISBN 0140554572

Handel and the Famous Sword Swallower of Halle by Bryna Stevens and illustrated by Ruth Tietjen Councell, ISBN 0399215484

Hilda Must Be Dancing by Karma Wilson and illustrated by Suzanne Watts, ISBN 1416950837

Hip Cat by Jonathan London and illustrated by Woodleigh Hubbard, ISBN 0811814890

How Music Came to the World by Hal Ober and illustrated by Carol Ober, ISBN 0395675235

I Hear America Singing by Walt Whitman and illustrated by Robert Sabuda, ISBN 0399218084

If I Only Had a Horn: Young Louis Armstrong by Roxanne Orgill and illustrated by Leonard Jenkins, ISBN 061825076X

Igor Stravinsky by Mike Venezia, ISBN 0613373995

In the Tall, Tall Grass by Denise Fleming, ISBN 0805039412

Inch by Inch: The Garden Song by David Mallett, ISBN 0064434818

Introducing Gershwin by Roland Vernon, ISBN 0382391608

Jazz Baby by Carole Boston Weatherford and illustrated by Laura Freeman, ISBN 1584300396

The Jazz Fly by Matthew Gollub and illustrated by Karen Hanke, ISBN 1889910171

The Jazz of Our Street by Fatima Shaik and illustrated by E.B. Lewis, ISBN 0803718861

The Lady with the Alligator Purse by Nadine Bernard Westcott, ISBN 0316930741

Lift Every Voice and Sing by James Weldon Johnson and illustrated by Elizabeth Catlett, ISBN 0809774423 ISBN 0606087990

The Magic Flute by Anne Gatti, ISBN 0811810038

Mama Don't Allow by Thacher Hurd, ISBN 0064430782

The Master Violinmaker by Paul Fleisher, ISBN 0395653657

Morning Has Broken by Eleanor Farjeon, ISBN 0802851274

Mozart Finds a Melody by Stephen Costanza, ISBN 0805066272

Musicians of the Sun by Gerald McDermott, ISBN 0689839073

Mysterious Thelonious by Chris Raschka, ISBN 0531330575

Night in the Country by Cynthia Rylant and illustrated by Mary Szilagyi, ISBN 0689714734

Night Noises by Mem Fox, ISBN 0152574212

The Noisy Book by Margaret Wise Brown, ISBN 0064430014

A Noteworthy Tale by Brenda Mutchnick and Ron Casden and illustrated by Ian Penney, ISBN 0810913860

The Nutcracker illustrated by Azat Minnekaev, ISBN 0810913933

Old Chisholm Trail: A Cowboy Song by Rosalyn Schanzer, ISBN 0792275594

One Grain of Sand: A Lullaby by Pete Seeger, ISBN 0316781401

The Orchestra by Mark Rubin and illustrated by Alan Daniel, ISBN 9780920668993

Our Marching Band by Lloyd Moss and illustrated by Diana Cain Blethenthal, ISBN 0399233357

Over the Rainbow by E.Y. Harburg and Harold Arlen, ISBN 0060295007

Peter and the Wolf by Sergei Prokofiev and illustrated by Charles Mikolaycak, ISBN 0140506330

Prince Ivan and the Firebird by Bernard Lodge, ISBN 1879085631

The Remarkable Farkle McBride by John Lithgow and illustrated by C.F. Payne, ISBN 0689833407

Rogers and Hammerstein's My Favorite Things illustrated by Renee Graef, ISBN 043941167

The Singing Man: Adapted from a West African Folk Tale by Angela Shelf Medearis, ISBN 0823412083

The Story of the Incredible Orchestra: An Introduction to Musical Instruments and the Symphony Orchestra by Bruce Koscielniak, ISBN 0618311122

Summertime from Porgy and Bess by George Gershwin, DuBose and Dorothy Heyward, and Ira Gershwin and paintings by Mike Wimmer, ISBN 0689850476

Sunshine on My Shoulders by John Denver and illustrated by Christopher Canyon, ISBN 1584690504

Swan Lake by Rachel Isadora, ISBN 0698113705

Take Me Home, Country Roads by John Denver and illustrated by Christopher Canyon, ISBN 1584690726

This Land Is Your Land by Woody Guthrie and illustrated by Kathy Jakobsen, ISBN 0316392154

Train Song by Diane Siebert and illustrated by Michael Wimmer, ISBN 0064433402

Troubadour's Storybag: Musical Folktales of the World by Norma J. Livo, ISBN 1555919537

Two Scarlet Songbirds: A Story of Anton Dvorak by Carole L. Schaefer, ISBN 0375910220

Ty's One-Man Band by Mildred Pitts Walter, ISBN 0590446444

A Very Young Musician by Jill Krementz, ISBN 0671726870

Violet's Music by Angela Johnson and illustrated by Laura Huliska-Beith, ISBN 0803727403

We All Sing with the Same Voice by J. Phillip Miller and illustrated by Paul Meisel, ISBN 0060274751

What Instrument Is This? by Rosemarie Hausherr, ISBN 0590446444

What a Wonderful World by Bob Thiele and George David Weiss, ISBN 15680136988

The Wheels on the Bus by Paul O. Zelinsky, ISBN 0525446446

A Winter Concert by Yuko Takoa, ISBN 0761304266

The Young Person's Guide to the Orchestra by Anita Ganeri, ISBN 0152013040

Zin! Zin! Zin! A Violin by Lloyd Moss and illustrated by Marjorie Priceman, ISBN 0689835248

Recommended Picture Books: Theatre

All the World's a Stage. R.P. Davidson. Illus. A. Lobel. 2003. Greenwillow.

Drama School. M. Manning. Illus., B.Granstrom. 1999. Larousse Kingfisher Chambers.

Mouse Theater. M. Cartlidge. 1992. Dutton.

Theater Magic: Behind the Scenes at a Children's Theater. C.W. Bellville. 1986. Carolrhoda.

The Year I Didn't Go To School. G. Potter. 2002. Atheneum.

Recommended Picture Books: Dance

A Young Dancer: The Life of an Ailey Student. V. Gladstone. 2009.

A Very Young Dancer, J. Krementz. 1976. Knopf.

Baby Dance. A. Taylor. Illus., M. van Heerden. 1999. HarperFestival.

Baby Danced the Polka. K. Beaumont. Illus., J. Plecas. 2004. Dial.

Barnyard Dance. B. Boynton. 1993. Workman.

Bea at Ballet, R. Isadora. 2014. Nancy Paulsen Books.

Beautiful Ballerina. M. Nelson. 2009. Scholastic.

Brothers of the Knight, D. Allen. 2001. Picture Puffin.

Dance! E. Cooper 2001. Harper Collins.

Dance by Bill T. Jones and Susan Kuklin.

Dancing with Degas. J. Merberg. Illus., S. Bober. 2003. Chronicle.

Dancing Wheels P. McMahon. 2001. HMH Books for Young Readers

Giraffes Can't Dance. G. Andreae., Illus., G. Parker-Rees. 2002. Orchard.

Kitchen Dance M. Manning. 2008. Clarion.

The Little Ballerina. H.L. Ross. 1996. Random House.

Maria Tallchief, Prima Ballerina. V. Browne. 1995. Modern.

My Mama Had a Dancing Heart. L.M. Gray. Illus., R. Colon. 1996. Orchard.

On Your Toes: A Ballet ABC. R. Isadora. 2003. Greenwillow.

Rap A Tap Tap: Here's Bojangles—Think of That! L. Dillon. and D. Dillon. 2002. Blue Sky Press.

Recommended Picture Books: Visual Art

The Art Lesson. T. dePaola. 1997. Puffin reprint.

The Art of Eric Carle. E. Carle. 2002. Philomel.

A Bird or 2: A Story about Henri Matisse. B. Le Tord. 1999. Eerdmans.

Camille and the Sunflowers: A Story about Vincent Van Gogh. L. Anholt. *1994.* Barrons Juveniles.

A Child's Book of Art: Great Pictures, First Words. L. Micklethwait. 1993. DK Publishing.

David's Drawings. C. Falwell. 2001. Lee & Low.

DaVinci. M. Venezia. 1989. (Getting to Know the World's Greatest Artists series.) Children's Press.

Diego Rivera (Life and work of ...). A.R. Schaefer. 2003. Heinemann.

Dinner at Magritte's. M. Garland. 1995. Dutton.

Dreaming Pictures. J. von Schemm. 1997. Children's Book Press. (Adventures in Art series.) Prestel.

Family pictures/Cuadros de familia. C. Lomas Garza. 1990.

Frida. J. Winter. Illus., A. Juan. 2002. Arthur A. Levine Books/Scholastic Press.

Frida Kahlo: The Artist Who Painted Herself. M. Frith. Illus., T. dePaolo. 2003. Grosset & Dunlap.

Grandma Moses (Life and work of ...). A.R. Schaefer. 2003. Heinemann

Harold and the Purple Crayon. C. Johnson. 1981. 50th anniversary ed. HarperCollins.

Harriet and the Promised Land. J. Lawrence. 1997. Aladdin reprint.

Henri Matisse: Drawing with Scissors. J. O'Connor. Illus., J. Hartland. 2002. (Smart about Art series.) Grosset & Dunlap.

I Spy an Alphabet in Art. L. Micklethwait. 1992. Greenwillow.

In the Garden with Van Gogh. J. Merberg. Illus., S. Bober. 2002. Chronicle.

Katie and the Mona Lisa. J. Mayhew. 1999. Orchard.

Katie and the Sunflowers. J. Mayhew. 2001. Orchard.

Katie Meets the Impressionists. J. Mayhew. 1999. Orchard.

Landscapes. C. Delafosse. Illus., T. Ross. 1996. (First Discovery Art series.) Scholastic.

The Legend of the Indian Paintbrush. T. dePaola. 1996. Puffin reprint.

Liang and the Magic Paintbrush. Demi. 1988. Henry Holt.

A Magical Day with Matisse. J. Merberg. Illus., S. Bober. 2002. Chronicle.

Marianthe's Story: Painted Words and *Marianthe's Story: Spoken Memories.* Aliki. 1998.

Mary Cassatt: Family Pictures. J. O'Connor. Illus., J. Kalis. 2003. (Smart about Art series.) Grosset & Dunlap.

Michelangelo. M. Venezia. 1992. (Getting to Know the World's Greatest Artists series.) Children's Press.

My Name Is Georgia: A Portrait by Jeanette Winter. J. Winter. 1998. Silver Whistle.

No Good in Art. M. Cohen. Illus., L. Hoban. Greenwillow.

No One Saw: Ordinary Things Through the Eyes of an Artist. B. Raczka. 2001. Millbrook.

Picasso and the Girl with a Ponytail: A Story about Pablo Picasso. L. Anholt. 1998. Barrons Juveniles.

A Picnic with Monet. J. Merberg. Illus., S. Bober. 2003. Chronicle.

Pictures for Miss Josie. S. Belton. Illus., B. Andrews.

The Starry Night. N. Waldman. 1999. Boyds Mills.

Vincent Van Gogh: Sunflowers and Swirly Stars. J. Holub. Illus., B. Bucks. 2001. (Smart about Art series.) Grossett & Dunlap.

What Is an Artist? B. Lehn. Photog., C. Krauss. 2002. Millbrook.

When Pigasso Met Mootisse. N. Laden. 1998. Chronicle.

Willy's Pictures. A. Browne. 2000. Candlewick.

The Year with Grandma Moses. W. Nikola-Lisa. and G. Moses. 2000. Henry Holt.